A Gloucestershire Diarist

Lt. Col. A. B. Lloyd-Baker of Hardwicke Court

The Early Years 1897–1919

edited by introduced by Joyce Popplewell

Thornhill Press

To
Mrs Kitty Cobham

First published in 1993 by Thornhill Press Ltd., Gloucestershire

© Diary extracts, The Estate of A. B. Lloyd-Baker

© Original material, Joyce Popplewell

ISBN 0-946328-52-8

Typeset in Monotype Ehrhardt by Carnegie Publishing, Preston
Printed in Great Britain by The Cromwell Press, Melksham, Wilts.

Contents

The Lloyd-Baker Pedigree

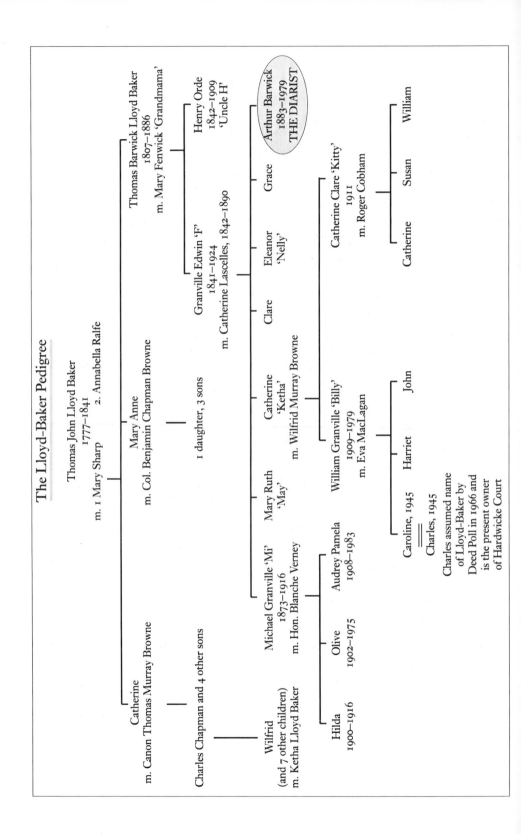

Thomas John Lloyd Baker
1777–1841
m. 1 Mary Sharp   2. Annabella Ralfe

Catherine
m. Canon Thomas Murray Browne

Mary Anne
m. Col. Benjamin Chapman Browne

Thomas Barwick Lloyd Baker
1807–1886
m. Mary Fenwick 'Grandmama'

Charles Chapman and 4 other sons

1 daughter, 3 sons

Granville Edwin 'F'
1841–1924
m. Catherine Lascelles, 1842–1890

Henry Orde
1842–1909
'Uncle H'

Arthur Barwick
1883–1979
THE DIARIST

Grace

Eleanor 'Nelly'

Clare

Catherine 'Ketha'
m. Wilfrid Murray Browne

Mary Ruth 'May'

Michael Granville 'Mi'
1873–1916
m. Hon. Blanche Verney

Wilfrid
(and 7 other children)
m. Ketha Lloyd Baker

William Granville 'Billy'
1900–1979
m. Eva MacLagan

Catherine Clare 'Kitty'
1911
m. Roger Cobham

Audrey Pamela
1908–1983

Olive
1902–1975

Hilda
1900–1916

Catherine   Susan   William

John

Harriet

Caroline, 1945
══
Charles, 1945

Charles assumed name
of Lloyd-Baker by
Deed Poll in 1966 and
is the present owner
of Hardwicke Court

Foreword

MY great-uncle Lt. Col. A. B. Lloyd-Baker came from a family who has lived in Gloucestershire for over two hundred and fifty years, first in Uley and for the last one hundred and seventy five years in Hardwicke. They had always done much in the county, amongst other things, acting as High Sheriffs, county councillors and magistrates. With this background Arthur Lloyd-Baker grew up and lived at Hardwicke Court for almost his whole life. He was born in 1883 and died in 1979. He never married.

He was educated at Eton and New College, Oxford and he remained devoted to both as long as he lived.

He had many interests. He was a competent cricketer and played for New College, a great reader, a keen traveller up to his nineties, an enthusiastic party-goer—in his young days a great dancer—and a keen follower of the Berkeley Hounds. Like the rest of his family he was a collector and, in his case, of books.

When he came down from Oxford he went to Paris and Vienna to learn French and German. He became English tutor to the young Prince of Hanover in Austria. He remained a friend of the family to the end of his life, visiting them for the last time when he was ninety three.

In 1913 he went to Cheltenham College where he taught modern languages and was housemaster of the day boys until he retired at the age of fifty five. There a number of boys owed their education to his generosity in paying their fees, but few people ever heard of this. He served in the First World War in France and Italy and was awarded the D.S.O. and the Croce di Guerra.

He enjoyed his retirement. Till he was in his seventies his life was spent mainly in public work. He was a magistrate and a county councillor and for many years was chairman of the County Education Committee. It was typical of him that he retired much earlier than he need, because he knew that his deputy chairman, who was older than my great-uncle, wanted very much to be chairman.

His life spanned nearly a century of change; one could say from the age of the horse and cart to the age of men landing on the moon. The wonderful thing about him was that he welcomed and enjoyed change. He never spoke about the "good old days."

What I think summed him up as a person was a remark he made on his ninetieth birthday. One of his nieces asked him how he felt. "Very old and very tired and very happy," he answered. It was so like him to say this—he always faced facts and never complained.

I hope these diaries will give readers a picture of a delightful and interesting person who lived through an extremely exciting period of history.

I am very grateful to Mrs. Popplewell for all her hard work in editing these diaries. It is a task which has involved much time consuming research and editorial skill.

C. G. M. Lloyd-Baker, October 1993
Hardwicke Court, Gloucester

Acknowledgements

Mrs. Kitty Cobham of Uley has been of immense help in explaining many complexities of names and relationships, and she has lent the photographs. As the only surviving niece of Colonel Lloyd-Baker her advice and encouragement have been invaluable. Mr. Brian Frith has drawn most generously on his fund of knowledge and experience and has expended much time in finding the solution to a variety of difficult problems. Mr. and Mrs. R. Alton, and Mrs. Caroline Dalton, Archivist of New College have given expert help with the Oxford section. Mr. David Smith, the County Archivist, initiated the engrossing task which has been so rewarding; and the staff at the Gloucestershire Record Office have been unfailingly helpful and kind, not least in repeatedly producing the uncomfortably heavy boxes in which the diaries are contained.

Brackets and Abbreviations

Round brackets in the text are the diarist's own.

Square brackets are the editor's and are used to add further information, to clarify relationships and to link excerpts which are separated by time, so making a more coherent whole.

Italics in the Notes sections indicate an achievement or appointment realised after the time span of the relevant section.

Family names and their abbreviations: other abbreviations

F	Father	H	Henry [*Uncle*]
Mi	Michael	Bl	Blanchie [*Blanche*]
M	May [*Mary Ruth*]	K	Ketha [*Catherine*]
C	Clare	N	Nelly [*Eleanor*]
G	Gracie [*Grace*]	Ch	Church or Chapel
M	morning	A	afternoon
E	evening	Kt	knighted
HC	Holy Communion	Bn	Battalion
k	killed		

In 1911 Mr G. E. Ll. Lloyd-Baker assumed by Royal Licence the surname of Lloyd before that of Baker. Since William Baker's marriage to the granddaughter of Bishop Lloyd 'Lloyd' was frequently given as a third Christian name and by the end of the nineteenth century the two names were used together. Readers will find rare examples in the Eton section of Baker being used alone.

Sources

Glos. R. O., D3549, Boxes 112, 113.

Introduction

WHEN Colonel Lloyd-Baker died in 1979 his private papers were deposited at the Gloucestershire Record Office in accordance with his wishes. Amongst this very large collection were his diaries, and in 1982 an opportunity arose to study the series which began in 1897, the year in which the diarist went to Eton College at the age of thirteen, and which continued until the year of his death.

At the suggestion of the County Archivist a calendar of selected entries was prepared, spanning the years 1897–1945. Held at the Gloucestershire Record Office this provides a concise but limited source of information; about events both local and national: about people, close personal connections as well as public figures: and, though rarely, the diarist's own attitudes and opinions. So much interest was shown at this stage by people who had known the diarist personally that it seemed appropriate to make the diaries more generally known.

A wider-ranging selection of entries drawn from the first twenty two years has been chosen as much to illuminate his own developing personality in late Victorian and Edwardian times in an essentially Gloucestershire setting as to chronicle events and recount anecdotes. Readers will be intrigued to discover considerable overlap and continuity with other published diaries kept by Gloucestershire figures. The young Arthur Lloyd-Baker dances happily at county balls and parties with descendants of the Reverend F. E. Witts, and he is at Eton and Oxford with Edward Birchall, youngest son of Dearman Birchall of Bowden, a firm friendship cut short by Birchall's death in Flanders.

At the centenary dinner of the Bristol and Gloucestershire Archaeological Society in 1970 when his extreme deafness meant that all communication had to be by means of his notepad and pencil Colonel Lloyd-Baker was full of lively interest in the proceedings, confirming one of the most striking features of the diaries, the enormous zest for life shown throughout. The early years especially have a particular attraction in their spontaneity and the obvious enjoyment he derived from all kinds of diverse experiences. Two major lifelong enthusiasms were for the theatre and for sport. Visits to plays, concerts, recitals, reviews and all manner of entertainments are described in detail. The theatre itself, in England or abroad, the cast or the performers, a critical and informed assessment of all these and of the merit of the work itself are combined with an occasional note of distinguished members of the audience. For example George Bernard Shaw's presence is recorded at some of his own first night performances when the diarist happened to be present.

Sport was almost an obsession. The minutiae of matches, teams and noteworthy scores made by anyone and everyone from W. G. Grace to Evans mi., all are set down and some even corrected in pencil at a later date. Hunting too is dealt with exhaustively during the first twenty years or so; two or three times a week when at home at Hardwicke in the season he is out with the Berkeley and gives full descriptions of the day, the weather, the countryside which he came to know so intimately and the horses which he rode with such panache together with their particular equine foibles.

A family tradition recorded by the diarist's sister May describes their great-great-grandfather William Lloyd Baker driving with his wife along the Owlpen road in 1785 and seeing sunlight glinting on the windows of a comfortable house across the valley. This was Stoutshill, which they decided to buy, thus beginning the family's settlement in the Uley area which still continues today. William's father was Thomas Baker, Rector of Bibury. He had married a granddaughter of that Bishop Lloyd who had defied James II in 1688 and with six other prelates was imprisoned in the Tower of London accused of sedition. The Lloyd family owned considerable property in Clerkenwell and Islington including the site of the Sadlers Wells theatre and the New River Head, areas which were to be developed later, about the year 1830.

The only child of the Stoutshill Lloyd Bakers was Thomas John. He bought Hardwicke Court in 1816, the former home of the Trye family. The fabric of the house was so severely attacked by dry rot that it had to be demolished and rebuilt. Sir Robert Smirke who had been working on the new Shire Hall at Gloucester was the architect for the new house. Thomas John married Mary Sharp, granddaughter of the Venerable Thomas Sharp, Archdeacon of Northumberland, in 1800. Mary brought property in Durham and Doncaster into the family as well as some interesting mementoes of the Sharp family to which the diarist refers. She appears as a beguiling little girl of about two years old, nursing a kitten, in a charming Sharp family conversation piece by Zoffany, now on permanent loan to the National Portrait Gallery. Her husband's portrait as a sporting squire with gun, dog and bundle of documents still hangs at Hardwicke Court.

Their family consisted of a son, Thomas Barwick, and two daughters who married brothers named Browne, one a Canon and the other a Colonel. Numerous Browne descendants pepper the pages of the diaries for many lived locally in Gloucestershire. Thomas Barwick was the founder, in 1852, of the Hardwicke Reformatory a pioneering enterprise in the treatment of young offenders which created much interest and served as a model elsewhere in England and also in Europe. His death in 1886 is commemorated by a wall monument in the south transept of Gloucester Cathedral. His wife was Mary Fenwick, the 'Grandmama' of the diaries. Their two sons Granville Edwin and Henry Orde were the diarist's father and uncle; 'Uncle H' never married and lived at Hardwicke Court all his life.

After Granville Edwin brought Catherine Lascelles to Hardwicke as his wife in 1868 family connections were vastly increased. Catherine was a niece of the third Earl of Harewood and one of ten children most of whom married and had extensive families. Our diarist Arthur Barwick was the youngest of seven children, separated by five sisters from his elder brother, Michael Granville. When Arthur was six years old his mother died and Grandmama came up to the Court from the Cottage, a most inappropriate name for the handsome Georgian house on the estate to which Michael would in due course take his wife Blanche, the eldest daughter of Lord Willoughby de Broke.

Until the 1914–18 war the diaries unselfconsciously reveal the normal life and upbringing of a younger son in a privileged family, but one with a particularly strong sense of duty and social awareness. Church affairs and county service had long claimed the energetic attention of the Lloyd Baker family and both Michael and Arthur followed these traditions, though Michael's contribution was tragically terminated by his death in action in 1916. Arthur survived the war having served with great distinction in the Oxford and Buckinghamshire Light Infantry, in France and Italy. He rose to the rank of Lieutenant Colonel, was awarded the D.S.O. and Croce di Guerra and was mentioned in dispatches three times. When his father gradually relinquished his county commitments after the war Arthur took his place. He served as County Councillor and Alderman for 47 years, and was appointed Deputy Lieutenant of the County in 1922.

Arthur seems always to have had the happiest of relationships with his family, escorting his sisters to parties and dances and the theatre, later arranging excursions for them in his succession of unreliable motor cars and obtaining invitations for them to attend functions at Cheltenham College when he became a schoolmaster there. He was delighted to become an uncle to a nephew and four nieces, and later in life extended this role to innumerable young people all over the county so that today totally unrelated adults of distinctly mature years speak with warm affection of Uncle Arthur. It is more than a little sad that despite his evident appreciation and enjoyment of feminine company he never married.

A great problem has been that of selection from the abundance of interesting material. Changes in format of the diaries themselves vary with the circumstances under which they were written and this suggested a chronological division into four sections. Each of these has its own introductory passage and some explanatory notes at the end which are intended to enhance the interest and relevance of the extracts. The notes are brief and idiosyncratic; a fully comprehensive reference list is quite outside the scope and intention of this work. Further information will be found in the Personal Names Index which accompanies the Calendar at the Gloucestershire Record Office.

Eton College, 1897–1902

I N 1897 Arthur Barwick Lloyd-Baker had left his preparatory school at Malvern Link and went on to Eton where his father, uncle and elder brother had preceded him. He was thirteen years old. The diaries for this period of his life are small leatherette pocket books with one exception; that for 1898 is a sizeable desk diary in which entries are atypical in their length and content, and it is interesting that this volume was omitted from the main collection and was thought to be lost. Some years after the diarist's death it was found on the library shelves at Hardwicke Court.

Typical entries for this time consist of irregular notes and jottings, many days and even weeks being left blank. Much attention is given to sporting activities. Daily games of fives from January until Easter, cricket in summer and football in autumn with precise details of partners and opponents, teams and scores, all make very dull reading in themselves. They are, however, enlivened by later annotations which often bring up to date the subsequent careers and achievements of those mentioned. This re-reading and up-dating continues throughout the whole series of diaries and in addition to increasing their interest is of the greatest help, especially at this stage, in identifying boys named simply, for instance, Wilson[1] and Lyon[2].

The Etonian régime around the turn of the century shows up indirectly as it touches the schoolboy's day by day experiences. The headmaster was Dr. Edmund Warre who remained a remote figure, preaching on the first Sunday of each half and on such momentous occasions as the death of Queen Victoria. It had been intended that the boys should line the route to be taken by the funeral cortège but this was forbidden by Warre because of the intense cold; the veto was revealed by the sergeant of the Volunteers. 'My tutor' was R. W. White-Thompson, though both father and elder brother had been under the care of the redoubtable Miss Evans, last of the Eton Dames. Academic demands bore heavily on a conscientious pupil though it was quite possible to take life more lightly than did the diarist in 1898, when the longer entries made in that year show him valiantly trying to keep up with the work in order to demonstrate that his remove to the fifth form was deserved.

Few Sundays pass without reference to church attendance at home or chapel at school, with a note about the sermon, even if in the early Eton days it is often 'man I didn't know preached'. Cash accounts are kept meticulously; accurate to a halfpenny they show the schoolboy's perennial yearning for an edible treat, 'sock' being the Eton term for tuck. Sometimes 'sock' is itemised, bacon and eggs being a winter favourite and raspberries a summer indulgence. Borrowings and lendings, mild wheeling and dealing in minor items such as pencils contrast with the occasional large outlay, financed by a loan from 'my tutor' for skates during a time of hard frost. The expenditure of 2s od. on mourning notepaper in the week of Queen Victoria's funeral indicates in a small way the national feeling of involvement, as do the references to the relief of Ladysmith and Mafeking.

Some events of great family significance, however, are simply not mentioned. For instance the marriage of Michael, elder brother and heir, to Blanche Verney on 13 April 1898 is reported at inordinate length in the *Gloucester Journal* and from the guest list it is clear that 'Master Lloyd Baker' was present and joined with his sisters in the wedding gift of silver candelabra. No reference appears in the diary, but three weeks later he mentions having special short leave

The brothers: Michael and Arthur in 1897 when Arthur went to Eton

for the 'homecoming', and helping to pull the bridal carriage along the main drive and up to the Court, before returning to Eton by noon the next day.

The diarist so seldom reveals his inner feelings that it is hard to tell to what extent he enjoyed his schooldays. He revelled so transparently in his four years at Oxford that it seems likely that Eton did not quite suit his temperament, and possibly he felt overshadowed by Michael's more brilliant performance there. However he returned with obvious pleasure in future years to attend Fourth of June and Old Boy celebrations in November, and wherever he travelled in this country, in Europe or in North America and especially during the war years 1914–18 he met Old Etonians with whom there was an immediate bond.

The Eton Diaries

1897

January

1   To Gibbins [sic] Al. Rather crowded.[3] G to Darells[4]

4   To Gloucester in morning. Hair cut. Sunday school treat afternoon. About 70 there out of 78. Magic lantern.

13   Beresford-Heywood's party. Al. Marcus rather funny.[5]

18   To Gloucester to dentist. 1 small place stopped. Didn't hurt.

20   To Eton. First to arrive. Then Boxall[6] and Stewart.[7] Am messing with S. Have forgotten to learn holiday task.

21   Nothing much to do.

22   Holiday task 4.30. Not hard. Think I have passed.

23   Snow quite deep. Mr Mellor[8] put me on for 9.15 Sat and 6.15 Mon. My tutor[9] horrified.

24   Ch M & A. Man I didn't know preached

25   Went for first music lesson with Mr. Mellor. Rather nice. Snowballing.

27   Went to look at skates. Wrote to F for 6/–.

February

7   Daman[10] preached M. Floods still rising. Finished *poena*[11] Wells[12] gave me for being late. Wrote to Father.

20   Run with Christie[13] A. Were pelted by cads[14]. C got insane idea of telling a policeman. Did not find one. Began my fortnight of mess fagging

23   Received wire from E. Sebright[15] to say he was coming down in afternoon. Went to St. George's Windsor. Beautiful singing. [*note in weekly accounts records 5/– received from E. Sebright*]

27   Many boys going for long leave. Only 6 left at my tutor's. Began being *Praeposter*[16]

March

15 E. Sebright with Australian friend down. Went over State Apartments. [*accounts record 5/– from E. S.'s Australian friend.*]

27 House sports. Did *not* distinguish myself

28 Bowlby preached M[17] Walk up to Windsor. Cousin Edgar down to morning chapel, Staying with Vaughan.

April

3 Birthday presents: Father 10/– Grandmama 10/–[18] N. Day[19] Stamp hinges and picture Stewart Pen.

9 Home!!! Travelled with Wilson. Met by M and F

10 Miss Josslyn went [*sisters' governess*]
Ch M & E. Mr Hayward both times. Grev Verney & Mrs[20] over from Cottage

May

5 Was given a watch & chain (Silver watch & chain from Father: I had never had one). To Eton.

9 Ford preached M, 17 mins. Walk with Stewart A to Windsor. Saw Queen!!!!!

June

4 M & Mi E & K & F down. Match v. New College: draw.

8 Went for short leave to 91 Ebury Street[21] to F etc. Saw Royal Academy M & Military Tournament A.

20 Jubilee[22]

23 2 Rehearsal, torchlight manoeuvres.

25 Winchester match. Torchlight procession in evening. Hervey Bathurst's people took me to tea A.

July

20 I am top of my French div.

23, 24 Trials[23]
[*A long interval without any entries*]

December

21 Hunted Whitminster. Moor Farm blank. Got reared off by pony while drawing.

28 Drove with M & Uncle H to Piers Court[24] leading Nigra behind. Meet at Stinchcombe . . . From Ashton Playne coursed by a dog. Group of cads lectured by R. I. Tidswell[25] who said he didn't care whether it was their dog or not, it was somebody's dog. Round Stinchcombe & killed at Dursely. Tea at Piers Court.

1898

January

11   Hunted at Matson. I did more jumping today than I can remember doing before in one day. Cornishes[26] dance at Goddards Rooms. Mi.C G & I went. Al. [*list of dances and partners follows*] Sat out with Christabelle whom I took to supper, and Marianne.

12   Tidswells party. Tea, conjuror & dancing. Conjuror good. Some tricks & paper-folding & shadows. The last two were explained in Strand magazine a month or two back.

14   Beresford-Heywood's party. Tea. Dancing. Managed to persuade Vere Heywood that I was at Eton. Marcus eat [sic] I don't know how many oranges . . . Put my foot in it by asking Aline Tidswell if the conjuror at their party came from Gloucester. Found he came from London.

15   Ought to have gone back to Eton but as Ina[27] is down with measles Dr. W said I mustn't. Went to stay at the Cottage to be out of the measles house.

28   . . . B. Verney came.[28]

29   Blanchie to luncheon at Cottage

30   Mrs White-Thompson writes to say I must not go back to Eton till Wed. Feb.2nd instead of Mon.Jan.31st. Also that I am in 5th form.

February

2   Went back to Eton. New boys at RWW-T's are Lyon [see note 2] & Fitzwygram[29] Am up to Bowlby

3   Bowlby asked if I was any relation to Mi. He thought I was cousin & much surprised to find that I was brother. Also that Mi was to be married. Took a long time over my Alcestis this evening. Learned my grammar paper for tomorrow early school. Hope I shall pass. Bought Lilleywhite's Annual.

4   Didn't do much of a grammar paper. Up to Bowlby all the morning. Up to Carter for Math. Did History questions E. Private [*study*] 7–8. Didn't go down for supper.

5   . . . Have got grammar paper to do again. In E began work at 6 & only got through one Greek construe & extra work by 9.15. Worked continuously

6   First Sunday in Upper Chapel.

8   . . . Did extra work in evening. Couldn't do last four sums. Hope Carter will pass it but doubt it.

9   Carter passed my extra work after all. Coode couldn't make out whether you divided sq. ft. by 9 or 3 to get sq. yds.

12   Wanted to watch final of school & junior mile after 12. Couldn't find cap. Got Luck's as he was on leave. Found afterwards that Christie had Howard-Vyse's cap[30] expect H-V had mine. Found it put back when I got back to my tutor's.

18   At private this evening my tutor said 'Draw a square 3 inches by 2 inches'. I don't think anyone saw the joke but me.

March

3   . . . playing at the Old Courts . . . we saw Lord Roseberry [sic][31] walking about watching the fives.

6   Went up to Castle with Fitzgerald & saw Queen.

17   Did 130 lines of Vergil after my candle expired.

18   Did 130 lines of Vergil after my candle expired.

19   Did 100 lines of Vergil in school library with Scholfield, written in darness [sic]

28–30   Trials.

31   Reading over. At absence Bowlby said an affectionate good-bye to each fellow as he called his name. I have got a 2nd class, Fitzgerald[32] & Fitzwygram got 1st classes, Fitzwygram his Trial prize.

April

1   Went home

28   Back to Eton. One new boy, Hargood-Ash.

29   No games owing to rain. Exit Hargood-Ash, being 14 and having taken third form.

May

2   Went to Hardwicke for Mi's homecoming. Special leave. Found out I could not get there in time & wired 'Will not be in time for homecoming, send bike or conveyance Gloucester 5.52'. Arrived at Gloucester & got into hansom as per telegram from M. Will Jones comes up & asks if I've seen anything of Mi & B. They missed their original train. Hansomed out & Mi. & B turned up a few minutes afterwards having come by the same train from Swindon. Unharnessed horses & dragged them up the drive. I ran behind. Cheers & speeches at Court. Tenants' dinner. Dancing.

3   Back to Eton by 12. Played in Mesopotamia. Made 4 b. Orealach. Fielded long slip

9   Got praeposter rules twice by two today for marking Carrgem in when he was staying out. Am very angry because they have shunted me from Mellor to Morsch a change I don't at all appreciate. Must get back to Mellor if I possibly can. (Mellor a pleasant & tolerant music master, Morsch an exacting & excitable German)

17   At Absence Brinton sent back all those wearing cricket or boating shoes or boots. I was sent back & so missed first Absence. At second Absence Brinton said 'You people must appear decently dressed at Absence, that's why I don't appear in my nightgown – not that I've got one as I always were pyjamas'.

18   I had received an invitation from the Henrys whom Mi. met while honeymooning to go up & spend tomorrow with them. I asked my tutor for leave. He began writing on a 'short leave' form. I said 'Sir mine isn't short leave'. He said 'What is it then?' I said I didn't know that leave to Windsor & off Absence would count as short leave. He read father's letter again & said 'Oh I see, that's all right' & wrote it out on an ordinary form. I was sincerely thankful as I did not wish to spare my short leave.

19   To the Henrys with Joe Henry after Chapel. We had an awfully jolly time. They said I was ridiculously like Ketha. Joe seems to have been immensely struck & amused by B & Mi. They are nice. <u>Mr. Gladstone died.</u>

22   Mr Donaldson preached. A good deal of the sermon about Gladstone.

25   Completion of our Junior v. Aingers. We didn't get the runs, myself being bowled Hodgekinson O which gave me a pair of spectacles.

29   Weldon [sic][33] headmaster of Harrow, preached.

31 My short leave. In the morning I went to Madame Tussauds & saw two tableaux new to me ie 'Dargai' & 'Death of Gordon'. Saw also in Chamber of Horrors the original knife and lunette of guillotine of the Revolution. To military tournament in afternoon. Head & posts, lemon-cutting, tent-pegging, tug-of-war, Scots Guards beat Royal Marines. Then there were displays by 8th Hussars, bareback riding by Canterbury depot, RA & RHA driving competitions & RHA musical drive. Pageant called 'Shoulder to Shoulder' . . . display of 'Capture of Benin City' . . . Alexandria, a representation of the 'gallant 28th', the Gloucestershire regiment . . . El Teb, had the band of the Gordon Highlanders. After the drum major came Piper Findlater, the man who got the VC for sitting under the rock & piping with both legs shot through.

June

4 May, Father, Ketha & Nelly down. Didn't got to speeches. I & K & N lunched at my tutor's, M & F at Miss Evans . . . Tea at Miss Evans. Procession of boats very good. My tutor's have four in boats this year. Supper with Henrys at their house. Fireworks very good as usual.

18 My long leave began. I went to Westminster Abbey in the afternoon & to 'White Heather' in the evening. Beautiful scenes of a Scotch [sic] loch, grouse moor, in & outside the Stock Exchange, in a Thames lock, & under the sea where the second best hero cuts the villain's air pipe, both being diving.

19 To St George's Chapel, Albemarle St, Piccadilly to hear the Waterloo Memorial service. Dead March with drummers of the Scots Guards. To Zoo in afternoon & Park in evening.

20 To British Museum in morning, Earl's Court afternoon. Extraordinary [sic] fine naval display with magnificent model ships. Bombardment of a town, searchlights & torpedo practice.

30 May & Grace down to try & let G have her first look at the Queen. We saw her.

July

2 The School v. I Zingari. I met the Arbuthnots[34] & the Guy Sebrights[35] on the field.

8 Lords. Eton v. Harrow. We had a bus in Block A in Arthur Winterbotham's name.[36] Loraine[37] at my tutor's has his eleven.

August

5 Went to Bristol. Saw Middlesex in, C.M. Wells made 77, hitting one or two on to the cycle path round the ground. I met him just as he was coming out & had a word or two with him. In the Pavilion I was greeted by old E. M.[38] with 'Hullo! been shooting any more tigers lately?' What he meant I can't imagine.

24 To Stow on the Wold or rather Wick Hill, to play for Mrs Godman. I made c. Wynter mi. b. Henderson 5, & c. & b. Henderson 13. Henderson and the two Wynters are Eton fellows. We lost the match. Back to Banks Fee[39] for the night. Played curling on the billiard table after dinner

25 Match at Chipping Norton junction on Heythrop Hunt ground. My side was beaten again. I made 7 & 18. In this match I kept wicket, catching 1 stumping 1 and running out 3

26   From Stow to Stroud to match got up by Mr Moreton Bell the Coroner. I made 9
       & 3 not out, having to leave early to get home.

September

15   Back to Eton. The new boys at my Tutor's are Campbell, Lyon mi. who is a cousin
       of the other [*ie of Patrick Bowes-Lyon*], Evans mi. & Balfour[40]

16   I am up to Benson[41]

23   Coming up from private Taylor was looking about for a lower boy. I said 'Hard luck'
       as I didn't see one anywhere. He said 'What's that you said?' I thought I was in for
       a smacking. I said 'I didn't mean anything' & he said 'All right, don't be frightened'.
       In spite of what Mosley's fellows may say there have been worse fellows in the world
       than Claude Taylor[42]

October

7   Benson caught Scholfield[43] & I ragging in his room before School. He told us to come
       to his pupil room after 12. He told us to bring something to do & I took my History
       questions. Outside his pupil room he met us & said 'You are dismissed with a
       warning, Baker'. I must take that warning.

8   Went to Industrial Exhibition at the Albert Institute where I saw living photographs
       of ballet dancer, shoeing a horse, fight between miller & sweep, a cook with a
       policeman & a soldier, an artist's studio with critics: the last three comic. Several
       train pictures, a balloon ascent & others. I also heard a phonograph (first 'flicks' I
       had seen)

14   Tyrwhitt[44] asked me if they had Foxe's Book of Martyrs in the Library. I said 'You're
       very keen on religious subjects all of a sudden'. He said 'Oh no I wanted the tortures'.
       In the Foxe's Martyrs he had seen there were 'coloured pictures with the blood all
       running down crimson'.

17   All Benson's division had to show up a piece of paper with the derivation of their
       name written on it. I put 'Baker: name derived from original trade of ancestors'.
       Benson said 'A very sensible answer & probably quite incorrect'. At pupil-room today
       my tutor translated a bit of Thucydides 'if the ships would not sail out to the open
       ground'!!!!!

18   Dean of Windsor preached about the best sermon we've had this half.

25   The crisis!!! Shall we have war with France?

26   Tremendous fight in French Chamber about Dreyfus.

31   I had made a great hash of praepostering yesterday & so expected to get the rules. In
       order to be able to play today I wrote them out last night. And now I've not got them!
       I suppose I shall have them soon.

November

1   Haven't got the praeposter rules yet.

3   Played in morning. No praeposter rules. Cherry is down with chicken pox &
       Warburton[45] had spots on his face this morning. He is going to see the doctor. I sit
       next but one to Warburton.

5 Warburton is in again & has not got chicken pox so I am pretty safe. Davies[46] preached a very good sermon on prayer. He quoted the prayer of one of Noll's generals before Edgehill: 'Lord thou knowest how busy I shall be this day. If I forget thee do not thou, O Lord, forget me'. H-Vyse told me afterwards that as he was coming out of the pulpit Davies got his gown caught up in it & tore it.

9 Whole holiday for the Prince of Wales' birthday

11 I got a piece of paper from 'Hoppy' Daman today with the following inscription 'Lloyd Baker has not learnt his Euclid more than twice out of the last 5 occasions. HD.' My tutor signed it after private adding 'Please see that he does it in future or he shall in PR'. [*pupil room*]

12 The chief event of today is the lecture given by Col. Rhodes on the Soudan. Very good indeed though sometimes one couldn't hear what he said.

17 Went down after 4 but there was no game. After kicking about for some time Ponsonby offered to dive & swim down Jordan for 2/–. The money was collected & he dived & swam about 9 yds down in full change!!! He came out streaming with water & next proceeded to take off his shirt & ring [sic] it out. Luckily nobody was coming by just then.

21 Whole holiday in honour of the appointments of Lord Minto[47], Mr Curzon [48] & Rev. Weldon [and see note [33]] [*All were Old Etonians*]

23 Bitterly cold today, a real wet Eton day. Steady downpour, not stopping for an instant. Did 100 lines of Vergil.

30 Uncle Henry, Ketha, Clare & Grace down here today. We went to lunch at Rowlands. We had oxtail soup, chicken, mince-pies, roll & butter & coffee also lemonade. We had Charlie Orde & Johnnie Warburton to lunch with us.

December

1 Dressing this morning I thought I saw a spot up by my neck. I thought it might be an animal & said nothing. In school I felt a spot under my hair on my forehead where Mrs Martin looked for spots the other day so as soon as I was out of school I went to her & she declared I had got chicken pox. And I have!!!

3 Up for an hour or two this evening. Read almost all the time.

5 Went for a walk today in playing fields. I am to go home on Thursday.

7 The usual walk. They can't have me at home so I shall have to stay here till heaven knows when. Gracie hasn't had chicken pox so that's why I can't go home.

13 Usual walk. Am not going away tomorrow as was intended but the next day. [*No further entries this year*]

1899

February

1 Just before 2.45 school I met cousin Edgar Sebright who asked me to breakfast tomorrow at Rowlands.

2 To breakfast with Edgar. The following were also there: Loraine, Kelly, Stephenson, E-Warburton, H. Lygon, C. Orde[49] Halsey. (The first 3 much senior to the rest)

3   Couldn't play fives today owing to chilblains.

5   Provost preached

6   We had a fine time of it with Impey this afternoon. People didn't know their saying lesson & so he said he would set an extra saying lesson of 20 lines of Homer & 5 lines more for everyone else who failed. But he at last retracted.

7   Got 'nn'[50] for verses today.

8   Went to Hargreaves this evening who is preparing me for Confirmation.

10 This evening at private Evans came in & said 'Oh please Sir I can't come to puppy-hole tonight!!! My tutor said 'Can't come to *what?*' Evans explained & retreated rapidly. We all laughed & my tutor laughed too. Impey lost his wool this morning owing to people failing in grammar paper.

18 Father down today. He lunched at my tutor's.

22 Was 3rd in my heat of the 100 yds out of 8 or so. Was also in for long jump where I didn't distinguish myself.

25 Very good lecture by Capt. Boisragan, one of the two survivors of the Benin massacre.

26 'Hoppy' Daman preached. Walked with Hamilton[51] in afternoon. Ford preached the first of his lectures on the catechism.

March

3   Rather an exciting time at early school owing to people not attending. It ended like most of Impey's blazes, in smoke.

13 Did 500 lines of Vergil for extra books in 1 hr 15 mins

23 Trials begin: 7.30 History & Geography
                10.30 Science
                4.30 Grammar

24 Trials   7.30 Arithmetic
                10.30 French
                4.30 Greek Translation
    Father staying with Miss Evans for Confirmation

25 I was confirmed by the Bishop of Oxford. I went up with Barker ma.

26 My first communion. I had it with Hamilton next me. The Provost gave me the bread & Davies the wine.

27 Trials   7.30 Divinity
                20.30 Algebra
                4.30 Latin Translation

28 Trials   7.30 Latin Prose
                10.30 Verses

29 Fives with Collier, H-Vyse ma. & Wilson mi. Collier lost his temper with Vyse in last game & went. Reading over, I got a class.

30 Home. Uncle A. G.[52] at Hardwicke.

April

3   My birthday, 16. Received £1 from Grandmama, 10/– from Father, 10/– from Uncle A. G.

4   Went to Worcester for a dance at Cousin Effie's. Stayed with the Brownes. The dance good & small.

5   Returned from Worcester. Was met by Michael who took me to Cuthberts[53] & then to Mrs Courtine's to have an operation tomorrow.

6   The operation performed. Ether not so nasty as choloroform.stayed in bed all day. (Chloroform for pleurisy in 1896)

12   Out of hospital.

24   Went to Beechwood, Edgar Sebright's place.

25   Edgar drove us ie myself, Uncle H, May & Ketha to Ashridge

26   Went to St Alban's, driving, & on by rail to Hatfield. Saw over Hatfield.

27   Back to Eton.

30   Head preached. Went to HC after morning service

May

1   Went to orderly room between afternoon schools to join the Volunteers.

2   Played after 4. Was introduced to Lord Belhaven by Hamilton at 3 Absence.

18   Went out to tea with Lady Belhaven

24   I tried to pass with the Morris tube in the Drill Hall. Did not pass.

June

4   Father Ketha May & Clare down.

5   On parade this morning the Volunteers were reviewed by Lord Roberts[54]

29   Went for short leave. Never put in my leave ticket so shall probably get my leave stopped. Went to Earl's Court 'Savage South Africa'. Very good

July

14, 15   Eton & Harrow. A draw as usual.

18   My first House match. My tutor's v. Ainger's. . . . myself 24 b. Scott

20   I played for Foster's scratch v. Tatham's Juniors. I made 21 not out.
     [No further entries this year]

1900

January

25   Back to Eton.

26   Am up to 'Toddy' Vaughan[55]

29   Head addressed us on raising strength of Volunteers, with great effect.

February

3   Played with Wilson & Lyon mi. & Balfour after clearing 4 ins of snow out of the court!!!!

21   All the Dorney road under water. Reported relief of Ladysmith (False)

A page from the Eton diary for 1900. Snow in the fives court: 'sock' a frequent item.

March

1   Field Day at Stoke. Just before it began we got the news: Ladysmith relieved. Cheers.

3   Played with Boswall, Scrimgeour & Vyse. Very good lecture on 'Union Brigade' by Somerville. Am in Beagles.

8   Field Day on Bagshot Common. Lot of marching but very good fun.

May

19   Mafeking relieved. Huge rejoicings. Made 12, run out, in rag game

25   G presented at Court by Lady Dorrington[56]

26   Went for leave. 'Messenger Boy'. Acting good, music not so good as usual.

June

2   Made 3 c. Gomm b. Hardy, & 18 c. Orr Ewing b. Vyse in game including several Lower Club fellows. Michael & Blanchie have a daughter, Hylda Blanche.

4   Father & G down. Roberts enters Pretoria.

13   Made 79 no out. Going on with same game tomorrow.

14   Increased overnight score to 104 not out. My first century, having carried bat through innings. Fielded long on & extra slip.

17   Dean Farrar preached.[57]

28   Made 109 in 3rd game after being missed first ball. No other chance. Fielded at point & long on & caught 2 in each place.

July

19   I passed in swimming!!

21   Inspection. Hamilton down[58]

29   Mumps. [*Isolated until August 1st, then home*]

November

10   Our Old Boy. Scored a rouge by myself, charging up on Johnson.

26   Got my shorts in House match v. Vaughans. We won 1 goal to nil. We played 10 extra mins to finish. Very hard game chiefly loose bullies.

30   Leave with Chamberlain. Went to Hertford House (Wallace Collection) & Albert Chevalier.

December

1   Beagles. Invitation meet. H-Vyse's first trial. Killed one & found another.
     [*A change in emphasis is discernible this year, from schoolwork to sport at which he is becoming markedly successful*]

1901

January

22   Hunt at Putloe. Very good day of 27 jumps. Splendid fun. Back to Eton. Queen Victoria died.

27   Head preached. M 'The souls of the righteous' E 'Blessed are the departed'

28   Heard Edward VII proclaimed on Windsor Bridge.

February

1   Practise [sic] for Funeral.

2   Funeral of Queen Victoria. We lined the Long Walk. Too beautiful for words. [*note in accounts this week: Mourning notepaper, 2.0*]

3   Bowlby preached. Very good sermon. Memorial service. Attended meeting of Council of Eton Mission this afternoon.

4   Did nothing in particular. We were invited to the funeral (at Frogmore) but Head (according to Sergt. Major) thought it was too cold.

16   Long leave to Father at cousin Frederica's. National Gallery A and 'Son Jolly' by myself E. Very good.

17   Church at St Peter's. Tea with Walter & Markie Rice.[59]

March

Inge preached[60]

April

11   Acting at Frampton. I acted Henry Sedley in 'Granny's Discourse' by Cotta Prevost who took the title role.

May

15   Heats of sculling. Riley fainted. Stewart swamped & got in again & finished.

June

2   Alington preached[61]

4   No celebration. Up to London. Saw George & Sybil Montgomerie married[62] Academy & Earl's Court.

11   Short leave. National Gallery M & Military Tournament A

28   Winchester match. Father & Nelly down.

29   Uncle H & Clare down. Eton won by 2 wkts.

July

12, 13   Eton v. Harrow match. Harrow won by 10 wkts.

17   Breakfast with Edgar (Sebright)

27   Very good concert in cloisters given by Ainger's & Luxmore's. Plunkett-Greene[63] accompanied by Stanford.[64] German & Irish songs.

21–27   Higher Certificate exam all week

October

5   I am a serjeant.

21   I was vaccinated for the 3rd time.

28   Short leave to Nelly at Lady Le Marchand's at Chobham. Good fun.

November

2   Short leave to Father. 'Emerald Isle' good but not surpassingly excellent.

4   Football in thick fog

11   Head preached. To Copper Horse[65] with Balfour after 4.

1902

January

28   Beagles at Salt Hill Ry. Bridge. WG out[66] had a word with him to tell him of hunting.

February

25   Dined with my tutor.

March

12   Father down. Dined at Evans'.

13   Public Schools Field Day. Head gave consent to my staying on if W-T can find vacancy., (He couldn't)

22   Confirmation which I did not attend.

23   My last HC at Eton. Bishop of Oxford preached. Dinner with Vaughan then on to selections from Messiah in Lower Chapel.
[*This is the final entry from Eton. No formal leave-taking is mentioned. Intermittent notes appear in this pocket book until the full Oxford entries begin in November of this year.*]

June

2   We heard of Peace.

5   Rice's ball.

6   Christie-Miller's ball[67]

8   Cathedral Thanksgiving for peace [*at Gloucester*]. Bands & splendid sermon from Dean.
[*In July and August scrappy notes mention coaching sessions with Mr Edwards in Bath on weekday mornings, with reading and tennis in the afternoons, and weekends spent with family friends.*]

July

10   London. Lady Meath's ball.

11, 12   Eton v. Harrow at Lords.

19   To Eton for Inspection.

20   Back from Eton where I enjoyed myself enormously.

August

15   [*Olive, second daughter of Michael and Blanchie, born.*]

29   To London with F for Continental tour

30   Queensboro', Flushing, Amsterdam. Was not ill
[*Some 6 weeks spent in sightseeing, visiting father's friends, father attends a Congress, visits to the opera. Venice, Padua, Milan.*]

September

27   Gazetted to 1st Bucks in papers today

October

16   To New College [*in accounts: Allowance £75.0.0*]

Notes for the Eton Section.

1. Wilson, Henry Maitland 'Jumbo' *Field Marshall 1944 1st Baron Wilson* His mother was a Kingscote of Kingscote where he often stayed as a schoolboy.

2. Bowes-Lyon, Patrick – Eldest son of Lord Glamis. Eldest brother of Queen Elizabeth the Queen Mother, and of John, Alexander, Fergus, Michael and David who in turn followed him to Eton. *15th Earl of Strathmore and Kinghorne, 1944.*

3. Gibbons, John Skipworth JP. Lived at Boddington House.
4. Darell, Sir Lionel E. H. M. 6th Baronet. Lived at Fretherne Court (now demolished).
5. Beresford-Heywood, Marcus – Eton. Lived at Eastington House, Stonehouse.
6. Boxall, Alleyne Percival *Secretary of cricket at University College, Oxford.*
7. Stewart, Edward Orde 'Ted' *see* February 1919.
8. Mellor, Mr., A kindly music master at Eton.
9. White-Thompson, Walter Remington – 'My tutor'. *HM Inspector of Schools.*
10. Daman, Rev. Henry 'Hoppy', Assistant master in mathematics at Eton.
11. *poena*, a punishment, probably lines to write out.
12. Wells, Cyril Mowbray, Assistant master at Eton. Played for MCC 1895–1909.
13. Christie, John Cambridge. Assistant master at Eton. Founder of the Glyndebourne Festival.
14. Cads, general term for unknown boys: otherwise if known, they are fellows.
15. Sebright, Sir Edgar Reginald Saunders 11th Baronet. A distant relative and Ketha's godfather. Lived at Beechwood, Beds.
16. *Praeposter*, a monitor of lowly rank, on rotation.
17. Bowlby, Rev. Henry Thomas, Assistant master at Eton. *Headmaster at Lancing College.*
18. Grandmama, Mary née Fenwick.
19. Nana Day, former nurse to the diarist and his sisters.
20. Verney, Greville. Brother of Blanche, Michael's fiancée. *19th Baron Willoughby de Broke.*
21. 91 Ebury Street, Belgravia. Lloyd-Baker family lived here for the London season. Later they lived at 36 Ebury Street and attended St. Peter's church.
22. Queen Victoria's Diamond Jubilee 1897.
23. Trials are examinations.
24. Piers Court, Stinchcombe. Father's first cousin Col. William Lloyd Browne lived here. In the 1930s Evelyn Waugh bought it.
25. Tidswell family of Haresfield Court.
26. Cornish family of Quedgeley. Rev. Stephen Cornish had three beautiful daughters, Cecily, Christabelle and Marianne.
27. Montgomerie, Geraldine 'Ina'. A first cousin: her mother was Aunt Nellie née Lascelles who married Cecil Molineux Montgomerie of Garboldishem, Norfolk.
28. Verney, Blanche 'Blanchie'. Eldest daughter of 18th Baron Willoughby de Broke.
29. Fitzwygram, Frederick L. F. *Killed in 1st World War.*
30. Vyse, Richard Howard – *General Sir Richard Howard-Vyse.*
31. Primrose, Archibald Philip, 5th Earl of Rosebery. Prime Minister 1894–95.
32. Fitzgerald, Gerald Milnes, *Cambridge*, An enduring friendship.
33. Welldon, Rev. J. E. C. Old Etonian. HM of Harrow 1885–98. *Metropolitan of India, Dean of Durham.*
34. Arbuthnot, Colonel George, Lived at Norton Court near Gloucester.
35. Sebright, Guy T. S., Brother of Sir Edgar. Olive Emily, his wife, and Ivo his son.
36. Winterbotham, Arthur, Lived at Cam near Dursley and owned Cam Mills.
37. Loraine, Percy L., *New College Oxford. 12th Baronet, s.1917.* Diplomat, finishing his career as *Ambassador in Rome in 1939.* Appears as Lord Bognor in 'Some People' by Harold Nicholson.

38. Grace, Dr. E. M. Brother of W. G. Grace. Member of the Berkeley Hunt.
39. Banks Fee, Longborough. Home of the Godman family. Mrs Godman was Blanchie's aunt and lent Banks Fee for Michael and Blanchie's honeymoon.
40. Balfour, F. C. C. Nephew of A. J. Balfour who was to be *Prime Minister 1902–05.*
41. Benson, Arthur Christopher, Assistant Master at Eton. F.R.Hist.S.
42. Taylor, Claude W. H. *Cambridge. DSO* and other European decorations in 1st World War.
43. Scholfield, Ailwyn, *University Librarian at Cambridge.*
44. Tyrwhitt, Gerald Hugh *9th Baron Berners.*
45. Egerton-Warburton, John – His aunt by marriage was Ruth née Lascelles, who was also the diarist's Aunt Ruth, his mother's sister. She married George Egerton-Warburton of Uckfield, Sussex .
46. Davies, Rev. George Sevier, Chaplain at Eton.
47. Minto, Lord, 4th Earl. Appointed Governor-General of Canada, 1898–1904. *Viceroy of India, 1905–10.*
48. Curzon, Hon. Nathaniel, Elder son of 4th Baron Scarsdale. *Viceroy of India* 1898–1904. 1st *Marquess Curzon of Kedleston.*
49. Orde, Charles William of Nunneykirk. A second cousin on the Lloyd-Baker side of the family.
50. 'nn' means 'need not make a fair copy', thus implying good work.
51. Hamilton, Ralph Gerard Alexander, Master of Belhaven. *11th Baron Belhaven.*
52. Lascelles, Arthur George, 'Uncle A. G.' Second brother of diarist's mother.
53. Cuthbert, Dr. Charles Firmin, Medical practitioner at 2 Barton St. Gloucester.
54. Roberts, Frederick Sleigh, 1st Earl Roberts. C-in-C of the British Army in South Africa.
55. Vaughan, Edward Littleton, 'Toddy', Housemaster at Eton.
56. Dorrington, Sir John and Lady, of Lypiatt Park, Bisley. Sir John was the first Chairman of Gloucestershire County Council.
57. Farrar, Very Rev. Frederic William, Dean of Canterbury. d. 1903. Wrote 'Eric, or Little by Little'.
58. Hamilton, Major-General Sir Ian S. M. H. *General.*
59. Rice, Walter Fitzurian, *7th Baron Dynevor.* Walter's wife was Margaret Child Villiers, 'Markie' elder daughter of the 7th Earl of Jersey. They had four children who gradually appear in the diaries, and Rice becomes 'Rhys'.
60. Inge, Very Rev. William Ralph. Assistant master at Eton 1884–88. *Dean of St. Paul's Cathedral from 1911.* Diarist calls him the Gloomy Dean.
61. Alington, Rev. Cyril A., Assistant master at Eton. Later, *Headmaster of Eton, 1916–33.*
62. Montgomerie, George, First cousin, and brother of Ina *see* above.
63. Plunkett-Greene, Harry – Professor of singing at Royal Academy of Music and at Royal College of Music.
64. Stanford, Charles Villiers, Professor of Music. Kt. 1902.
65. Copper Horse, An equestrian statue of George III in Windsor Great Park.
66. Grace, William Gilbert, Renowned cricketer. Younger brother of E. M. Grace.
67. Christie-Miller, Geoffrey – Showed athletic prowess at Eton, winning both steeplechase and mile events. *Trinity College Cambridge*

New College, Oxford, 1902–1906

ALACONIC ENTRY 'To New Coll' on October 16, 1902 appears in the Eton pocketbook for that year. It is a somewhat inauspicious beginning to the most interesting period covered by the diaries. During the first six weeks frustratingly scrappy entries appear in the old book. Then on November 30 the diary sequence starts in earnest and from this date it is rare for any day to lack an entry. Indeed some are many pages in length; and it is clear from a study of ink and handwriting that block entries were often made. Hard-backed quarto volumes with lines are used until the war years, with the date embossed in gold on the spine. Entries for a year extend to an average of about 200 pages; and this has posed great problems of selection.

During the Oxford years an underlying pattern of annual events emerges which is sustained until the outbreak of war and in some instances long afterwards. The Christmas gathering at Hardwicke was a long-term survivor. The routine was of church attendance followed by a large lunch party with present-giving in the evening. Grandmama's gift was always something special but the family exchange was restricted to books, prints and gloves until the next generation reached the age to receive sturdy toys. After Christmas came the January round of social festivities for which a Hardwicke house party was arranged, coinciding with the meet of hounds held at the Court. Eton visits for Fourth of June and Old Boy celebrations are part of the yearly pattern, and so was attendance at Lords for Eton v. Harrow, Oxford v. Cambridge and other cricket fixtures during the season, for which the Lloyd-Baker family took up residence in Ebury Street, Belgravia. There the diarist joined them to escort his sisters to various balls and theatres, to the Royal Academy and sometimes on a morning visit to Earls Court where the more robust amusements offered there must have afforded some light relief. Territorial camp occupied a fortnight in August, and in early September the Music Festival, later to become the Three Choirs Festival, took place. When it was the turn of Gloucester the family again organised a house party, taking their guests in to the Cathedral each day to attend performances at which original works were often given conducted by their composers.

As with the Eton section life at Oxford portrayed in the diaries reflects the times and customs then prevailing. Varsity life was leisurely as regards academic requirements and social aspects were of far greater moment. Brekkers, lekkers and not too much emphasis on collekers: the tight little group of special friends with their nicknames: an enormously wide circle of new and renewed acquaintances and distant relatives; and of course the dons, amongst whom must be mentioned Dr. Spooner the Warden of New College, Gilbert Murray and C. W. Holmes, with many others. All this was tremendously exhilarating and contributed to a rich undergraduate experience. New sports were enjoyed: golf, hockey, beagling, tennis and punting were good outlets for surplus energy, and in winter an exhausting bout of 'fug soccer' in someone's room often provided a safe release for confined high spirits.

Vacations were a foil to Varsity life and were if anything even more energetic. In winter the family attended a succession of balls and parties each of which is vividly described. The dance itself, the name of the tune played for it, his partner and often a flashing comment, nearly always complimentary: 'Violet Wynter is more beautiful than ever' but just occasionally a trifle acidic: 'Miss Agg-Gardiner will pretend she is only just out'. Hunting too was a family activity at this time, and the punishing twice or thrice weekly meets are described in such detail that the day's action can be reconstructed quite easily today, raising admiration for rider and horse alike. Cricket and tennis monopolised the summer vacations and the well-fought contests in both sports are re-lived in fine detail.

Academic achievement was not a high priority for the diarist, and he was quite satisfied with his modest Third in Greats though there is no doubt that his subsequent career showed how much better he could have done with even a little more application. Perhaps though he might not then have been able to sum up his appreciation of this period as 'four years of the most intense happiness, getting better and better as it went on'.

The Diaries at Oxford

1902

October

  16   To New Coll.

  29   Paderewski A. Moonlight sonata [*note in accounts: Paderewski 5.6*]

Lloyders' friends and their names

November

12   To Slough for Volunteers dinner. Went to my tutor's first

13   To 'Toreador' with Scrimgeour[1] Gibson[2] Tod[3] & Hallett[4]

14   Beagles at Heyford, Hall's place[5]
     [*New diary begins here*]

30   Early service M. Lunch with H. E. Butler the don[6] rather good fun. He told us that
     he knew of a man who used to distribute tracts with allegories from cricket, football
     etc. One of them had a picture of WG on the outside entitled 'Grace wins the day'!
     H. W. Holloway of Stroud called in the afternoon. He had seen me in Buol's but
     didn't know where I was up. He is at University whither he asked me to breker – or
     is it brekker?[7]

December

4   I played hockey today. A very uneven game including swells like Dickens & Cherry
     & duffers like myself. After hockey I went to tea with Woolley[8]. In the evening I
     went with Balston[9] & Whitworth[10] to a Morality play in the Town Hall. Benson's
     company acted extraordinarily well. Bitterly cold. Chilblains rather bad. This eve-
     ning we had an excellent 'smoker' given by the Glee Club.

7   Spooner[11] told us of a foreigner who when rebuked by H. A. L. Fisher[12] for writing
     an essay on Walpole without an appreciation replied 'I, so young, so small, so
     grotesque to write an appreciation of such a great man..' We had a long talk on slang,
     with instances eg quagger = Queen, kagger = King, pragger-wuggins = Prince of
     Wales. Spooner says that adding –er came from Harrow.

9   Letter from Grandmama telling me to get a stationery cabinet.

11   In the morning I had a logic collekers. In the afternoon I went to Town to choose a
     stationery case. Leukers of 166 New Bond Street hadn't anything I wanted so I went
     to the Stores, where after standing about some time admiring the masterly inactivity
     & indecision of the lady customers I purchased a very nice 'Grosvenor' case.

15   Divvers collekers in morning.

16   Went down. Nearly missed my train through being kept in Hall till 11, to go through
     the process of hand-shaking. I was called up after about ½ an hour. Dean[13] remarked
     that my Demosthenes paper wasn't up to much but didn't seem annoyed. Said
     goodbye to the Spoo, Dean, Joseph[14] and Butler. Nelly is down with mumps, has
     joined Clare & Gracie.

22   Gloucester M: tried to buy Christmas presents. Hockey in the afternoon. 14 there
     including Marcus Beresford-Heywood who has Porter's house colours.

25   Church M & A. There was to have been a carol service in the afternoon but they
     hadn't lighted the lamps & it got too dark. We had Michael & Blanchie up to dinner
     and present-giving afterwards. I gave Grandmama a Turner calendar, Mi – 'Uncle
     Remus' illustrated by J. A. Shephard, Bl – share of a dictionary, F – 'Rural England'
     by H. Rider-Haggard, May – 'On the heels of De Wet', Ketha & Clare – photo
     frames, N – 'English Pre-Raphaelites', G – 'Daddy Darwin's dovecote and Mistress
     Mary's window' by Mrs Ewing. I received from Grandmama 'Grosvenor' stationery
     case, Mi – Quorn gloves, Bl – Tennyson, F – 'Verona', M K N & G 'Ruskin in

Pictures', C – scrapbook. Blanchie heard today of Lord Willoughby's death from another stroke, 2 days after leaving Colombo on his way home.

27   Kennels. Drove on with Uncle H. No one else hunted but F had a ride on W. Canning's motor.[15] I rode Outlaw. He had got the haybin open in the night & blown himself out with hay. So he was not so skittish as usual.

28   I biked into Gloucester in the morning & did some things. On coming out I found a telegram from Davis of Cirencester to say he was to be in Gloucester at 3.15 to try on my suit so I had to go in again at once.

1903

January

2   Dance at Meredith[16] Miss Collier with whom I had no.7 and the last extra is a daughter of the artist John Collier. He is, she told me, painting Tree as Falstaff. She is pretty & charming. Miss Marling[17] came with Jock Wemyss[18] who introduced her to me. She was extremely ingenuous. She is off to Dresden to complete her education.

6   Darells' ball. About 360 there. The floor was excellent as was Iff's band. Before the last dance I met Mr Trower searching for his party. 'I got 'em all together once & now they're all over the place'. Mr. Green said 'Wait till the music starts, you'll know where they are then'. 'Wait till I get 'em by the leg' said Mr Trower. I got to bed about 5.45.

8   Hardwicke as usual [*for the meet of hounds*]. Nice bright morning. We drew Quedgeley, blank, found at Hunt Grove. The country very deep & the old mare over-reached herself. It was a deepish cut but would have been very much worse but for the boot she was wearing: the boot itself was cut right through just above the fetlock. When I got to the Bristol Rd..I met Charles Dunn (Uncle H's groom) at the Cross Keys & he said I could do any amount of trotting. I turned back towards Quedgeley & soon met the hounds. Mi met me & we went to the Cottage where he mounted me on Frocester, his new purchase. It was very kind of him as he wanted him on Saturday. Gloucester ball in the evening. Not nearly so crowded as last year, 230–250. We went in 2 flys & the bus.

[*The diarist includes a note from Father's diary about expenses*[19]]

9   Charity ball in the evening: it was fairly empty, only 180

14   To Biddulphs for Ledbury ball. A jolly little dance; nice room but the band was all cornet.

15   Rat hunt at Ledbury kennels. They killed 37, which was as nothing to last year's bag when in the same place they killed 120 in 2 hours. Gibbons dance in the evening. Very good fun. Michael went, the first festivity he's been to since Lord Willoughby's death. He was 30 at midnight, I went & drank his health.

16   Up to 'Varsity by 6.36 from Gloucester. Grandmama gave me £5.

19   I went with Whitworth to the pit for the Carl Rosa Opera company in 'Tanhauser'. Lekker on Oedipus Coloneus by Sidgwick.[20] In the middle of a very interesting part he broke off & addressed some unfortunate: 'That is a very good cat & will behave

very well if she is allowed to: as long as she does I will permit, nay approve of her presence: & I will ask gentlemen not to put temptation in her way'

20   Town for Regimental dinner. I went out & bought pictures at Franz Haufstaengl's, 16 Pall Mall. I got Bellini's Doge, Turner's Garden of Hesperides, Tintoret's Bacchus & Ariadne & Watts' Sir Galahad. All these were framed. I got Landseer's two Studies of Lions, unframed.

22   Sidgwick sends round a list at his lekker: at the bottom he has put 'The cat' He marks her in himself.

24   Brekker with Boxall of my tutor's. He seems very flourishing: he's sec of the cricket at University. He's reading History. There are some rather good original pictures in his room: a very small Hogarth, a rabbit by Linley Sambourne, pen & ink, & a nice little sketch by Cowper RA.

25   Chapels as usual. Anthem in evening 'As Saul journeyed' from Mendelsohn's 'St Paul'.

26   I went to the XX Club as Clarke's[21] guest. I spoke. I had a few facts from Ency. Britt. which I strung together very badly. I was put up for election at private business.

27   Read the big edition of 'Stones of Venice' at Union, but fell asleep. They have the first edition there, rebound I fancy.

29   The Warden[22] died at 2.30 this morning.

30   Vernon Harcourt's dance in evening: in honour of Simon Harcourt's coming-of-age. I consulted several people as to the propriety of going considering the Warden's death. But we thought it would be all right. A good many New Coll men went.

31   Beagles didn't go out because of Warden's death. Read first two chaps of 'Seven Lamps' also Cicero's 'Divination'.

February

1   Beethoven's Dead March in morning & Handel's evening. Read 'The notorious Mrs Ebbsmith'. Hung pictures in evening.

2   Walked to Iffley to see the church; its most lovely, chiefly Norman. Walked on to Littlemore & back by Cowley, about 6 miles altogether. We had a meeting of the Twenty Club to pass a vote of adjournment as a mark of respect to the Warden's memory. Clarke informed me I had been elected a member by the committee but I still have to be balloted by the members.

3   The Warden's funeral. We all assembled in Hall at 3.15, then marched in procession round the quad to the Chapel. We had the first part of the service in Chapel & then went out into the cloisters where the burial took place. Hymns 84 & 126. Our wreath was made chiefly of lilies

7   At the Spoo's lekker this morning a dozen of us answered some 40 names.

12   Had dinner with Woolley at 53 Holywell. Went on with Clarke to the Union where they were debating 'Disestablishment & Disendowment'. I came in time to hear Cadogan make a rather feeble attack on Dis etc. & Curran a vigorous defence. Then the great gun of the evening Lord Hugh Cecil got up & spoke excellently. He of course was all against Dis & Dis.

34 Feb 2.3.	Battels	
	Lent '04	Summer '04
University dues	10. 0	1. 0. 0
College dues	4. 3. 8	4. 11. 6
Rent & Taxes	6. 5. 11	6. 5. 11
Rent of furniture	12. 9	12. 6
Bedmaker	2. 10. 0	2. 10. 0
Buttery	2. 0. 10	2. 6. 5
Kitchen	10. 9. 5	12. 10. 11
Coals & Faggots	1. 19. 6	13. 6
Store Room	3. 14. 10	3. 13. 3
Electric Light	13. 4	7. 6
Laundress	1. 19. 8	2. 1. 8
Depreciating Furniture	1. 3. 6	1. 3. 3
Tuition	7. 0. 0	7. 0. 0
Common Room	5. 2. 1	6. 19. 6
Club subs.	1. 6. 8	1. 6. 8
Carriage account		2. 10
Bike shed	5. 0	5. 0
Baths	3. 4	2. 4
Fines		5. 0
	50. 0. 6	53. 17. 9

Battels: some archaic items. Was 'depreciating furniture' a result of over-energetic fug soccer?

13 Brekker with J. G. Hubbard[23] at the House. After hockey I ran with our first togger[24]. In the evening 'Oc' Asquith[25] came in: in his right hand he held a tumbler of whisky & soda, in his left a huge pipe. We had a very jolly talk.

14 I went to Gardner[26] to look over a Greek sculpture paper I did for him: he seemed fairly pleased. Gibson was to have answered my name & Tod's at the Spoo's lekker but forgot to go himself.

16 The Spoo sent for me today for cutting his lekker on Sat. I explained that I had to go to Gardner & he seemed quite satisfied.

18 A glorious day. Asquith Gibson & I went off from the Ashmolean after Gardner's lekker in a motor car. We went to the New College Grind[27] at Bledington. We did the 25 miles in 70 mins. We meant to come home in time to see the Toggers but had to stop for 20 mins to mend a puncture. Our I Togger stayed Head of the River & our II Togger bumped Corpus. So we are Head of the River in spite of all the gloomy prophets.

21 Father came down by the 5.30 to the Mitre. He came to my rooms after Hall.

22 Sunday. F came to both chapels. Before lunch we looked up Tom Parry[28] Charlie Ackers[29] and Fitzwygram. Had tea with Nowell Smith.[30] I gave dinner to F, Charlie Ackers[29] & Tom Parry at the Union.

26 After Hall I went to Gibson's room: he was entertaining Clarke & Asquith to supper. We stayed in there for 4½ hrs! We had a tremendous good rag, steeple-chases, charades, all sorts of things. Got to bed 12.45

March

5 Spooner was elected Warden today. He made a very nice speech. They say that seeing he had tired out his congregation by the length of his sermon, he said 'I see I am addressing beery wenches'

6 Saw in the Daily Mail an account of the foundation of the Bible Society by a meeting including Wilberforce, with Granville Sharp[31] in the chair.

9 Tried to gather some ideas of Logic. In the evening I gave dinner at the Clarendon to Guy Whinyates & Gibson: then we went to the 'Mikado'.

10 Logic colleker in morning. 'Mikado' again in the evening. Most of the afternoon was spent in writing a life of Cicero for Nowell Smith's edification.

11 Biked to Littlemore & Cowley with Gibson. Littlemore has a lovely east window by a disciple of Burne-Jones . . . the faces have more character than B-J's work. I gave a dinner at the Clarendon, then to 'HMS Pinafore'.

12 Dinner with Asquith in his rooms, a sort of send-off to Gibson who departs tomorrow for North Italy. A great assembly in Gibson's room from 10–12. We all took a weeping farewell of him. I left him finally at 12.30.

13 'Yeomen of the Guard' with Hallett.

14 Cicero collection: did a very moderate paper. Up to Eton for night attack. I had to change at Didcot where I caught a train that was very late, before my bike & luggage could get across: I thought it was the regular train & pictured myself turning up for the field-day without a bike. However I got out at Maidenhead & waited till the right train brought my bike. I was introduced to my section of cyclists & proceeded to drill them with the sergeant as prompter, I having not the least notion of any cyclists' drill . . . Afterwards we went back to Somervilles [*housemaster at Eton*] where I had my first whiskey & soda.

17 Came down after 'collections' in Hall. I was not in time to hunt at Frampton.

19 Walked to the Reformatory[32] with F & then to the Cottage. Hylda was very shy at first but afterwards we became great friends.

23 Uley. Mi lent me Prince. Uncle H rode Old Mare. A capital hill day. Found on the Bury, ran to Downham & then back to Westridge: drew Simonshall Firs, found at Twopence near Owlpen & ran to Kingscote.

24   Standish Park. I rode Outlaw.

25   Mi drove me over to Boddington races.

27   Corse. Mi mounted me on Frocester.

28   Nibley. I rode Outlaw, Uncle H his new mare Sappho. He got her from Anstey who is known as Ananias: Uncle H accordingly called her Sapphia but the family said it was an ugly name & too pointed so he promised to call her Sappho.

30   Nympsfield. I rode Pinwire.

31   Kingscote. I rode Outlaw.

April

1   Uncle H drove me to Hill Court to see old Jenner Fust who is 97. We drove Sappho as far as the Prince of Wales. Uncle H then thought she might break down at Hill Court and we should be stranded. So we got a wagonette from the Prince of Wales & drove on. Old Mr Jenner Fust was very cheery. He showed us his old bat inscribed '1829 from B.A. 1831'. It was made as far as I could gather from the stamp, by Dark. It was all in one piece, no splice, the front nearly as round as the back. It was not much broken & not bound at all. He made with it 173 on the Woolwich ground; this was his record score. (In about 1970 I was told that the bat was lost)

3   [*Staying at Banks Fee*] My birthday, 20. We all hunted with the North Cotswold at Norton, Mr Bruce's place. He is going to be High Sheriff this year. F & I called on his son at New College last term. They drank my health.

21   Went to see Cuthbert about my chronic stuffiness of nose. Lionel Darell married Nelly Heathcote at St Peter's Eaton Square

22   Redmarley steeplechase. I biked over. It is about 16 miles, I did it in about 1½ hrs, each way. On arriving home I had some food & then set off on F's bike, Uncle H's which I rode to Redmarley having punctured, to Standish for an entertainment there. First part was a concert: the second a play called 'Change Partners'.

25   'The Casino Girl': most of it was very boring, the only person who was really good was Gabrielle Ray. It is most annoying to see how every dance or exit has been infected by that pestilential cakewalk. Several people including Asquith with the invariable pipe & whiskey & soda came in afterwards.

26   Sunday. Sermon from the Spoo in the morning. Lunch with H. E. Butler the don, Clarke, H. H. Hardy.[33] Tea with Cotton[34] Clarke, Asquith, Montagu.[35] Anthem this evening from the Messiah.

27   Ketha here. We wandered through the House, then down to Magdalen & then to New College. Twenty Club in the evening. I spoke 'on the card' against Brodrick's Army Corps Scheme.

29   Tennis. Hallett & I went out in his canoe: the wind was blowing pretty hard across the Cher & we ran ashore twice. I have been elected to the New College Nomads.[36] Oc & Gibson have started a club called 'Puntsmen & Huntsmen'. Oc is President, Gibson Treasurer & I am the one & only member.

May

1   Played 'fug' soccer.

2 Gibson took me out in his punt to qualify me for secretary to Huntsmen & Puntsmen Club. G lost his pole 3 times. In the evening I went to hear Sir Edward Carson, Solicitor General, speak at the Conservative Clubs' dinner. The clubs are mostly composed of New College men. I met Todd of Malvern Link [*diarist's preparatory school*]. He appeared decently pleased to see me.

7 Wrote to Walter Wethered[37] about Vivian Birchall[38] who is meditating joining the Bucks.

11 Very cold. Twenty Club on Temperance Reform. While eating a piece of cake I became aware that something had run into the back of my mouth, just by the uvula. I examined it by the aid of a glass & could only see a black speck: rather painful but I couldn't get rid of it.

12 Went round to Dr Ormerod this morning. He was still in bed & also is apparently only medical officer & doesn't do odd jobs. So I went across to Mallan who extracted a beetle's leg from my throat. It was about half an inch long: I can't think how it got into the cake.

23 I bought a book of Ruskin's letters to Mary Gladstone & others. It was printed for private circulation but a few copies were put on sale at the Clarendon Press & I got the last.

24 A very good sermon from Rashdall:[39] heretical but attractive.

26 Town for Cunliffe's dance. In the afternoon May & Gracie & I went to the Academy. The dance was at 82 Eaton Square lent by the Sligos.

27 Went with Nelly Gracie & May to the National Gallery. Saw Pierpont Morgan's new Raphael, a very fine one. Rock Sand won the Derby. I came back just in time for the end of the bump supper. We went & cheered under the Warden's windows: he came out & made a splendid speech about the first time we were Head of the River.

June

1 Everything overshadowed by the awful disaster at Eton. Kindersley's house completely gutted & two boys suffocated.

4 All Eton celebrations were of course put off. Kindersley was a perfect hero apparently & utterly disregarded his own safety & belongings.

8 XX Club. 'That England is not sufficiently progressive'. I spoke fourth. My remarks, contrary to their wont, bordered on the intelligent.

11 The Warden's dance. I had twelve dances, one with Miss Spooner.

12 Gibson persuaded me, in spite of impending divvers, to come to Benson in 'Merry Wives of Windsor'. Benson himself was excellent.

13 The dread day of divvers. I got up at 6 & did about three hours work. However it wasn't at all terrible really. I ought to have passed if they only ask for a reasonable standard. I dined with Gibson, his mother & Asquith at the Mitre. We then proceeded to 'Hamlet'. Benson was very good again & Mrs. Benson was excellent when mad & dull when sane.

15 XX Club dinner. HAL Fisher spoke very well, the rest a trifle tedious. We had an 'after' in Peel's rooms. I danced with Eyre, the 'Varsity cox who is about 5ft 4ins tall & looks about twelve. People came in quaint garments for the dancing: Robertson put on a boating zephyr, flannel bags, white shoes & white cotton gloves.

16   Michael down for the night. He had lunch in my room & we then walked round the House. He showed me the alley near Pembroke where Scrimgeour tried to drive the team through. I gave a dinner at the Mitre to Mi. Then we went on to 'The School for Scandal' & supper at the Mitre afterwards. Bed about 1.15.

17   Went for a walk & saw Mi's old rooms. We had a Turkish bath at the Merton baths. It was my first: I liked it. We watched the first ½ hr of the tennis match to settle who was to represent the 'Varsity.

18   Viva voce of divvers. They only made me translate one verse & answer one question. I passed successfully. Poor Oc managed to fail somehow.

22   Gloucestershire v. London County at Gloucester. LCC started badly by losing WG for 8. WG played very badly, hitting his second ball straight back to Roberts who missed it. He then cut Roberts out of the ground into Spa Road. A ball or two later Roberts displaced WG's bail but didn't knock it off: & just afterwards bowled him.

23   WG went on & bowled 8 overs for 12 runs.

29   Town with N. We arrived just in time for a Serpentine party. We had tea at the Mosque in Kensington Gardens. N & I had to hurry to go to Faust.

July

1   F took Helen Lascelles[40] & self to a loan exhibition of Greek sculpture at the Burlington Club. Lunched with Mi at the Wellington. Then Mi took N & me to the Temple Rose Show which was beautiful but hot. Earl's Court party with Egertons. N & I dined with them then I went on to the Alhusens' dance.

4   Lords. N & I went through Turner at the Nat Gallery with the aid of 'Ruskin on Pictures'. In the evening M, N, G & I went to 'Mrs Gorringe's Necklace'

5   St Peter's M & A. In the afternoon they had their anniversary service including 'For all thy saints' & the Hallelujah Chorus

6   G & I to Lords for Gentlemen v. Players. F & K came up & N went down. K, G & I to 'The Admirable Crichton'. Henry Kemble, Gerald du Maurier, H. B. Irving.

7   With F to British Museum where Lawrence Binyon vetted some old prints for us. All were genuine but not valuable. An Albert Durer of about 1495 had been bought by F in Nuremberg. F, K, G & I went to the Contardons' concert which developed into a dance

9   G & I bought some tea things at Liberty's for my rooms. K & I to lunch with the Sebrights. Ivo has just been told that he will not pass his army exam from Cambridge. C, G & saw 'Cousin Kate' at the Haymarket.

10,11   Lords for Eton v. Harrow. C, G & I betook ourselves to Earl's Court where we played about on the chute.

14   Up at 6 & off by the 7.25 to Cirencester to play for Mi's team v. Tim Cripps.[41]

16   Did 2nd Aeneid. Went to Kennels [*at Berkeley*] to look at the new entry. Will Rawle showed us the hounds by twos & threes.

23   Banks Fee for Walter Wynter's team v. Mr Fenwick's team. In the evening we went to a dance at the Wynters who have taken Lower Slaughter Manor House.

24   Great bazaar for the Infirmary. Mi had a farm produce stall & did very well, £15. We helped there & at the Whitminster stall. The Duchess of Beaufort opened it.

29 VWH v. Heythrop match. I played for the former. Stayed at Banks Fee.

August

[*in camp at Shorncliffe*]

7 . . . we got to bed at 4 when the east was just getting light.

8 I got up at 6 to copy out the report. Got a good deal of it done but General went away by the 8.30 so I took it home to finish. It was rather hot & we were 10 in a 2nd class carriage. I slept a lot . . .

11 The great day. Godman's XI v. Baker's XI at Banks Fee. Mrs Godman forgot to order the brake to come to Broadwell to fetch us. We had begun a game of croquet, Fred Cripps & Evelyn Wynter v. Violet W & self. They were winning easily when Johnny Godman[42] fetched us. Ketha & Gracie came up by the 12.5. Mrs Godman met them in her trap in which she sent on Tim Cripps & Clark as they were playing. She then saw Lady Elcho coming to the station in a motor & asked if it might bring sisters up to the ground. It turned out to be Mr Balfour's [see Eton note 40] but he was most polite & tucked them all into it & sent them off. He was on his way to Hatfield of course.

[*The score card for this match is on p. 32*]

27 Our garden party. Mi & I marked out 3 croquet grounds, 2 on the cricket ground & one on the Round. The rain started about 3 & continued almost incessantly. However 133 people came & seemed to enjoy themselves. We had the Artillery band who played very well. Carpenter excelled herself in the tea.

28 Cub-hunting at Whitminster. I rode Outlaw. Ben Browne[43] walked to the meet from Piers Court starting at 4 am.

September

4 In the afternoon all the sisters & self went to tea with Sarah (nurserymaid who married Jim Smith)

5 Early this morning F & Mi left for a Dairy Conference in Brussels. It is the first time Mi has been abroad.

8 May & I to Wolverley, Eric Knight's place. Eric's children are Freddy aged 3 and Dicky aged 2. [*The latter plays a prominent part in later diaries*]

9 Eric took us to see Mr Tomkinson's collection of Japanese things. He is a Kidder-minster carpet man & had various sons at Eton & Winchester. I knew FMT at Eton. He showed us first his collection of miniatures: Evelyn the diarist, Charles I and Charlotte Corday, which had belonged to the first Napoleon. Then he showed us the books: 'Horae' bought from Mrs A. Severn with Ruskin's Ex Libris. R used to say the illustrations were by Mantegna. The first three folios of Shakespeare, several Caxtons & Kelmscotts. Then the Japanese things: workmanship simply marvellous, carving & hammering of cold iron being miraculous.

10 May & I started early for Hereford. We had seats in the north transept for the 'Dream of Gerontius' Elgar & 'Voces Clamantium' Parry[44] 'The Dream' was very fine indeed. Sir Hubert's was more popular & easier to listen to. We lunched at the Deanery. Home in the evening.

212

J. Godman's XI

Batsman	First innings		Second innings	
Capt O. Tritton.	not out	36	c M. Baker b T. Cripps	6
S.D.R. Byass.	c M. Baker b F.Cripps	4	b Bland	0
Rev A.H. Watson	c A. Baker b F.Cripps	9	c M. Baker b Bland	0
R. Low	c Nash b T. Cripps	4	not out	29
Rev S.W.B. Holbrook	b T. Cripps	0	b T. Cripps	13
J. Wynter	c Dennison b Nash	1	c F. Cripps b T. Cripps	5
J.C. Tritton	b T. Cripps	14	b Bland	1
J. Godman.	c M. Baker b Bland	5	c F. Cripps b T. Cripps	01
L.J. Tritton.	c & b F. Cripps	6	b T. Cripps	0
W. Wynter.	c & b T. Cripps	0	b Bland	0
Rev W. Verney	c T. Cripps b F. Cripps	2	b T. Cripps	2
	b6 n-b4	10	b1 l-b.	2
		91		**59**

1-$\frac{10}{3}$ 2-$\frac{24}{5}$ 3-$\frac{29}{9}$ 4-$\frac{37}{17}$ 5-$\frac{41}{27}$ 6-$\frac{64}{28}$ 7-$\frac{75}{35}$ 8-$\frac{83}{35}$ 9-$\frac{86}{49}$

M. Baker's XI

Batsman	First innings		Second innings	
M.G.L. Baker.	c & b Holbrook	0	run out	15
S.C. Dennison.	c Holbrook b Watson	11	b Holbrook	1
E.T. Cripps.	c J. Tritton b Holbrook	8	b Holbrook	0
W.W. Nash.	b Holbrook	15	c Watson b Byass	3
F.W. Cripps	b Low	8		
m. more	b Holbrook	0		
J.H. Birch.	lbw b Watson	5	b Watson	13
A. Bland.	c O. Tritton b Holbrook	5	b Byass	8
a.B.L. Baker.	not out	5	b Holbrook	4
J.P.H. Clark	c O. Tritton b Holbrook	2	not out	5
G. Cunninghame.	b Holbrook	1	not out	4
	l-b 2	2	b2 n-b1	3
		62	(for 7 wkts)	**46**

1-$\frac{0}{9}$ 2-$\frac{12}{14}$ 3-$\frac{33}{14}$ 4-$\frac{44}{19}$ 5-$\frac{44}{24}$ 6-$\frac{48}{25}$ 7-$\frac{53}{41}$ 8-55 9-57

M. Baker's XI bowling.

	O.	M.	R.	W.		O.	M.	R.	W.
F.W. Cripps.	16.1	6	20	4					
A. Bland.	12	2	27	1		12	3	26	4
E.T. Cripps.	9	0	27	4		11.2	1	31	6
W. Nash	4	0	11	1					

J. Godman's XI bowling.

	O.	M.	R.	W.		O.	M.	R.	W.
S. Holbrook.	17	5	25	7		6	0	16	3
A. Watson.	12	2	32	2		3	0	9	1
R. Low	4	2	3	1					
d. Byass						8	0	16	1
J. Wynter						1	0	2	0

'The great day,' Godman's v. Baker's team at Banks Fee, August 11, 1903

11 Nelly & I to Hereford for 'Messiah'. The artists showed great want of restraint in certain passages, making them more theatrical by singing penultimate notes high when they were written low.

27 Biked to Gloucester. Bishop Mitchison[45] preached & we had 'Give thanks O Israel'. The voluntaries were Toccata in C, Arne & Andante from the Symphony in C minor, Beethoven. The three services I have been to lately in the Cathedral have impressed me with the fact that the choir boys want a sound smacking all round. They loll about & giggle & slam their books & don't half sing.

October

8 Had to bike to Stroud to do my class firing once more as I have only done the new system & the Adjutant says I must do the old one as well. It poured all afternoon & though I kept fairly dry the light was beastly. I only got 55 marks out of possible 112.

9 Col. Wingate & Mrs came[46]

14 K, N & self came to Cottage. F. G & May to Lampern[47] owing to drains being completely altered at Court.

15 Went up to pack at the Court. Blanchie took 89 degrees out of the rain gauge for the last 24 hours.

17 Odyssey colleker

22 Went to the Union debate 'That this House would welcome Mr Chamberlain's scheme for Preferential Tariffs'. W. Temple[48] of Balliol spoke third; he was very amusing & original.

November

4 Hall & Whitworth invited me to join a new dining club, the Comus Club. To dine once or twice a term but not to have any uniform.

10 OE dinner at Taphouses Rooms. About 180 there. We drank King & Floreat Etona.

13 Greek Sculpture almost all day. Did a paper for Gardner on 'Gods on the Parthenon Frieze'. Went to a very interesting lecture by Evans[49] on his excavations at Cnossos in Crete.

14 Conservative dinner at the Randolph organised by the United Club of London. Principal guest was Lord Percy the new Under Secretary for Foreign Affairs. The toast of His Majesty's Ministers was proposed by one Remnant MP. 'The University' was proposed by W. W. Grantham who described Gavin Simonds as a great man at Mods & a moderate man at Greats. Simonds replied rather well but took a very gloomy view of the Conservative cause at Oxford.

16 At a public meeting on Fiscal Reform Winston Churchill who was quite unexpected & had to speak ex tempore has a very curious lisping delivery & a trick of suddenly opening his eyes wide. He was good & conciliatory.

18 Beagles. Very long run, 45 mins without a check. I caught the brake that was going home early to get back for the first dinner of the Comus Club. All the members were present: it was a great success.

21 Down to Eton for Old Boy. I played corner. The House was captained by Jock Lyon.[50] We stopped with the score a goal & two rouges to three rouges in favour of

Old Boys . . . the rest of us went by turns to wish my tutor goodbye & by saying we were not going till 9.30 rushed him for dinner, quite contrary to his intentions.

December

3   'E' Coy dinner at Slough. I stayed too late for the 9 o'clock train . . . & arrived back at 2.30. Rang & knocked till I roused Honey . . .

4   Warden sent for me. I had to explain what he wanted me for as he had quite forgotten. He was very jolly & said he thought he could get me off.

9   Warden writes

> Dear Lloyd Baker
>> We were glad under the circumstances to remit the fine
> you had incurred.
>> Believe me, yrs truly
> W. A. Spooner

Can you come & have some tea with us between five & six next Sunday evening?

13 Sunday. Tea with the Warden. Only two or three men I knew were there: no-one to announce me, everybody very shy. I talked to Mrs Spooner & escaped as soon as possible.

20 Read Murray's[51] translation of 'The Frogs' to Nelly.

25 . . . I gave Grandmama a Calendar . . . Hylda a picture book & Olive a wooden horse. She takes to horses more than Hylda does & comes & rides on the old rocking horse every morning.

30 Hylda's party. Great fun. Hylda consented to dance at last & then wouldn't leave off at all.

31 Shooting round Hawklow in the morning . . . Rent dinner in the afternoon. In the evening I chaperoned May to a Fancy Dress ball at Shire Hall. May helped to judge the childrens' cake walk & the grown up dresses. The children, all girls, made the cake walk into a quite fairly graceful dance but very unoriginal.

1904

January

3   I took Mi's boys in Sunday School . . . reading 'England's Roll of Glory'.

7   Meet here as usual. [*Berkeley Hunt meets at Hardwicke on the day of the Gloucester Ball*] I rode Spirit, one of Uncle H's new ones. Spirit carried me splendidly but we had a fall below Monkshill. I fell on my nose & bent the vomer bone. Gloucester Ball in the evening. It was very good but we only had old Iff's brother who is accurate but not exhilarating. At the ball Cuthbert put the cartilage that was sticking up in place, in the supper room, to the great surprise of the waiters. Further operations postponed until tomorrow.

8   Spent most of the day getting our new fire engine to work. In the afternoon I went in to Cuthbert who doctored my nose. The vomer was bent over to my left: he bent it straight & put in a plug of flannel to support it.

12   Fancy dress dance. I went in one of the old court suits, with wig, rather a success. The girls were all domino & before 11.30 there was no introducing so I got little dancing. Afterwards I got on much better.

13   I made another visit to Cuthbert. He pushed a fresh plug far up my left nostril, painful at the time but only uncomfortable afterwards.

15   Sunday School treat in the afternoon, tremendous fun. The children enjoyed themselves greatly.

16   Meet at Woodford. I rode Pinwire. We had a nice run up to the top of Cam pitch . . . many people fell, Michael & Ketha. Tom Matthews had a rather bad fall.[52] Uncle Bryan came.[53] I haven't seen him for more than 2 minutes together for years. He's very interesting & amusing & we talk Greek sculpture.

17   Cuthbert took the plug out & finally finished with my nose. It is now almost straighter than it was before the accident.

19   To Highgrove,[54] the Mitchells, for Tetbury ball at the White Hart [*now the Snooty Fox*]. The band was Iff's . . . they had 8 men for a rather small room & were much too loud.

20   I had to ride to Tetbury to catch the train to Cheltenham, to the George Witts'.[55] There were in the house Mr, Mrs & Sybil Witts, a Miss F. Witts from Stow & a Miss Vavasour, daughter of Mrs Witts. The ball was in the new Town Hall at Cheltenham which has just been built by Waller.[56] It's a fine though distinctly municipal building. The floor is excellent. The band was Godfrey Holbech. He was at Eton, as was a brother in my time.

21   To Tate's Hotel, Cheltenham, where I met F K & C & Charles Prevost[57] for the Ratcliffs' ball at Southam.[58]

23   [*At Oxford*] An assemblage to discuss a coming of age present to Scrimgeour. Great dispute on relative merits of 'Tantalus', cigarette box, ditto case or simply silver box, claret jug, or decanter. Discussion removed to my rooms continued till 12.30.

26   Scrimgeour's 21st birthday. He chose the tantalus. I was to have gone to dinner with him but his people descended on him & took him home. His would-be guests dined together at the Clarendon.

February

9   Somebody (Convocation?) has abolished Greek for Smalls . . . Blackwells had in their window a number of old editions of the classics and an inscription 'Morituri te salutant'.

11   Coffee at 10 in my room. It was meant to be one of the short intervals of relaxation that we Mods men take during the evening. It developed into a most delightful rag . . . no damage done.

12   Breakfast with Joseph the don. Also there Mouse & 2 Eton freshers, Soends & Coventry. The former I knew fairly well at Eton, the latter is a brother of Coventry of Jameson Raid.

13   Beagles & blizzards at Cuddesden. It's almost all plough there. The wind was too high for there to be much scent. Dinner at the Clarendon. Monty rode a bicycle all round the coffee room in amongst the tables. We ragged about a good deal outside & inside College but got to bed by 12.30.

24   Great Bump Supper. I sat at a table with all the Comus Club except those that were rowing, who of course had separate tables.

27   Carron & Ben gave a combined twenty-firster at the Randolph. We had most tremendous fun. I gave Ben Clough's works.

March

5   'Patience' matinee: 'Yeoman of the Guard' in the evening. Nancy Freyne forgot her words: in the encore Scott Russell pointedly impressed them on her; everyone laughed & clapped.

8   I tried to read the Georgics but my eyes began to ache so I walked to Littlemore & saw the church window once more. Played fug soccer. During the day I managed Georgics II & III.

9   Bags announced that Greek plays were to be tomorrow afternoon. Consternation tempered by incredulity. The Moderator admitted the soft impeachment – 'hinc illa lacrimae'. However Ben, Carron, Buller & I went for a great drive in a motor to Henley & Marlow. We had an absolutely splendid day.

10   Mods! 9.30 l. Demo [*Demosthenes*] & Homer. I did a poor paper but the pieces were easier than I had hoped for. 2. Greek plays. They set rather bad gobbets ie not very difficult & therefore just the ones one hadn't got up. Did a fair paper. Everybody in tremendous form: the actual crisis & the beautiful weather have bucked us all up.

11   Virgil & Cicero. Did fairly well in Virgil & very moderately in Cicero. Unseen: did fairly

12   9.30 l. Latin Verse, moderate. 2. Aristophanes, the best I've done so far

13   Sunday. Did Horace.

14   9.30 Latin Prose, fair.

15   9.30 Greek Prose, poor. 2. Horace, fairly good.

16   General Paper, very hard & I did a poor paper

17   Logic, poor

18   Sculpture. I did a very fair paper I think. In the evening Nowell, Butler & Matheson gave a dinner to Mods people in Senior Common Room as per plan

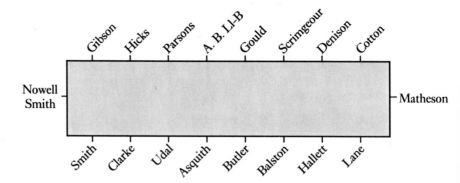

We adjourned to Butler's room afterwards & had a very good time. About 11.30 we went & danced in Mouse's room.

20 Sunday. Today the anthem was 'O rest in the Lord'. Most appropriate to Mods.

31 To Town to meet Walter Wethered. I bought a pair of Zeiss no. 8 field glasses, Grandmama's birthday present. (They cost about £6 & were still in use at the Front, Oct '17, cleaned in 1940 & used in Home Guard, 1959 cricket etc., & in 1975 & 1979). Then went to Tate Gallery & looked particularly at Watts with the help of Cook's handbook. At 5 I went to the Automobile Club, 219 Piccadilly, & found Walter, Cluckie & the Kid. We dined there, joined by Capt. Johnson of the Hampshires & Lieut. Easton of 26th Middlesex, a most objectionable bounder. We discussed plans for manoeuvres until 5th April.

April

3 Easter Day & my 21st birthday. We had Church Parade & a very good sermon of 4½ mins. At mess Walter, Cluckie, Hammy[59] & others drank my health.

11 Wilfrid Browne came to lunch.[60] Full of horses as usual.

12 Owlpen on Pinwire. We saw Father who has gone up to Lampern. He's not been very well & wants a change & rest.

18 Boxwell with the Duke [*of Beaufort*] on Outlaw. We went to the Gists. Lord Fitzhardinge was out. He was in great form. He presented Major Gist with a spring of myrtle from Miss Trotter to comfort the Major because 'Mabel wasn't out'.

19 In Fry's magazine for May there is an article by Warre Illustrated by Eton photos. One of these is officers & sergeants in 1902 in which I figure: also Vivian Birchall & Harold Butler.

21 Bazaar at the school for the church restoration [*Hardwicke*]. We cleared about £50. I framed some pictures from odd numbers of Burlington, Connoisseur etc. in some old frames I had at Eton. They sold very well.

22 Up to 'Varsity. Travelled with Vivian Birchall. Churchill the porter greeted me with the news that I have got a Third in Mods. I am well satisfied as it is a pretty good Third & so many good people have got a Second, eg. Mouse, Ben, Buller.

26 Tennis. To 'Floradora'. To a lecture by Myres on the Homeric Age with special reference to modern discoveries.

30 Tennis. Dined at the Clarendon, then went to 'Floradora' again. Carron got chucked out for practically nothing, as did Roger Hall. Everyone most awfully sick.

May

1 Lunch party on the Cher. Monty gave the lunch. Whitty Mouse & self in canoe. 7 others in punts. Luncheon above Marsden, very jolly. Tea at the Union. Twenty Club 'That this House would welcome the abolition of workhouses'. I had been rushed to speak & didn't take long in supporting the motion. Poor Carron & Roger got fined £5 & gated for half the term by the Proggins.[61]

3 . . . Whitty & I went to the pit to hear Ellen Terry & company in 'Much Ado' She was quite wonderful. Her voice is extraordinarily flexible & clear.

4 Gussie gave me a dinner at OUDS & we proceeded to hear Ellen Terry & Co.

7–27 Theatres & dinners: XX Club & cricket. In one match Jowett, later Lord Chancellor bowled very mechanically.

28 Father came by the 8.30. He stays at Pembroke. Bp. Mitchison is away, however we had supper at Pembroke & much talk of everybody. Edward Lyttelton[62] was just going when we came. F & he had a little talk. Lyttelton said that his eldest girl is doing Latin verses 'better ones than Michael ever did for me'.

29 F lunched with me, also Gibby. We went to call on various people but only Mrs Temple was in.[63] F dined in Hall at Pembroke. I went to the Balliol concert. Anthem: Hallelujah Chorus.

June

2 Roger Hall & Whitty's twenty-firster at the Randolph

4 To Eton for IInd (New College) v. Eton II. I hit a four & a single off Methuen[64] & a three off Jock Lyon. For lunch we all scattered to the different houses. Jock took Parr & self to my tutor's. Some relation of Mrs W-T had died so there was no big lunch. Neither my tutor nor Mrs were very cheerful.

5 My lunch up the Cher, horrible situation at 12 o'clock – no punts! However we managed to borrow. 9 came.

12 Great Common Room in the evening. Introduction of Gibby who has just been elected Steward for next year.

13 Ben gave me 'The Florentine and the Venetian Painters of the Renaissance' by Berenson in 2 volumes. XX Club dinner at the Clarendon. Very many toasts.

14 Owing to people being in for 'Schools' etc. I squeezed into the first eleven v. Malvern College.

22 Went to Monty for the Winchester match. He lives at South Stoneham House, Hampshire. Sir Samuel & all the family are up in Town so Monty, Buller & I had the house to ourselves. It's a very nice house with beautiful gardens down to the Itchen. We had a magnificent seven course dinner, all Jewish food.

23 We rowed up the Itchen, then paddled & punted & shoved & pushed up a backwater. After dinner we trained to Southampton & went to the Royal Palace of Varieties.

24 Monty went away by an early train for Commemoration at Clifton. Buller & I went to the Winchester v. Eton match. I just waited to see the end then drove off to catch the 6.18. I wired to say when I would arrive [*at Gloucester*] but there was nothing at 11.15. I went to the Bell, they had heard nothing & I concluded that the carriage would meet the 12.26. However no carriage. I went to the Wellington & Gloucester hotels which were still open but neither could lend me a bike. I asked the policeman at the Cross & while I was talking to him the Inspector came up & lent me his, a beautiful machine. I got home about 1.45 a.m.

26 It appears that Ketha sent me a card to say they could not meet me which must have taken a day & a half to get to Stoneham. In the afternoon I drove May to the Cathedral service & took back the Inspector's bike.

29 To Ampney. Michael's XI v. Tim Cripps'.[65] We had lunch at the house. Hilda Cripps & baby boy came & looked on, also Mrs Fred & her boy & girl. It was about the most exciting match I've ever played in & a very sporting finish.

July

3 St Peter's in the morning, Nat Gallery in afternoon where I discovered several pictures I had never noticed before, notably Pisarro's Vision of St Eustace.

5 Nelly & I to His Majesty's for a performance for the British Opthalmic Hospital at Jerusalem. Tree's make-up as Falstaff was wonderful. Kubelik was amazing doing anything he liked with his violin. Albani not at her best.

7 I went to Hertford House . . . I had been there a few years ago, up for short leave with Chamberlain [*3.11.1900*] . . . disappointed to find only one Corot & no Millet. I liked the Meissoniers very much. I loafed in Bumpus' & bought some pictures at Mansells.

12 I went down by the 5.50 train to do a drill at Marlow. Frank & Walter Wethered there. The Colonel[66] turned up to inspect the company so Walter & I did nothing but look on. Gilbey has heard a rumour that Major Willy Grenfell is going to be offered Canada when Minto gives up. Frank Wethered gave me dinner. I caught the 9.20 from Marlow & got to Town by 10.47 & then proceeded to dress & go to Major Paynter's ball at the Hyde Park Hotel. It was a nice ball & well done but too many men. A great many Eton & Oxford men there whom I knew or half knew.

13 I slept till 12 o'clock & then went to the British Museum armed with E. T. Cook's handbook. In the evening Clare & I went to see 'Lady Flirt'. Cyril Maude was wonderful as the little French Count, a little beast.

14 I went to the Victoria & Albert to see the Ionides collection which has been left to the Museum. It includes several delightful Millets.

15 British Museum, looking at vases. My people went on to Syon garden party. Clare & I consoled ourselves with Earl's Court. The water chute was nice & empty. The grotto of Capri, late Canton River, vice Styx, was good fun. I took Clare to 'The Duke of Killiecrankie'. It was quite as amusing second time round.

19 Agricultural show at Gloucester. Mi won a second prize in Hunters over 5 years old. He showed Serge. The Beachs[67] were there very jubilant because Ellis has a daughter, Rachel.

24 London boys who are staying at Madam's End [*a farm on the estate*] came up for tea: very jolly & frightfully sharp.

30 To camp at Sway.

August

1 Lce.Cpl. Walter of Wolverton was run over by a motor driven by a lady. The motor passed right over his body & the occupants never turned to see what had happened. No bones were broken due to Walter's superb physique.

3 Subaltern for the day. Pelting rain all the morning. We sweated to get everything into order against the visit of Maj. Gen. Montgomery RA CB etc. When he came he rushed hastily round the outside edge, praised the kitchen & didn't see the inside of a single tent. The battalion came in thoroughly sopped.

22 House party at Escrick.[68] I was received by Helen Lascelles. Billiards with Miss Stewart Wortley, daughter of MP. Later, Jack Stewart Wortley of the Warwickshires came in.

25   Races with Bertie Grosvenor. I pleased myself by picking the winner of the Great Yorkshire Stakes out, by his looks. Castello, 100 to 8. Racing both days was very amusing though disastrous to backers. It was the first flat racing I had seen.

29   Jack & Miss S-W, Helen & Miss Lindsay trained to York & we went to the Minster. We found our way to the Crypt & Chapter House. There are several pieces of columns in the crypt with patterns deeply incised; I don't remember anything of the kind before.

September

3   Winifred, Violet & Willie Orde came; the latter turned up about 9 o'clock, only just arrived from Norway [*for the Music Festival*].

4   Opening service in the Cathedral. Willie & I had great times with a miniature score of the Brahms symphony, as we did not know they were only going to play the last two movements: we were however in at the death.

6   The best performance of 'Elijah' that I've heard. Ffrancon Davies, bass, magnificent & looked the part, sang without book. Albani better than 3 and 6 years ago owing to a visit to S. Africa. Sobrino didn't turn up owing to some misunderstanding: Daisy Beach not to be found, so the boy[69] was hauled down to sing. John Coates, tenor, has a fine voice but was unsympathetic. I lunched at Bishop Mitchison's. Tea at Maggie Bowers.[70]

7   Parsifal prelude was quite divine. 'The Time-Spirit' was noisy & very secular, 'The Organ Concerto' was supposed to represent a midnight meditation on the Cathedral organ. Sir Hubert's thing was very good [*'The Love that casteth out fear'*]. It was a little difficult to follow the sequence of thought in the words. The Brahms' 'Requiem' was of course lovely: soloists very good [*listed*] Helen Lascelles at Cottage. Walked there in the evening to get photos of York. Miss Stewart-Wortley & J S-W sent me a photo each of the Minster.

8   'The Apostles' by Edward Elgar who conducted was perfectly glorious. Plunkett-Greene as Judas was inaudible on the lowest notes & rather too melodramatic. Whole work more of an opera than an oratorio.

9   'Messiah'. Not such a good performance as 'Elijah'. Ffrancon-Davies sang everything very softly & seemed rather played out . . . trumpet was brought down to stand by conductor & was very successful. Cuts unnecessarily large. Walked over to Cottage after tea to see Helen Lascelles, she accompanied me back as far as the Long Orchard.

10   Party dispersed. Ordes started by the 9 o'clock train in order to arrive at Nunneykirk in time to take choir paractice!

12   F M & N start abroad aiming at Rome by easy stages. Uncle H also starts tour of inspection of various hunts.

13   Tennis at Tidswells. [*list of players & partners, as usual*] Court was soft & slow, badly wants rolling: play rather poor. Blanche[71] very pretty.

19   Cheverells. Mi B K & self. In Town went to Hatchards where bought books on painting & on to the Stores for hat irons.

20   Drive to Gaddesden Hoo which is to be sold tomorrow. Ramshackle old place, would cost an enormous lot to put in order. Thence to Whipsnade to see beautiful view from Chilterns.

23   Home via London. Hatchards again where I bought 'Six Lectures on Painting' by Clausen which Blanchie afterwards made a present.

26   Cottage to see Olive, just 2, who has a rash: there is not much wrong with her judging by her spirits. She speaks of me as 'Mr Arthur'. She suddenly announced she was going to say her prayers, sang 'Onward Kissy Sojers' & other hymns & ended up with Georgy-Porgy.

October

3   Coming out of Gloucester I found a man who had fallen from a bullock cart on to the road. Unconscious, head & neck bleeding. Crowd about 12. Nobody has any plan. Finally I put man, my bike & self in bullock cart already occupied by 2 sheep and start to Infirmary. *On dit* that the linch pin is out of the wheel: delay while piece of metal is brought from the gas works. Then I drive bullock cart to Infirmary, slow but majestic. Man revives & expresses desire to 'go home'. Cart belongs to Joe Vick of Quedgeley, horse to Sir Lionel Darell, man & sheep to Turner of Arlingham. I forced him most unwillingly to leave his cart & enter Infirmary: I go to Albion & leave cart & message for Vick & Turner. Return to find man progressing favourably.

6   Thucydides most of the day. Thunderstruck on looking at the score of 'The Runaway Girl' that the part of Leonello the head of troupe of musicians was taken by John Coates. I always said he was a Christy Minstrel. From the Gaiety to the Cathedral!

7   Thucydides again. Slimbridge concert. Miss Mabel Clifford sang several times.

14   Up to 'Varsity. Everything much as usual except rooms which have changed hands considerably. Monty is opposite me. [*ie on the diarist's staircase; a diagram of the old & new arrangement is given*]

16   Sermon from Spooner. Anthem in evening 'Remember now thy Creator'. Jock Lyon of my tutor's is up, also Carron's brother.

17   Was elected treasurer of XX Club.

21   Mouse & I to Hinskey after Joseph's lecture to try & get instruction from Sherlock [*a golf professional*]. Biking down road leading to club house suddenly came on a hansom round the corner. Jammed on front brake as left hand was engaged: result, turned somersault into road. No damage except a little scraping & bruising. Sherlock was engaged so we played 3 holes. After Hall, Rashdall's informal talk. About 30 there. Subject 'How far is the belief in Immortality necessary to Morality or Religion'. [*exhaustive analysis & criticism by diarist*]

24   First news of the 'Baltic Outrage'. Trawlers off Dogger Bank fired on by the Baltic fleet. Seems pretty serious.

28   Lesson from Sherlock at Hinskey. He coaches well. Showed me how to cure slicing . . . instruction with driver, mashie & lofter. He was rather encouraging.

November

10   Great event at 7.45. Buller & I gave a twenty-firster at Randolph. A good evening. Gibby proposed our health. I proposed beagles & Gibby, Buller the soccer team, Denny the Twenty Club. Dancing in big room afterwards. On return to College Roger hurled plate through my window & Gore broke a lamp. Roger also broke Rickard's window. Otherwise no damage done & a great success.

11   I went to Nowell Smith to get leave to go to Old Boy on Saturday. Long talk about last night. He hummed & hawed as usual. I accepted responsibility for damage: he exonerated me personally: we parted friends: he gave me leave all right.

12   To Eton for Old Boy. Very jolly meeting people again. We were beaten by 2 rouges to O. Conspicuous of our house were Alec & Fergus Lyon.

13   Buller & I discussed twenty firster bill which has made its appearance: slight item of £10.18.0. for damages, including an immense quantity of glass. Bill for actual dinner & wine quite moderate.

14   Buller & I protested against Randolph bill, pointed out that glass was put down in round figures: waiter admitted to having calculated from fragments. I imagine stem & bowl counted as two glasses! Union at 5. Roseberry [sic] unveiling bust of Salisbury. He was very clear, gave a concise appreciation of Salisbury.

21   Hinksey to buy a new brassey. Sherlock however told me my present one was exactly right & that I only needed practice.

December

5   Visitors' debate at XX Club 'That this House disapproves of the Socialistic tendencies of modern politics'. Best visitors' debate we've had in my time. President of Union was not good: best were Livingstone, Corpus don & member of XX Club, & A. E. Zimmern[72] New Coll don, old member of XX Club. Mouse also spoke.

7   Newly founded Housman Club met in Whitty's rooms. As constituted at present it consists of T. Balston, President: Committee: R. Page,[73] Treasurer: ABLIB, M. B. Hallett who couldn't come: G. A. Whitworth, Secretary.

12   Down . . . First to Pantheon, Oxford Street. Gilbey's office, for meeting of Officers. Christmas shopping, including fur coat, Grandmama's present to me, at International Fur Store, Regent Street.

13   Up to the Pratts at Great Rissington for the Stow ball. Banks Fee had a large party. Miss Violet Wynter more beautiful than ever. Lady Celia Milnes is very nice: we talked of Fitzgerald, her first cousin, whom she knows very well.

20   Meeting in the school [*at Hardwicke*] addressed by Mickey Beach[74] the new Conservative candidate. F in the chair. Mickey spoke very well, principally on South African war, Chinese labour in SA & fiscal reform. He follows Balfour to Retaliation but not Chamberlain to Protection. The audience was enthusiastic. Plenty of farmers. Sir William Guise Vernon of the Bacchus, G. Witts, Mr Sinclair of Hempsted, Canon Nash, Cecil de Winton, Uncle H, Col. Curtis Hayward, Mi, Col. Metford.

21   Cirencester to try on some clothes at Davis'. Lunch at Kings Head. Had to wait ¾ hr at Kemble, train late owing to fog.

23   Very foggy so gave up Ledbury & went to Lionel Darell's beagles at Arlingham.

24   Kennels on Pinwire. Rawle [*huntsman*] very unwilling to let hounds go out because of frost. However we hunted at 12. Nice gallop & then some muddling, & the Old Man stopped us at Berkeley Heath at 2.0: he said fog was too bad but presumably he meant frost.

25   Service M & E. Present giving after supper. Received musquash & beaver coat from Grandmama, sheared rabbit gloves from Mi & B. Reinach's 'Story of Art through

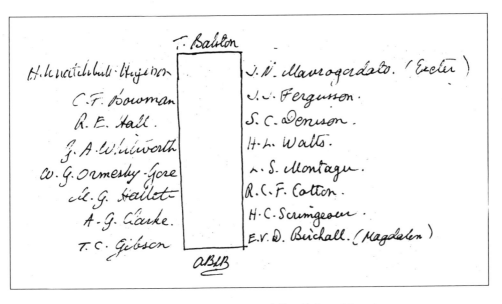

Seating plan for the shared twenty-firster with Tom Balston, November 10, 1904

the Ages' from M K C N & G. Gave Turner calendar to Grandmama, share of cabinet to F, & books to sisters & Hylda. Cockatoo to Olive.

29   Tortworth on Pinwire. Robeson[75] out. We discussed the headmastership at Eton. He says Rawlins would be popular with the dons: Benson also but would introduce many reforms. Sydney James too bad mannered. Lyttelton quite a good chance, not nearly so 'faddy' as represented. Ford not popular with the dons. Everyone agreed that some changes are needed: too many subjects taught.

30   In the afternoon we heard hounds at the back of the house. Biked to Arklow but could see nothing. Later we heard that the Ledbury had crossed the river, Carneby Fisher & his whip crossed in a boat, swimming their horses alongside. Don Vick & another farmer joined in on this side.

1905

January

3   Party for Darells' & Gloucester balls came . . . Edric Kingscote,[76] a nice towzley haired person . . . Inigo Thomas an architect. Kingscote not over intelligent but takes a cheery view of life. I talk about St Marks & architecture in general to Thomas: he very soon guessed I had been reading Ruskin. He told me the true cause of the fall of the Campanile [*in Venice*] ie the uric acid eating away the mortar on each landing. Darells' ball: the Yeomanry band, not very good. Floor excellent. Very great fun, not a single bad partner. Bed at 5.

7   Kennels on Outlaw: not so fresh as usual. Uncle H took May & self to gruel at Eastwood.[77] The first time I had been inside it: everything very handsome, but rather too many plants & china fruits.

[Facsimile of a handwritten ball programme:]

284   Dec 13.   **Stow Ball.**

1	Valse 1001 Nights	Miss Pratt (eldest)	poor dancer.
2	„ Caressante –		
3	Polka My Little Topsy	Claudie Tritton.	Banks Fee.
4	Valse Down the Vale	Miss Skeen	
5	Lancers The Orchid	Miss Witts (Sybil)	good sett.
6	Valse Beautiful Lilies.	Miss Hermione Wynter	see p 279. introduced Lady C.C. Miln.
7	„ Schatz	Miss Waller (?)	v. good
8	Two Step Mosquito's Parade	Lady Celia Crewe Milnes.	1st cousin of Fitzgeralds: welcomed him thoroughly. v nice v good dance.
9	Valse Choristers	Miss Pratt (younger)	better dancer than sister
10	„ Enchantée	Miss Pratt (elder)	
1	Valse Rosen aus dem Süden	„ : Supper	
2	Polka Wandrin' Walter	„	
3	Valse Veronique		
11	Lancers Earl's Girl		
12	Valse Eton Boating Song	Lady Celia Crewe Milnes.	v good.
13	„ Wein, Weib and Gesang.	Mrs Arnold Butler.	v good
14	Barn Dance First Love	Miss Hankey	
15	Valse Contrasse.	Miss St	
16	Two Step Hiawatha.	Miss Witts (Stow)	
17	Valse Frau Luna.	Miss Violet Wynter	she had torn her dress so we sat out: staying at Banks Fee.
18	„ Frou-Frou.		
19	„ Love's Secret.	Miss Pratt (younger)	
20	Galop Royal Ascot. Post Horn.		
21	Valse. Frau Luna (?)	Miss May Verney	v. good.

Ball programme at Stow on the Wold, December 13, 1904

8   Tea at the Cottage. Olive had a choking fit: Blanchie, Bussell & self held her upside down & shook her etc. & got her right: all three of us very frightened as Olive grew quite stiff & black in the face. Ten minutes afterwards she was as cheery as anything.

. . . Grandmama had an attack of breathlessness last night and didn't go to church: better in afternoon.

9   Grandmama died this morning at 7: heart failure. She rang her bell for Boles who fetched Uncle H. He fetched Ketha & Father: she coughed for a little while & then became unconscious. She had no pain the whole time & passed off quite quietly. Cuthbert had been sent for & came about 8. He said he could have done nothing if he had been there.

12   Said goodbye to Grandmama: she looked very peaceful & younger. Cousin Benjie came.

13   Grandmama's funeral: glorious day: frost, sudden mist came down about 9.30 but went an hour later. Cloudless sunshine & not cold. The wreaths entirely covered the bier. Reformatory boys in their working suits with black bands lined the paths. Canon Nash took the first part of the service, cousin Charlie & cousin Bevil the second.

14   Took wreaths to the Workhouse: the first time I had been inside it. We saw the old men & old women & then the tramps breaking stones.

February

5   Lunch with Rashdall: also there Nowell Smith. Walk with Rasher to Port Meadow. Discussed all ecclesiastical subjects I could think of including Gloucester See coupled with the name of Archdeacon Sinclair, the appeal to the first six centuries, the Bishop of London's accounts, the Archbishop of Canterbury's diplomacy etc.

9   C. J. Holmes[78] had invited anyone to come & see him at the Ashmolean the day after his lekkers. I persuaded Whitty to come. Holmes started by showing us the Chinese bronzes: we eventually spent two hours with him: he took us all round the pictures with Macdonald, Ruskin's drawing master. Incidentally told us of his only meeting with Ruskin. Holmes was about 12 at the time: rowed with his brother across the lake & landed on the Coniston side: pulled in a night line to see if there was anything on it. Hearing steps threw it back into the lake. Enter Ruskin, whether he had seen the deed or merely regarded them as trespassers on the sacred shore is not known: anyway he addressed them as they hastily put out from shore 'in the most fearful language' & they departed under his curse. Historic meeting of two Slade Professors!

10   I'm progged for the first time! Met Blagdon of Christ Church coming back from Union about 9.45. Cap & gown business.

11   Paid my fine at the House

12   Buller had a lunch party of females today. Seeing that his window was open & a cold wind blowing Gussie & I sent in the following note 'think perhaps you had better ask your lady guests whether they are polar bears or if they like a draught'. He was rather sick.

March

3   Fitzgerald over from Cambridge. After lunch, all fish as Fitz is RC, we went to Ashmolean, the House, top of the Radcliffe. I gave him & Buller dinner at the Clarendon. Went to the 'Clouds'. Parry's music an extraordinary jumble of motifs from Wagner, Strauss, Beethoven etc. mixed with 'Rule Britannia', 'We won't go home till morning' & motor horns. E. M. Compton Mackenzie of Magdalen was very good as Pheidippides, voice excellent . . . Gibby very good as Coryphaeus, very clear

words & led the singing well. Archaeological details by J. L. Myres of Christ Church.[79]

4   Managed to get Fitzgerald off without missing his train: his punctuality is what it used to be. Father came to stay with Bp Mitchison for the 'Clouds'.

5   Lunch with Bp Mitchison: also there Bp of Manchester & Mrs Knox. The former is a trifle ponderous, the latter clever & delightful. Called on Mrs Temple.

12 Was elected to committee of Nomads cricket club.

14 With Buller & Page to see 'Hamlet' without scenery at the Town Hall. Tree & his company, excellent of course. Tree with an imperial [*beard*]. He only pretended madness & loved Ophelia to the last. Miss Forbes Robertson as Ophelia quite excellent in the mad scene.

18 Woolley turned up. He's been mastering at Hereford Choir School & has just failed for British Museum. We walked round the garden & talked Oscar Wilde etc.

April

4   To the Malt House, Little Stretton, where reading party consists of Bags, B. S. Gould, Mouse & Helm.[80]

5   Golf & reading. Perfect blizzard while we were playing.

6   Hardy of New Coll came with a dear bob-tailed sheepdog, Mop.

8   [*At Hardwicke*] Bob Bateman came, Oxford friend of F's. Amusing: dry cutting style. Dresses artistically. Has exhibited at RA. No opinion of Impressionists & not much of Whistler . . . he greatly admired 'Man with a Gun', our portrait of Thos. J. Baker but didn't at all like 'Granville Sharp' by Maddox Brown. He says that 'William Sharp' is not by Gainsborough, a myth that F had dropped into: it is too 'slick' & not enough brush 'niggling'.[81]

20 To Gloucester where I indulged in a new bike. Rudge Whitworth, two-speed gear. Runs very nicely but I may find the gears too high.

22 Golf with Sydney How & Reginald Penley[82] at Stinchcombe. Played all right in morning but rather bad in afternoon. Hunt going on while we played but Outlaw is going to be fired [*farrier's treatment*].

23 Easter Sunday. Biked to tea at Whitminster: service there very nice. Teesdales[83] run the whole thing, no-one else has any say.

29 Gibby & Murray Hicks in Greece last vac. For three days they travelled with escort & were received by mayors. This owing to Murray's other name being Frederick, which appearing on his portmanteau induced the belief that he was Eitel Frederick, German Emperor's son, known to be coming to those parts. The more they protested the more people thought they were trying to preserve their incog. At the end of their journey they could not change a £5 note so had no tips for the escort who thought them the poorest princes they had ever set eyes on. The donkey man . . . insisted on coming with them to the next station where they changed the note & sent back tips to the escort. The whole story perfectly true though it sounds like the wildest farce.

May

6   Captained Nomads v. Headington Quarry. We only made 52, & lost 4 for 4, self O again.

9, 10, 11,   Mikado, Gondoliers, Patience, Yeoman of the Guard, Pinafore & Trial by Jury,
12, 13   Iolanthe.

22   Met WG at the Mitre: he seemed cheery. Gents v. Varsity, which I watched for a short time. Watched WG & Marshall put on 140 for no wicket in Gents second innings. WG made 55 not out not very carefully but extremely well.

29   Whitty tight tonight: rushed into Buller's room where Zimmern was: afterwards to Page's salon with an armful of boots collected from the passage outside.

June

3   Eton. Played for New Coll II v. Eton II. Saw the Head (Warre) read his last Absence. Viewed the procession of boats for about the 8th time I suppose. We adjourned for lunch. I didn't go to my tutor's as I thought he would be full up. Lee took me to Stone's: he has got Lowry's old house, at the end of Cow Lane. Lee himself was most awfully cheery & nice & very refreshing after four weeks of would-be blasé Varsity life. During a whole hour & a half he didn't try to say one smart thing. Supper with Wells whom I was up to my first two halves. He was in great form, full of fun: he gave us an excellent supper & champagne. He is pleased with Lyttelton, doesn't anticipate much faddiness. During the day there was a good deal of talk about Buller who is going to tutor Paul Methuen in the Vac.

8   I have had headaches & diarrhoea since Monday. I find that I was poisoned on Saturday. The Daily Mail says forty boys are down with ptomaine poisoning, thought to be the salmon. Denny who also lunched there has got it slightly.

14   Doctor says I had better go home for about a week, on Friday.

16   Went into College to pack a few things, then home. Clare & Ketha at home & father at home for one night. We live, move & have our being in the Study owing to Spring Cleaning.

18   Church M. Hylda there. Drove over to tea at the Cottage.

23   To Eton by the 7.55. Lunched with Vaughan who is putting me up until Monday.

24   Chapel: much as usual, but seats on altar steps taken away & level of floor changed. The usual Voluntary, mixture of Carmen & Domum. Lunch at my tutor's. Mrs W-T was having a private luncheon of children so only he appeared. He was quite agreeable & gave us the usual mutton & suet & treacle on one of the hottest days we've had! Got away in time for the cricket . . .

25   Chapel. Archbishop of Canterbury preached. Vigorous & well delivered but naturally not very profound. After Chapel I met Buller & his brother Montagu. We retired into Heygate's & ate strawberries. Up to Windsor. Life Guards & Coldstreams bands played. Chapel in evening, very crowded. Anthem: 'Hear my prayer': head boy having cracked his voice 'O for the wings' was sung as a duet. Tea at Tap, very good strawberries etc. After supper the house came for hymn-singing. Toddy suddenly seized me by the arm & said 'Here is a boy who knows you'. Small rough-haired child had demanded an introduction. He turned out to be Sidney Parry's boy Michael who had met me shooting at Highnam. We talked & then Toddy sent him to fetch three others to sing part songs. Parry brushed his hair in the interval.

27   Gracie & Nelly up for Commem by the 4.50 & F followed later. Dinner at the Mitre. At 9.0 went towards our ball where we found things in some confusion. Workmen

had gone on strike & floor was still in process of completion. However all went well. We kept it up till about 6 & then trooped off to be photographed. I then took the girls back to the Mitre. Returned to Page's room: cocoa & strawberries. At last to bed 7.30 – 10.

28   Lunch in Monty's room. Girls went home by the 2.15.

30   Down to Weston-super-Mare via Bristol. Blanchie met me at Weston. She & the children are at 3 Churchill Terrace. Nice lodgings. It was rainy when I arrived & I thought the place looked rather dismal.

July

1   Rainy again. We walked about during the day, mostly along the sea front. Children very jolly & looking very well. High tide about 6.30

2   Church & walks.

3   Back in time for cricket at Gloucester

5   Up to town for Portmans' garden party. [*Long list of relations & friends present*]. Met Carron at Paddington. He had the motor & took me up to his place Parkfield, Highgate. Beautiful drive looking over Hampstead Heath. Parkfield looks out over town on one side & over pure country on the other. The occasion of my visit was the Highgate Bachelors Ball house party: a number of curious people but plenty of nice ones: very few good dancers however. It went on till 3 & we got to bed about 4.30.

6   Up by 9, when we were told there would be breakfast. After ringing 3 times in search of bath or information as to whereabouts of bathroom, did cat's wash & went down. Nobody down yet so I took the unwilling Tip for a walk. Breakfast came on with a rush. The carriage took me to Lords, the Varsity match. To Albert Hall with May to hear Chamberlain. Although at the top of the hall we could hear nearly every word: he speaks wonderfully well & clearly.

9   Sunday. Bp of Stepney at St Peter's. Brit. Mus. & Nat. Portrait Gallery in afternoon. Called on the Belhavens: a long talk with Lady B about Ralph, Harry Lascelles[84] etc., including a full discussion of the ragging row. The whole matter from beginning to end was a mass of misunderstanding & mismanagement: but whereas Harewood 'lay low' Belhaven fussed about so that Ralph had to resign while Harry, just as much concerned, was able to stay. Lady B admits that all the junior subalterns had got above themselves owing to joining while their seniors were at the front in S. Africa.

13   Pictures all the morning: Fine Arts Society, Tayler's 'Empire's Cricketers' chalk drawings, good of Tyldesley finishing cut, Warner on-driving; Grafton Galleries, especially noticed Millet 'Donkeys on Heath' & 'Angelus', & J. E. Millais 'Orphans'; Royal Academy, only skimmed it . . . Alexander Macdonald's Lady Margaret Rice' [*'Markie'*] was horrible: Poynter's 'Mrs Guy Sebright' was very nice but not pretty enough for Olive. Walter Cave's 'Proposed Memorial Buildings at Eton' a rejected design, horrible beyond conception: red brick-built Methodist chapel. Lunch with the Walter Lascelles[85]: Aunt Ellen very jolly. I hadn't seen any of them for a long time. To British Museum to be shown Chinese paintings. I found Laurence Binyon in the Print Room, also Holmes. Binyon, looking the minor poet all over, was awfully kind & showed me a few of the best.

17 Went to see the Titian at Conalghi's, 'Pietro Aretino': very fine, magnificent old gold silk sleeves. In the afternoon I had tea with Fitzgerald at Charbonnel & Walkers, Bond Street. Then New Gallery: Collier Smithers' 'F. Cripps Esq.' a good looking portrait of Fred C. Dance at Alhusens'.

18 Up Westminster Cathedral tower to see the view which was misty. V. & A. & Imperial Institute. Then drill at Marlow. Frank Wethered being at Bisley I commanded the company. No dinner as I hadn't the courage to attack Frank's maiden sister.

19 Lunch at Piccadilly Lyons. 1/6 lunch, swelled to 2/10 by sweets, drinks etc. Not bad but not very cheap.

25 Garden Party at Haresfield. Blue Hungarian band played awfully well. As we were departing Michael rushed in from the station: he, Uncle H, Ketha & Henry Clifford had broken down near Berkeley Road. Mi had come on by train, others waited for the motor to be repaired & eventually arrived.

26 Tennis Club at Wallsworth, the James Dorringtons. The house & gardens are extremely well looked after. We had some good tennis: amongst those there were Nelly, Gracie & self, Blanche, Muriel & Wilfrid Murray Browne, Col. & Mrs & Miss Metford.

August

2 Garden party at Fretherne to introduce the new Bishop.[86] Tennis.

9 [*During annual camp, at Sway*] Message-carrying from 2–6 am. Parade at 1. The men turned out wonderfully quietly. It appears that last night some of the company headed by Sergt. Clelland made a fearful row during drum-beating at tattoo: a sort of band with tin buckets etc. The Adj. talked to Clelland this morning & reduced him to tears. I paraded the company & talked to them with considerable vehemence: in fact I was very rude. They quite took it to heart & were very repentant.

10 Subaltern for the day. Got through the guard mounting parade without a hitch though I did form fours with open ranks!

24 Muriel Browne married to Claud Going at Hucclecote. I was groomsman & conducted Blanche from the church. Very jolly, any number of Brownes about, from all parts.

29,30 Gloucestershire v. Australians . . . Jessop & Dennett played out the last 15 mins amidst desperate excitement. Jessop was so steady that Trumper came silly point: Jessop drove one at him with his usual vigour & Trumper made a wonderful effort to hold, falling on his knees to avoid instant death: he seemed to have got it but it forced his hands apart. Of course we were eventually quite outplayed.

September

4 Orde Brown came over to say goodbye previous [sic] to going to Canada.

6 Marianne Cornish married to Gerald Simonds at Quedgeley. I gave her 'The Oxford Book of English Verse'. Rain till after the ceremony, when it cleared up completely. Marianne looked lovely. The bridesmaids were all dressed in different colours, a not very successful experiment. They were Cristabel, [*sister*] Aline Tidswell, [*of Haresfield*] Toffee & Baby Darell, [*of Fretherne*] & Nancy Hill.[?]

9　　Pouring rain after 11. Before, I had prepared a pitch which was already in such a condition that the light roller brought up the water. Of course there was no play. [*at the Hardwicke garden party*]

11　　The party went to Berkeley on the motor, Gardiner Bazeley & Mrs, Sir John & Lady Dorrington came. Bazeley took Sir John & me for a drive on his motor to Stonehouse.

12　　Worcester Music Festival. 'Dream of Gerontius' very fine indeed. Lunch & tea with Cousin Effie.[87] Violet & Valentine Orde there.

20　　Tennis Club at Hucclecote. We had a general meeting in which we decided to go on as we are instead of hiring a central court in Gloucester: we also decided to get 1/– instead of 9d balls.

21　　Travelled home with Mabel Clifford . . . talked about new hockey club: it is decided that girls are to wear skirts of white house flannel which causes great opposition.

22　　Cub-hunted around Owlpen, very thick. I did over 30 miles. Drove Violet Orde in to Gloucester to see the Cathedral: we hit upon Precentor Fleming who took us over & showed us lots of things not in the usual round.

October

1　　Church M & E. I read the lessons in the evening for the first time. Church absolutely packed as it is the continuation of Harvest Festival.

7　　Tom Balston came by the 5.30. He had lost most of his luggage but was cheerful as usual. Played 'Pit' in the evening.

9　　Beagles at Arlingham. Tom, May & I went out. Very amusing hearing Lionel & Guy [*Darell*] quarrelling from each side of the hedge. About teatime Cecil & Daisy Battine[88] came. He has just leapt into fame as author of 'The Crisis of the Confederacy'.

11　　Up to 'Varsity. Arrived at our digs, 52 High. I selected what appeared to be the best room, looking towards New Coll garden. Tom came later & quite late Gussie arrived.

12　　Doing the collekers that I missed last term. Gussie similarly occupied. All attempts at settling down postponed.

20　　I beat Roger by 1 up in 14 holes. We each had only one club: he chose a mashie, I a driving iron. His theory was that with a mashie you could always get out of a hole: mine was that with a driving iron you need not get into one. I also had enormous advantage in putting.

21　　Nelson Day: the Evening News came out with his signal in flags as a hand-bill. I bought one & presented it to Page to match his 'Fall of Port Arthur' news-bill, a red & yellow rising sun.

22　　G. K. Chesterton on 'the Chief Danger to the Church of England' at Queens. He was less brilliant but more serious than I had expected. Large, fat, smiling, unkempt: laughed at his own jokes & generally behaved with boyish good humour. The chief danger according to him is the idea that a clergyman must be a gentleman.

25　　'Tommy' Lascelles[89] to dinner. Later we talked family shop. He anticipates that Harry Lascelles my cousin & contemporary at Eton will sell Harewood on the slightest provocation. H's debts amount to about £35000.

November

2   Old Boy at Eton. RWW-T's Old Boys v. CM Wells'. House captained by Alec Lyon. Old Boys consisted of Christie, in very good form & much quieter than of old, Jock Lyon, Parr Lees & self for Oxford.

6   Houseman dinner, given by Page & Whitty. For the first time guests were introduced, namely Zimmern & Scott. The whole thing was a very partial success till the visitors went. Zim was not in good form & Scott was feeling chippy. Tom brought in Alec Cadogan to tea, the first time I had seen C to speak to since Eton days when I only knew him slightly.

9   Holmes on Rembrandt. Only Page & self got in of the New Coll push. Gore & Whitty got shut out by the man at the door in response to a primaeval order of Herkomer's that the doors were to be shut directly on the stroke of 6. The room was very hot & I slept a good deal.

14   To 'Veronique' with Page. Veronique & Denise were good, especially the latter played by Peggy Primrose. (P.P. became the beloved mistress of Horatio Bottomley).

21   Dinner with the Warden. I sat between Farmer, rather dull, & the 2nd Miss Spooner with whom I got on excellently. Bridge afterwards in which I did not join.

25   Essay Club. Gilbert Murray read part of his 'Electra' which is to be published on Monday: it was splendid, he read very beautifully though the tragic accent throughout the play grew a trifle monotonous. He afterwards had an informal discussion of the play.

26   Lunch with H. A. L. Fisher. I met Mrs Fisher at a dance in the summer. I sat next to Hal & enjoyed myself enormously. He told us stories eg. Haldane MP was invited to meet the King of Greece the other day. After dinner all the Royalites were put on one side of a rope & all the other people the other side: the latter including ladies had to stand the whole evening. The Lord Chamberlain came up to Haldane & said that the King would honour him with a reception & added 'May I suggest that you will find His Majesty interested in the subject of pheasants?' Every soul in the room had to follow suit: the King must have got sick of pheasants before the evening was out.

30   Eton with Tom, Carron & Ben. Travelled in the saloon engaged by many tugs who were going to College Pop Jubilee. Wallgame a draw. Tea at Heygates with Tom's minor: also Tom, Clive Bowman, Paul Methuen. An excellent tea but it was difficult to get the boys to talk when Methuen was talking: he was very nice, cool & collected: he doesn't seem a bit stupid: rather appreciates an attentive audience.

December

4   Everything overshadowed & everyone upset by Ralph Brassey's death. Riding an open race at the Cambridge Grind he fell & not being hurt he rose from the ground just as another horse came over: he was knocked down & taken from the ground unconscious.

6   Clare, Nelly & Gracie up for the day. Lunched with me, Tom & Carron being there also. Walked about town & to top of Radcliffe as usual & then tea: after which they went.

7   Ralph Brassey's funeral: the JCR sent a wreath: about 30 went from New Coll. At about 10 pm a whole host of men came in to gamble. They played roulette & after Ben had satisfied his curiosity having never seen the game before, he & I retired to my sitting room.

8   Chamberlain at Town Hall: not as good as in the summer. No argument at all, skirked economics, made a few remarks on empire: he was at his best on the new Liberal administration. I sat next but one to Oc who was not altogether pleased. He made a few rather good repartees to groans & hisses. No particular rowdyism. Shedden is said to have organised a corps of 60 chuckers-out but they weren't wanted.

10   Tommy Lascelles to dinner at the Grid. Blanche has just been made Maid of Honour to the Queen, receiving £300 for 6 weeks waiting. Most of it is spent on dress, so that she will be a trying companion for Helen & Maud in Town.

11   Home. Train 1½ hrs late owing to fog. Micky Beach staying here for electioneering purposes.

19   Whitminster on Special, who tumbled down & broke his knees again. He did it once with Uncle H. He stumbled again on the way home & seems very unreliable.

20   Kennels on Outlaw. Capital day, plenty of jumping, mostly large dry ditches, some very blind. Outlaw went excellently. Mellersh[90] to tea. He seems a nice man & rather clever. He recommends F to vaseline all the book bindings in the library. Friend of Ketha's chiefly over gardening. (We believe he subsequently proposed to Clare)

28   Children's party here : about 40 children came: great fun.

1906

January

1   May & I to the Charlie Godmans in Sussex. Bertie Godman has stayed at Hardwicke several times: quite nice, very full of horses.

2   Crawley & Horsham ball. I got plenty of dancing, I think May did too. The floor, laid by the Army & Navy Stores, was excellent. J. N. Taylor of Malvern Link recognised me. He took a 1st in Law Tripos.

3   Home via Town. At Agnews I saw the Rokeby Velasquez 'Venus & Cupid'. The exhibition was closed but I was allowed to see it: the glass had been removed so that I saw it better than those who saw it in the exhibition. It is quite beautiful. The curtain at the back is red & the drapery on which the figure lies is greyey-purple. The Cupid has got delightful brown hair & the Venus has a sort of silvery sheen. A man came in with a friend & talked about the picture in a way which suggested that he was Sir Thomas Agnew: he said offers were coming in from all over the world but that the government would not produce enough.

4   Hardwicke meet as usual: on Outlaw. Huntsman Thompson had a very bad fall over a gate near Hunt Grove & has concussion . . . Gloucester ball: Florence Teesdale came under our chaperonage.

5   Hospital ball, taking the place of the old Charity ball. The old system of supper tickets by which county people get in before the town, roughly speaking, was expanded. Probably this was an improvement: at least it transferred some of the jealousy to a

section of the town instead of heaping it all on the county. Obviously it is right that the mayor should go in first & that the procession should be formed but any other distinction seems to me most dangerous to the success of the ball.

10   Up to Lampern with F, May & Nelly: later Robeson joined us. Chavenage ball, the Lowesley-Williams. They've just built out a ballroom, & several other rooms: most beautiful floor, as springy as possible yet not too jumpy: plenty of room & lots of room to sit out too. About the best done ball I've ever been to.

11   Lunch with the Mildmays at Stoutshill.[91] They've made it beautiful inside.

16   Star Hotel Worcester to stay with the Gibbons for the Worcester Hunt ball. Danced with Miss Agg-Gardner: rather pretty with mole on cheek: *will* pretend that it is her first season.

18   To Southam Delabere with F & Grace . . . the naval boy [*Ratcliff*] who starts for China in a day or two made a most efficient host. To Horlick's ball at Cowley. Everything magnificent but the whole house is decorated like an hotel, lots of plate glass & swinging doors: the ball room is crimson, very trying to hunt coats, & has large panels with painted cornucopias, flowers etc: hot water pipes gilt.

21   [*At Varsity*] Woolley & Whitty to tea. Woolley is working in the Ashmolean at present arranging Cypriot vases.

23   Down for election. My first effort as free & independent elector of the Tewkesbury division. I arrived about 2.30 & recorded my vote for Mickey Beach. Hung about the school all day taking slips from the school to the Committee Room & marking off those who had voted on the register . . . we had two motors, one from Mrs Wayle which did excellent work & one from Horlick which broke down about 2 o'clock & never reappeared. Everyone nervous & anxious tonight.

24   Io triumphe! Mickey in by 127 votes. We had windows at Mrs Gibbons opposite Shire Hall where we waited with Curtis-Haywards, Darells & Nashes. At 1.30 Harry Brocklehurst[92] came out with Mickey on his right & Lister[93] on his left. The Crowd below was abut 500. As soon as silence was procured the result was given out & after a great deal more cheering, the figures. We had speeches mostly inaudible from both candidates. Lister ended up '..and I hope he will have as distinguished a career as his father & grandfather'. We then carried Mickey to the Conservative Club where he first spoke in the big room below & then addressed the crowd from a window. Back to the Varsity with much joy at heart.

February

9   Walk with Joseph: we discussed Eton v. Winchester, their system of houses, art, Tennyson, inter alia et inania. Roger won £20 on the turf & gave Denny, Gussie & self dinner at the Mitre.

10   Roger lost £20! Glad I've had the dinner. [*Study time is now given weekly: 38½ hrs*].

11   Tea with Joseph: also there Clermont Witt, secretary of National Art Collectors Fund. I had sent £1.1s towards the Rokeby Velasquez. Witt was a youngish man & amusing: he said the King gave nothing himself but he made Lord Michelm subscribe £8000.

18   Dinner at Clarendon with Whitty Page & Tom. Quite like old times when we used constantly to dine here. William the German head waiter delightful as usual & we

Stoutshill, Uley. The family's home before moving to Hardwicke Court

sat at the old round table at the far end. We all agreed that we felt younger than for many a day.

21   Holmes showed me Goya's 'Bull Fight' & 'Caprioso' at the Ashmolean: a mixture of aquatint & dry point. Wonderfully powerful, any amount of motion & grotesque caricature: almost as brilliant as Hogarth.

March

2   Went to hear Maurice Woods of Trinity tried by Vice Chancellor for being on roof of Warden's house at 2.25 am on Monday 'supposedly for an unlawful purpose'. Woods looked about as washed out as usual: the whole trial was conducted very well: the Warden gave his evidence very nicely & did everything to make it easy for Woods. He was eventually handed over to proctors to deal with: he pleaded guilty to being on the roof but not guilty to the 'unlawful purpose'. As a matter of fact Woods belongs to the Alpine Club which emanates from Balliol & Trinity. L. S. Amery, a friend of May, of All Souls was a member: there is a series of well-known routes over the roofs of Oxford.

3   Biked to South Leigh to see frescoes in tempera in church: 14th & 15th century. The best is 'St. Michael weighing souls': magnificent composition, by no means primitive: spacing & cutting of lines excellent. I've managed to do 43 hours work this week which I should think is as good as I've ever done, an average of 8 hrs a day.

4   Called on Hal Fisher. Paul on Disraeli at Essay Club. Hal spoke very well, telling the story of Sir Bartle Frere.

15, 16,   Down. Collections in the morning, when Warden told me I ought to get a second.
19, 20   Told him I thought not.

23   To Gibby at Hindley House, Stocksfield on Tyne [*At York*] I had just time to go inside the Minster: they are repairing the two East towers, with red brick apparently: it will be faced with stone.

25 Snow early: we walked to Corbridge. Gibby showed me a Ruskin notebook which was found in his pocket when he died: it contains some splendid studies of birds, notably a toucan in pencil & a cockatoo in colour, also views of Coniston. [*Visits to Housesteads, the Roman Wall, Chesters, Hexham, all described vividly*]

April

7 To Nunneykirk [*the Orde family of cousins*] Everybody at home. All except Charlie went to choir practice. The house is larger than I expected, the manners & customs of the inhabitants strange. I remember Ben Browne's description 'No one speaks except when Willy addresses a remark to the dog': . . . fairly accurate

8 Church at Netherwhitton. Very large choir including all Ordes, & very small congregation. Cantata in the evening in which Charlie took a solo. Winifred plays the organ. Memorial window to Willy's father.

11 Saw over the Mauretania, the new Cunarder: biggest ship in the world, just under 800 ft long, full weight 40,000 tons: she is built under cover, a novelty. Met Edward Browne's fiancée.[94] She is very tall, pretty, rather shy. Edward & I . . . got on capitally tonight: he is amusing, brusque & caustic. He is all for linguistic education.

12 Home. Stopped at Sheffield to see the Ruskin museum.

May

2 Jamieson showed me where to buy Fullers' peppermints in Oxford. I have been searching for a place all my four years!

5 XX Club dinner. Toasts: 'The King'. 'The Visitors' proposed by Paul & replied to by H. Belloc: he was jolly & amusing: talked at random, almost impromptu. I was afraid it was going to be too noisy but tho' everyone talked their loudest there was no riot.

10 Trinity II v. New Coll II. I got 37 & 52.

30 Motor drive: Eynsham, Burford, lunched at Northleach, Bibury, Fairford, home via Faringdon. At Fairford I led the party to the top of the tower . . . it's a rather perilous ascent for bad heads like mine.

31 Schools at last! [*Final examination for BA degree*]

June

6 I should think that my best papers have been Roman & Ancient History though the latter was bad & I wrote off the point. Roger gave a dinner at the Mitre.

7 Played for the Dons v. the Boating Men. I felt very ill when fielding & didn't go to the Greats dinner this evening, much to my disappointment.

9 Boojum dinner. Unfortunate incident was breaking of Zuluetta's window: he came out & slanged the company. Gibby answered him back & they had rather a row. Oc & Scott then went to smooth Zulu down but I don't think they succeeded as Zulu went across to the Dean.

11 Work for special subject. The people at 23 gave a big dinner. We went into College afterwards where someone fell foul of Zuluetta[95] who is having a rather rough time now: he's very nervous & irritable.

13 Greek sculpture papers. Gibby & I both thought the papers a bit stiff.

15 Farewell dinner at the digs. Went off very well: round to College about 10 where Ben & I talked to Zimmern. Then back to digs where we talked some time . . . I then saw Ben home & came back. Sat talking to Tom until about 2. Denny came down to see how we were getting on & talked some time: but went to bed before we did . . .

16 Home. End of my 'Varsity career. I've had 4 years of the most intense happiness. I think, in some ways, it got better & better as it went on.

Notes for Oxford Section

1. Scrimgeour, Hugh Carron. Eton, New Coll. *Coldstream Guards. Partner in family firm.*

2. Gibson, Thornley C. 'Gibby'. New Coll. *Became a professional singer.*

3. Tod, Arthur H. A. Charterhouse, New Coll.

4. Hallett, Maurice G. 'Mouse'. New Coll. *ICS. Governor of United Provinces. 1939–45. Kt. 1937.*

5. Hall, Roger E. Winchester, New Coll. *Colonial service in Africa and Far East. Chief Justice, Malay States. Kt. 1937.*

6. Butler, Harold Edgworth. Tutor and fellow New Coll. *1901–11. Professor of Latin 1922–43 and Public Orator 1932–47, both at University of London.*

7. Brekker, breakfast: lekker, lecture: colleker, collection ie examination: hence for example divvers colleker, divinity examination.

8. Woolley, Charles Leonard. *Archaeologist. Excavator of Ur, inter alia. Kt. 1937.*

9. Balston, Thomas 'Buller' New Coll. *Writer. Expert on wood carving.*

10. Whitworth, Geoffrey A. 'Whitty' New Coll. *Secretary to C. J. Holmes (see below), Founder of National Drama League.*

11. Spooner, Rev. William Archibald 'The Spoo'. Warden of New Coll. 1903–24.

12. Fisher, Herbert Albert Laurens Winchester, New Coll. Historian. *Fellow and Warden of New Coll. 1924–40. Minister of Education. OM 1937.*

13. Matheson, P. E. Dean of New Coll.

14. Joseph. H. W. B. Fellow of New Coll. Junior Bursar. *Lecturer in Philosophy University of Oxford 1927–32.*

15. Gordon-Canning, William James – the family lived at Hartpury, now the Hartpury College.

16. Meredith. Home of the Wedderburn family.

17. Stanley Park, Stroud. Home of the Marling family.

18. Colchester-Wemyss, John Morris – 'Jock'. Younger son of M. W. Colchester-Wemyss of Westbury Court. The house has been demolished but the gardens have been restored by the National Trust.

19. A note from F's diary: 'Fretherne & Gloster balls. Jan 5–12 incl. Montgomeries'

Waiter	2–12–6
12 bottles cham	3–0–0
& Port, Sherry, Hock	1–0–0
Oysters	1–7–6
43 head extra at 3/6	7–10–6
12 servants at 2/6	1–10–0
48 selves extra 1/–	2–8–0
cabs	9–3–0
Tickets, 5.8 & 2.18	8–6–0
	36–10–0
[should be 36–17–6]	

20. Sidgwick, A. Reader in Greek University of Oxford.

21. Clarke, A. G. 'Bags' *K. in 1914–18 War.*

22. Sewell, J. E., Warden at New Coll. when diarist went up. Died January 1903.

23. Hubbard, John Gellibrand. Eton and Christ Church, Mi's old college. Lieut. 1st Bucks. Regiment, Ox. & Bucks. Lt. Inf. *Succ. as 3rd Baron Addington.*

24. 'Toggers' are the sculling races properly called torpids, in spring on the river Cher to see which college becomes 'Head of the River'.

25. Asquith, Arthur M. 'Oc'. Son of H. H. Asquith. *DSO & Croix de Guerre, 1914–18 Member of Council, Ministry of Labour 1919.*

26. Gardner, P. Professor of Classical Archaeology at Oxford. Numismatist.

27. Grind. A steeplechase.

28. Gambier-Parry family lived at Highnam: they usually appear as Parry. Diarist shoots with Sidney, is up at Oxford with his son Tom and meets young Michael at a later date on a visit to Eton. *See* note 44 for Sir Hubert Parry.

29. Ackers, Charles P. Lived at Huntley Court.

30. Smith, Nowell (Charles) Fellow, New Coll. *Headmaster of Sherborne School.*

31. Sharp, Granville. Diarist's great great uncle who worked with Wilberforce for the abolition of slavery. He is shown in Zoffany's conversation piece 'The Sharp Family'. He holds the double flageolet which is still at Hardwicke Court and his clarinet rests on the piano.

32. The Hardwicke Reformatory was a private institution founded by T. B. Lloyd-Baker in 1852 where compassionate principles together with education and hard work were used to rehabilitate young male offenders. It was visited and approved by penal reformers from Britain and Europe.

33. Hardy, Henry Harrison. Rugby, New Coll. *Headmaster, Cheltenham College 1919–32. Headmaster, Shrewsbury School 1932–44.*

34. Cotton, R. C. F. 'Ben' Rugby, New Coll. Lived at Brydone, Bitterne, Hants. *Died of wounds 1918.*

35. Montagu, Lionel Samuel 'Monty' 4th son of 1st Baron Swaythling. A large family who lived at South Stoneham House near Southampton.

36. Nomads. A New Coll. cricket team.

37. Wethered, Major Walter. CO 1st Bucks Regiment. Lived at 'Blounts'. His brother Frank became Lt.Col. R. Warks. Regiment.

38. Birchall, Edward Vivian Dearman. Known first as Vivian, later as Edward. Eton, Magdalen. Youngest son of Dearman Birchall of Bowden and brother of Jack, Percy, Violet and Lindaraja. *K. in France 1916.*

39. Rashdall, Rev. Hastings 'Rasher' Fellow, New Coll. *Dean of Carlisle 1917.*

40. Lascelles, Helen Margaret. Daughter of Frederick Canning Lascelles and granddaughter of the 4th Earl of Harewood. Diarist was particularly fond of this distant cousin. In 1913 she married Eric MacLagan, son of the former Archbishop of York and had two sons. Her sisters were Blanche, Maud and Margaret and her brother was Alan Frederick 'Tommy', qv.

41. Cripps family of Ampney Park, Cirencester. Frederick William Beresford Cripps elder son of F. C. Cripps lived there: Egerton Tymewell Cripps 'Tim' younger son, lived at South Cerney Manor.

42. Godman, John. Eton. 15/19 Hussars. Grandson of 9th Lord Willoughby de Broke and a cousin of Blanchie. Lived at Banks Fee. *High Sheriff of Gloucestershire 1942 and Chairman of Gloucestershire County Council 1946–56.*

43. Browne, Benjamin. A second cousin, living in Northumberland, who often stayed in Gloucestershire: frequently with his uncle at Piers Court, Stinchcombe.

44. Parry, Sir Charles Hubert Hastings of Highnam. Composer: often conducted his own works at the September Music Festivals. Professor of Music, University of Oxford. Kt. 1898.

45. Mitchison, Rt. Rev. John. Bishop of Barbados and the Windward Islands. Canon of Gloucester Cathedral. Master of Pembroke College. Great friend of Father's.

46. Wingate. Mrs Wingate was a distant cousin and mother of of Orde Wingate (*Orde of the Chindits 1939–45*).

47. Lampern was a family rural retreat in deep woodland above Uley.

48. Temple, William. Undergraduate at Balliol. After a brilliant and varied career became *Archbishop of Canterbury 1942–44.*

49. Evans, Arthur John. Son of Sir John Evans. Harrow, Brasenose. Archaeologist *Excavator and restorer of Knossos. Keeper of the Ashmolean. Kt. 1911.*

50. Bowes-Lyon, John Herbert – 'Jock'. Eton & Oxford. Brother of Patrick, *see note 2,* Eton section.

51. Murray, George Gilbert A. Fellow, New Coll. *Regius Professor of Greek, Oxford, Founder and Chairman of League of Nations Union OM 1941.*

52. Matthews, Tom and Olive. Brother and sister: hunting friends. Lived at Newport Towers, Falfield: now a motel.

53. Lascelles, Brian Piers 'Uncle Bryan' (diarist). His mother's youngest brother. Librarian at Harrow.

54. Highgrove, the home of the Prince of Wales.

55. Witts, George Backhouse, 3rd son of Edward Francis Witts, mentioned in 'Diary of a Cotswold Parson'. Lived at Hill House, Leckhampton with his wife and only child Sybil who appears quite often, dancing with the diarist, and with other Witts cousins. GBW was a JP and noted amateur archaeologist.

56. The dance floor was said to be laid over chains to give springiness.

57. Prevost, Sir Charles Thomas Keble, 4th Baronet. Son of Archdeacon Prevost. Lived at Yercombe Lodge, Stinchcombe, now a short-stay nursing home and day centre.

58. Southam. A most interesting house, now the Delabere Hotel. *See* 'Gloucestershire: the Vale and Forest of Dean' by David Verey for an excellent description.

59. Cluckie and Hammy: McClaughlin, 4th R.Berks Regt. Berners, Hamilton Hugh, Irish Rifles. Both died in 1914–18 war.

60. Murray-Browne, Wilfrid. A second cousin. He married the diarist's sister Ketha in 1909.

61. Proggins: the University proctors. 'Progged' – to have one's name taken.

62. Lyttelton, Rev. the Hon. Edward. Assistant master at Eton 1882–90 during which time he taught Michael. *Headmaster of Eton 1905–16.*

63. Mrs Temple was the wife of Frederick, Archbishop of Canterbury 1897–1902 and mother of William. *See* note 48 above.

64. Methuen, Paul. Oxford. Corsham Court, Wilts. *4th Baron Methuen.*

65. Cripps, Mrs Frederick née Constance Wykeham. Children: Joseph & Freda, + *3 boys* Cripps, Mrs Tim née Hilda Gambier Parry. Son: William Parry, + *daughter.* All at Ampney cricket match.

66. Gilbey, Lt.Col. Alfred. CO Bucks Regt.

67. Hicks-Beach, Michael Edward. Statesman. 9th Baronet. Lived at Williamstrip Park. *1st Earl St. Aldwyn.* His only son, Michael Hugh, *Lord Quenington Conservative MP for Stroud, 1906* was *K. in 1916. Michael John,* posthumous son of the last, became *2nd Earl St. Aldwyn.*

68. Escrick Park, Yorkshire, was the seat of Lord Wenlock who had married Constance Lascelles, daughter of the 4th Earl of Harewood.

69. 'The Boy' was Ivor B. Gurney who sang soprano in the Cathedral choir. Better known as Gloucestershire's wartime poet.

70. Bowers, Mrs Margaret. Wife of Canon Bowers Lived in College Green.

71. Murray-Browne, Blanche. A second cousin, sister of Wilfrid. Married Neville Langton.

72. Zimmern, Alfred Eckhard. Fellow, New Coll. After 1919 pursued an international political career. *League of Nations; Professor of International Relations at Oxford; UNESCO 1945–50 Kt. 1936.*

73. Page, Reginal Exhibitioner, Winchester. New Coll. Not at first closely involved with the diarist's group of friends but after Oxford he shared with Tom Balston.

74. Hicks-Beach, Micky *See* note 67 above.

75. Robeson, Frederick Eden. Assistant master at Eton where he taught languages and advised the diarist about his career. A member of the Berkeley Hunt.

76. Kingscote, Edric Thomas. Elder son of T. A. F. Kingscote of Kingscote.

77. Eastwood Park, Falfield. Home of Sir George Jenkinson, 12th Baronet.

78. Holmes, C. J., Editor, Burlington Magazine. Slade Professor of Fine Arts, Oxford, 1904–10. *Director, National Gallery 1916–28. Kt. 1921.*

79. Myres, John Linton. A mature student at Christ Church 1895–97. Archaeologist. *Chairman, British School at Athens 1934–47. Kt. 1943.* Father of J. N. L. Myres.

80. Helm, G. T. Exter College. *Padre of 5th Gloucesters 1914–18 war. Vicar of Dursley.*

81. Pictures at Hardwicke Court included the portrait of T. J. Lloyd Baker 'Man with a Gun', the conversation piece by Zoffany 'The Sharp Family' now to be seen in the National Portrait Gallery, 'Granville Sharp' by Madox Brown, and 'William Sharp' attributed at one time to Gainsborough but now with some uncertainty.

82. How, Sidney and Penley, Reginald were to marry sisters Constance and Geraldine Murray-Browne, second cousins of the diarist. *See* Wilfrid & Blanche and five other Murray-Browne cousins.

83. Teesdale, Rev. F. B. and family, especially Florence. Lived at Whitminster House.

84. Lascelles, Henry George Charles. 6th Earl of Harewood. Eton & RMC. Married the Princess Royal in 1922.

85. Lascelles, Walter. Eldest brother of the diarist's mother.

86. Gibson, R. Rev. E.C.S. Bishop of Gloucester.

87. Cousin Effie Browne was the widow of Walter Browne, 3rd son of Archdeacon Thomas and Catherine Murray Browne. She lived at Worcester and was most hospitable especially during the Music Festival when this was held at Worcester.

88. Battine, Captain Cecil. Married Margaret 'Daisy' Orde, one of the Nunneykirk cousins.

89. Lascelles, Alan Frederick 'Tommy'. Marlborough & Trinity. *Asst. Private Secretary to the Prince of Wales: Secretary to Governor General of Canada:* [*other intermediate appointments*] Secretary to Queen Elizabeth II. *See* 40 above.

90. Mellersh, W. Lock. Gloucester solicitor. Author of books on birds and gardening.

91. Stoutshill. The home of the Lloyd Baker family before moving to Hardwicke Court. The other Browne family [*cousins*] lived there afterwards. Later it was leased to the Mildmays. It next became a preparatory school at which Captain Mark Phillips was a pupil. Today it is a time-share establishment.

92. Dent-Brocklehurst, Henry – of Sudeley Castle.

93. Lister, Robert Ashton. Unsuccessful Liberal candidate in 1906. *Later, Labour MP for Stroud.*

94. Browne, Edward. Born at Stoutshill. Eton, Cambridge. Read Medicine & Oriental Languages. Held the Thomas Adams Chair of Arabic Studies 1902–26. Married Miss Blackburn-Daniell, 'Lally'.

95. Zuluetta, Francis de. Fellow of New Coll. *Regius Professor of Civil Law Oxford, 1919–48*

Transition

1906 (July) – 1914 (August)

AFTER THE SUSTAINED EXHILARATION of Oxford the next phase is, with some notable exceptions, in a lower key during the eight year interval until the outbreak of the Great War. On
coming down from Oxford the diarist plunged as usual into family and local events. He must
however have been considering the direction his future life should take. While at Eton on a
visit in July the first clue is found and it is a surprising one. He sought advice about
schoolmastering but with a complete change from Classics to Modern Languages. 'Father
agrees to four years' we read in September, though without any particular parental enthusiasm.

Acting on recommendations from Byrne and Vaughan at Eton he first joined the acclaimed
Hénaut establishment in Paris, which specialised in training young men for the Diplomatic
Corps, Foreign Office, Indian Civil Service and similar posts, and where in addition to language
proficiency a knowledge of the appropriate social *mores* was instilled. Here and later at Hanover
and Dresden the diarist meets many lively interesting and eventually influential men busy in
laying the foundations of their careers. The Hénaut ménage was particularly successful and
revered though Harold Nicholson, a contemporary of the diarist, later criticised it unkindly in
Some People.

The abortive offer of a temporary appointment at Eton in January 1907 is one of the very
rare occasions where deep inner feelings are expressed in the diaries. It is impossible not to be
affected by the disappointment and chagrin caused by raised hopes, so soon to be dashed. This
is counterbalanced by a completely unexpected and extraordinarily flattering offer made in
September of the same year by the Duke of Cumberland: to travel to Gmunden in Austria for
a weekend, in effect on approval for a six months appointment as English tutor to his two sons.
This remarkable interlude deservedly receives greater coverage for the glimpses it gives of a
completely different way of life and for the great success achieved by the diarist in fitting himself
into this wholly German setting, establishing a happy relationship with his pupil and imparting
enough English to 'satisfy the examiners' even though it was rather a borderline affair. When he
left in April 1908 the affectionate links forged with this likeable minor German royal family were
to last through two world wars; he came away loaded with gifts including a ducal crested tiepin
as a special memento which is still in the possession of his niece, and an invitation to return
whenever he liked, a graceful gesture which he was happy to recall in years to come.

When the time came to start teaching in earnest it seemed surprisingly hard to find a suitable
niche. Eventually he settled in at The Grange, a preparatory school at Folkestone, and plunged
with his usual energy into prep-school life with games well to the fore. He found hospitable
and congenial relatives close by, and London was conveniently accessible for free weekends and
half days so that we find an outburst of theatregoing, always a favourite interest, at this time.
Family events crowd in: the happiness of his sister Ketha's frost-sparkled wedding to cousin
Wilfrid Murray-Browne in January 1909; the death of his beloved Uncle H in a hunting
accident later that year; and the joyful arrival of Ketha's two children Billy and Kitty, both of

whom make innumerable appearances throughout the diaries, Kitty becoming a much-loved surrogate daughter as the years passed. A popular master at the Grange died there suddenly and the boys needed much help which the diarist evidently supplied, to come to terms with this shock. The difference in his adult attitude to the death of King Edward VII in 1910 (and his assesssment of King George V, borne out in later diaries) and to that of Queen Victoria when he was an impressionable Eton schoolboy is interesting.

Changes in ownership of the Grange increased a gradual realisation that prep-school life was too restricted to be permanently acceptable. Again, his applications for other posts were unsuccessful for many months, and finally the diarist gave notice of his intention to resign in July 1913, and arranged an ambitious and extensive tour of Canada and the United States with his old Eton and Oxford friend Edward Birchall. This tour is written up in fine detail and standing alone would make an enthralling period travelogue of North America. Crossing the continent twice the diarist visits all major places of interest, Niagara, Yosemite Valley, Grand Canyon, the Civil War battlefields and then spends time in Washington and New York where he has introductions to influential people and places difficult of access. A skeletal outline and a very few longer extracts have had to suffice for this section and scant justice has been done to its historical and topographical value.

No sooner had this tour been finalised than the Principal of Cheltenham College wrote to suggest that the diarist might care to apply for a forthcoming vacancy there. Too late to withdraw from the tour, Waterfield agreed to hold over the diarist's starting date until January 1914. He was thus in post for only seven months before the Great War burst upon an ill-prepared and largely unsuspecting country.

Travels in Europe and America,
1906–1914

[*The three month interval between Oxford and the first major step towards establishing a career is not without interest. The diarist is soon engrossed in family and local affairs, taking his appropriate part in each. After coming down on 16 June the next four entries epitomise his activities at this time.*]

June

17   Sunday. Read the lessons M & E.

18   Town. 36 Ebury Street. F, May & Gracie, Uncle H. Clare later.

19   Uncle H took Clare & me to Ascot & paid everything as usual. We went into the 10/– stand. Lunch at Guards Club. Uncle H & I to the Empire . . . very good ventriloquist, Arthur Prince. The ballet Coppelia very good all through, the chief attraction being Adeline Genée . . .

20   Tate Gallery with F & Whitty. The newly discovered Turners are splendid . . . the more unfinished they are the more suggestive they seem, full of light and colour . . . Edward Browne married to Alice Blackburn-Daniell at St. Mary Abbot's Kensington. Afterwards great meeting of cousins in the Empress Rooms.
      [*Amongst the well-established routine of cricket matches, tennis club meetings, visits to friends and to local events can be seen distant glimpses of future responsibilities, introduced by his uncle at this time.*]

July

2   Assizes for first time with Uncle H. The only two cases which were really fought were both rather beastly. Cranston defended one splendidly, pulling the prosecution to pieces . . .

4   Assizes: Heard Counsel's speech & part of summing-up in Leckhampton riot case: Sturges (defending) & Cranston (prosecuting) were both good. John Lawrence's summing-up wearisome to a degree.

9   Got home in time to see Lord St. Aldwyn enrolled as a freeman of Gloucester. [*The mainstream account continues.*]

13   Lords. Eton v. Harrow . . . I never noticed so much the distinction between the bright effective Harrow hitting & the beautiful though slightly academic Eton style: our men down to no. 11 batted admirably but unless the style is coupled with power to 'place' it is not conducive to quick scoring. During the day I met Monty Balston who gave me a ticket for the Eton stand. I sat with him, Pat, Jock & Fergus Lyon. As I was going to tea with the Jervoise Smiths [*a Lascelles connection*] I was accosted by Birrell of Vaughans accompanied by his father (who is at the moment the object of much blasphemy over the Education Bill).

16   Went to see Whitty at the offices of the Burlington, which he has just entered as Holmes' secretary. He is a long way the first of us to get to work. Holmes had been greatly struck with the Zoffany from Hardwicke Court, exhibited at the Whitechapel Gallery. Oxford for viva.

17   Viva. Wells of Wadham gave me 10 mins of sculpture, churches, Lysander. Said farewell to various friends especially Ben.

19   To Eton, to Toddy Vaughan. Drill at Slough . . . after which I descended on Byrne[1] to ask his advice about learning languages with a view to schoolmastering: he gave me much that will be useful.

The sisters: May, Ketha, Clare, Nelly, Grace. Date unknown, but before 1908

20   Chapel. Went over the State Apartments which I only visited once while at Eton: fine Rubens & Van Dyke but got rather tired of Zuccarelli.

21   Inspection of the Eton Collect Volunteers by Oliphant.² For the first time the inspecting officer told them what he thought of them: that they slouched, that they ought to walk as if they had a sovereign in their pocket. I think the 'Eton walk' aggravates the evil. Monty Balston [*brother of Tom*] is disgraceful as I pointed out to him. (next saw him at Bihucourt in June 1917).

27   Today came out the Schools List. I was very fairly contented though I had hoped for a second.

August

26   Tea at Cottage when Blanchie gave me a beautiful waistcoat she had worked herself.

28   Gloucester to settle going abroad.

September

3   Packing for abroad whither I go to learn French.

4   . . . only got as far as Cheltenham! where I remained all day. Much wiring to Gloucester, Worcester, Birmingham, Derby and finally Southampton whither my luggage had arrived safely. I back to Hardwicke & had another 'last night'.

5   Off all right this time. Met by Ben Cotton & Monty who put me into a motor car & took me to South Stoneham . . . This time the family were at home, rather formidable. Sir Samuel & Lady M., very cheerless & a number of large sons & daughters. After dinner I watched Sir S., Monty, Ben & a brother play bridge till it was time for me to catch the 10.56 at Swaythling. Got onto the boat at Southampton & got a saloon berth on the main deck.

6   Only woke up just in time to dress before we got in. Splendid passage. No qualms at all. [*In Paris*] By cab to 174 Rue de la Pompe where dwell Mdme & Mdlle de Hénaut³ whose address was given me by Vaughan & Byrne. Batten-Pooll⁴ of Hare's is here finishing for the Diplomatic. Ronald Campbell of Haileybury⁴ᵃ came tonight. B-P walked me round the town, i.e. Place de l'Etoile, Champs Elysées, Place de la Concorde, Rue de la Paix, l'Opéra, Tuileries & then home by Metropolitain. A wonderful town, big streets, fine houses & shops & hotels.

7   . . . I went to the Louvre today, a short hasty visit. I specially examined Leonardo's Bacchus, a haunting evil, & of course the Venus de Milo. She is very beautiful & yet she is not inhuman.
     [*The diarist describes his progress at length, in grammar, pronunciation, dictation &*
     translation & enjoys his increasing prowess: 'I'm getting on a bit already' he notes
     cheerfully, on his second day there. But the great adventure is in his exploration of the
     city, alone or in company with his fellow students, and his theatre visits. To omit or cut
     short so much of his enthusiastic & vivid writing is quite painful; 'sampling' while
     preserving a coherent account of events has been the aim.]
     12 Mdlle tells me that if I want a good place, perhaps Eton, I must be prepared to give not 2 but 4 years to French & German. This is rather a blow: but I'm quite game for it myself: have written home on the subject.
     My day in the Rue de la Pompe
     9.45, 9, or 9.15: breakfast; bread & butter & egg, usually with Pooll.

10–11, 10.15–11.15 or 11.30: lesson, varying from 1 hr to 1½ hrs

12. déjeuner: 2 courses & dessert

Afternoon, sight-seeing, almost always by myself

Tea. 4.30 or 5

7. Dinner: 2 courses or 3, & dessert. Smoking afterwards.

Apart from lessons & meals we don't see Mdlle or Mdme: hence meals or rather the smoking afterwards is prolonged for purposes of instruction.

17   F writes agreeing to 4 years: also to my going on to pension at Hanover, recommended by Campbell, when Mdlle can no longer have me.

19   Biked to Montmartre. Most of the streets are cobbled & hilly, the worst possible place for a bike. The most characteristic inhabitants hide by day & the whole place looks quiet & respectable.

20   . . . I was aiming at the Eglise du Sacre Coeur. I was much impressed by the church. The sculpture inside is better than usual, especially the founder offering the church, behind the high altar. I ascended the dome . . . the day was not very clear so I could only study the geography of the town: it is much larger than I thought, especially eastward.

23   American church: very nice church & service: the first time I had seen an American prayer book. Lunch at Duval & then walked & trammed to Bagneux Cimetière Parisien where I laid a few flowers on O. W.'s grave (Oscar Wilde) pure sentimentality & I was much too ashamed to tell anyone. The grave was in great disorder, a bunch of withered flowers evidently very old: I removed several thistles.

24   Bibliotheque Nationale, but was much too frightened by notices to go in: so strolled down to Hachette & bought a history of France for Florence Teesdale.

25   Clare & cousin Fanny came by the 5.45 from Bâle. They have been touring in Switzerland with the Penleys. They stay at the GFS Lodge. Sightseeing & a splendid tea at Rumpelmayers.

29   Reading the papers at Smiths I find that Mouse was 12th in the CS exam.

October

2   Invalides: the tomb [*Napoleon's*] is fine. The blue light is rather a trick but is certainly effective.

4   Louvre: a farewell visit. I discovered a whole series of rooms of Greek ceramics etc. back to back to the set I knew. What a place it is. Departed for Hanover by the 10 pm from Gare du Nord: Mdlle can't have me any longer. Fair journey . . . to Cologne at 8. Excellent breakfast, then to see the Cathedral & Bishop's museum. Returned to the station for the 10.14. I had left my dressing case with money, hat box, aquascutum & stick & umbrella in the carriage, having understood that I should continue in that same carriage. However that was now well on its way to Berlin while I was dumb on the platform. A guard, friendly though contemptuous, escorted me to the restaurant car where the head waiter acted as interpreter. Together we concocted a telegram. I fortunately had my place ticket so that we could give the exact spot . . . good lunch on the train & arrived at Hanover where I was met by Fraulein Lily: she had warned 10 porters & a guard, all apparently particular friends, to ask any young Englishman whether he wanted the Alte Döhrenstrasse [*the Abbenthern pension, recommended by Campbell in Paris*]. The men in the house are: Tyrwhitt Berners, *see* Eton note 44 of

Somerville's, once in my division. He is very musical, jolly, rather smart, talks in short incisive sentences with a good deal of wit. Kenny: Foreign Office: pleasant & clever but rather effeminate: I don't quite take to him. Algy West: no exam: was at Bowlby's: left last Christmas. He is known as Rebecca. Hugh Whittaker: Diplomatic: Eton & Magdalen: very rich, has been taking the party about in his motor: unfortunately he goes tomorrow: a good sort.

6   Walked in the town: clean & pleasant but dull after Paris.

8   Went with West to arrange lessons with Fraulein Matilda Abbenthern. My health has been steadily improving for the last week: at first I had bad constipation. I put it right with Cascara & Huniados-Janos water but that didn't effect any permanent cure. I took several doses of Listerine & after about the 2nd day began to get better.

14 West, Tyrwhitt & self to Church. 'Die Walkure' in the evening. Not nearly so good as Dresden where I saw it with F in 1902.

19 Tyrwhitt departed for Rue de la Pompe.

24 Walked with Hans, Frau Hermine Abbenthern's son, aged 14. He knows a lot of English: when we can't get on in German or English we speak Latin. My German consists of a fairly accurate use of the auxiliary verbs coupled to a very minute vocabulary.

November

1   Haircut at Koch's in the Theatreplatz. They cut it fairly well. Then I was rash enough to ask for a shampoo. They conducted me, arrayed in flowing white robes, to a subterranean chamber. There one man regulated the water supply tho' never certain whether it would be hot or cold & the other man scrubbed my head with a scrubbing brush & yellow soap . . . Cecil Blake, Evan's & Trinity came. I had known him slightly at Eton & Oxford. A trifle dull.

4   Blake & self to Church. 'Siegfried' from 6.30–11 pm! It was perfectly glorious. I had never heard it before & liked it much better than 'Die Walkure'. It is much brighter, full of youth & life.

11 West & self to Church. 'Tannhauser'. Much better than I had seen it in Brussels in 1902.

17 Chief event, sending off Kenny at 2 o'clock Sunday morning. We had a great excitement provided by Nicholson (naval brother of Harold) who seized on 2 flasks of cognac from the piccolo's tray. There was a great ado & Nicholson was hauled before the Bahnhofwache: but he had laid the flasks down on the platform where they were found by a guard & all passed off well. Most people were amused: not so the boy.

21 Blake & I to Hildesheim by tram. It is perfectly beautiful: the old houses have immense steep roofs with windows at impossibly frequent intervals, one above another. Some of the houses are coloured, notably on the market place. The Dom . . . contains the rose tree of Ludwig the Pious, long since dead but the root is said to remain: the present tree is about 100 years old. Batten-Pooll has arrived, following me from Paris. He talks our heads off but it's his only vice.

28 B-P & I to a Thee Abend given by a dancing class. All the men except one were young fellows just waiting for their commissions. They were in uniform, well

buttoned up to the neck, full of beer: & the windows were hermetically sealed. About 12 we moved on to the Hotel de Wien where the Anglo-American ball was on. We went in just as we were but didn't dance.

December

2 'Die Gotterdammerung' with West. The last moments are very grand if one knows the story but as performed tonight the end was unintelligble: we could not see Brunhilde on the fire, nor Hagen drown, nor the Rhine maidens secure the ring.

14 Blaking went. Great grief. Lily on the verge of tears all day.

18 My last lesson. B-P & I went by the 3.49 both bound for Town . . . Owing to fog we were nearly two hours late, in London where I was met by dear Page who is putting me up for two nights. We had breakfast then went out to see Agnew's exhibition . . . it included a Vandyke, a Lawrence, 2 good Reynolds & 2 Franz Hals. Mouse came to lunch, very cheerful. He is learning Hindustani & Persian for the ICS, also riding. Page & I went to Paternoster Row to satisfy my craving for religious literature. I eventually contented myself with one of the 'Essays for the Times' and a book on ritual. In the evening P & I dined in Old Compton Street. The talk French, the dinner was quite good & only cost 1/6. Then on to 'Yeomen of the Guard' revived at the Savoy.

20 Visit to Times Book Club in morning, then to Whitty at 'Burlington' offices. Holmes was out but W & I lunched at Hotel d'Italie. P & I & Whitty to Oxford House on the invitation of Bags where we found a large assembly enjoying itself in various harmless & non-alcoholic ways

21 Departed after a second visit to Times Book club where I found them selling remaindered reviews at 1d each. Travelled home with F who had been up for dentist. The Cottage party are here & we are all home except May, touring with Mabel Seymour in India.

25 Presents: I gave to F: Cripps' 'Silver Plate' (share) [*was this a picture? ed.*] Bl: writing case (share) Mi: Archaeological handbooks.

[*With this incomplete entry the diary for 1906 closes.*]

1907

January

1 Our party for the balls consisted of [*inter alia*] Lady St. Aldwyn[5] and Daisy Beach[6] both rather tremendous though very nice: Edith Alhusen, much the nicest of her family, taking after her mother: 'Blaking' of the Alte Döhenstrasse. F discovered him to be a relation through his mother: Tom Gist of Kingscote whose name appears to be really Frank. He was a tremendous success, pleasant & quiet, his clothes however are rather given to shouting: Richard Lascelles,[7] he hasn't been here for 5 years & has smartened up enormously in the interval: Farquharson, architect friend of F's . . . Haresfield was great fun: they had built out a room & passage: the floor was nice & springy though sticky at first. The 'cello player had smashed his instrument or himself so there were 3 violins & a piano which made a superfluity of fiddles.

3   Ball meet as usual. Each year we think his lordship[8] is going to refuse us but he never actually does. I rode Special. Uncle H complimented me on getting him to go so well . . . it was one of the very best of days. At Gloucester ball Iffs band returned after 2 years absence: they played gloriously under the leadership of the German-looking pianist with glasses: we never had a better band. During no. 17 dance I talked with Robeson as to foreign languages mastership.

9   To Ben Cotton's. Mr, Mrs & Miss all at home. Everything cheery & pleasant as usual. Ben & I talked theology & other Greats shop this evening. I had brought Inge's 'Truth & Falsehood in Religion' with me which began the conversation. Ben tells me that Bags has abandoned not only taking Orders as I had heard but Christianity itself after reading 'God & the Bible' and 'Ecce Homo'. He is going to train for a school inspector now.

12   Golf. In the evening more theology in which Miss Cotton joined. She reads a good deal of solid stuff, much to her father's disgust. I have begun Rasher's 'Christus in Ecclesia'. It seems very good, it is practical & marked by his common sense: it is very characteristic of his pigeon-holey mind & it is not dogmatic.

20   One of the most exciting days of my life. I received a letter from Robeson beginning thus: 'I have just had a wire from Somerville[9] stating that he has written to you about acting as my substitute at Eton for a bit'. It was rather sudden. I couldn't do anything till I heard from Somerville.

21   Letter from Somerville definitely inviting me. I wired acceptance, & wrote to explain how little I knew of the languages.

22   Home early [*from hunting*] to go to Banks Fee for Abbotswood dance . . . quite fair fun but there were no programmes which always makes things difficult for strangers. Danced with Witts of sorts & one Miss Fenwick.

23   Freezing hard. Home, where I found the children's party in full swing. I had to pack up & make off to Oxford to take my degree. I found a letter from Robeson at home saying that Somerville had told him he shouldn't have a substitute. So it is all off. Arrived late at Oxford. Harold Butler is putting me up. He lives in the Dean's house & has the second floor.

24   Took my degree with all ceremony . . . Dinner with Butler in Hall. I sat between HAL Fisher & Butler & was of course frightened to death of the former.

25   Lunch with Woolley. He hopes to go excavating in Tangier & enlarged on the number of vacant posts in archaeological work. He tried to persuade me to enter for a British Museum post vacated by Yeames. Walk with Gibby who is up reading History with a view to an All Souls Fellowship, but doing more music than reading I think. Gathorne Hardy[10] came to stay with Butler tonight. We kept it up for some time. Among other tales: one Tutton came here as a Don for a short time, rather a poor sort who soon went. One night he dined with the Warden [*Spooner*] who after struggling with the joint for some time remarked 'Oh my dear you've given us this muff Tutton again'.

26   Lunched with Chute.[11] He lives with Vivian Birchall in 50 High. He's recommended me to Frau Lürman at Dresden. He gives a promising account of Dresden.

30   Town. I met Ben. To 'The Doctor's Dilemma', Bernard Shaw's new piece . . . The acting certainly as brilliant as I have ever seen. Caught the night boat Queensborough

to Flushing . . . succumbed to a rather rough passage. Couldn't breakfast but ate a hearty lunch on the train.

31 Arrived Hanover about 3 & found Rebecca West waiting for me at the Lahmeyers.

February

5 Left Hanover for Dresden where I arrived at 8.30 at the Lehnhof Villa, so called in memory of the old home of the Lürman family. They were all playing 'Flinch' an American importation. The family & students are Herr Lürman, a friendly person: Frau Lürman, pleasant & ladylike, quite understands a joke but is rather strict & almost prim. Reminds me of a governess. Lore Lürman, 16, not pretty but very jolly: always in a state of suppressed revolt against her mother's strict system. Miss Foss, an American girl of 23. She is intelligent, or stuffed, I'm not sure which yet. Talks German with a pronounced American accent and rather bad German too. My room is 2nd floor, long & narrow, heated by hot air as is all the house. One window at end, opposite the door.

6 Slept badly last night on account of electric trams. Lost no time in making a visit to the Picture Gallery. Spent most time in the Holbein room & before the Sistine Madonna. I remember I was not much impressed with the Sistine in 1902: now I think it one of the most beautiful of all pictures. The little room is a perfect casket of gems.

[*Throughout his 6 weeks' stay in Dresden the diarist continues to visit galleries & collections, and to give informed opinions & criticisms of their quality.*]

7 Called on Fräulein Gottschald to whom I have been recommended by Eton masters.

8 1st lesson. Asking questions to probe my knowledge, or rather ignorance.

11 My first attempt at skating since '97 when I skated on Jordan at Eton . . . It must be 10 years almost to a day. Nobody laughed which was truly polite: one small boy with whom I conversed burst out laughing but that was because I addressed him as 'Sie'.

18 Frau Lürman took me to watch Lore's Tanz Stende this evening. All the mothers including me! sat up in the gallery & the children ages about 16–18 had the floor to themselves. They danced very oddly; the time was slow & the dancing stiff and angular. Men & girls very decently dressed, men in smoking jackets & black ties.

21 'Lohengrin' with Miss Foss. I had heard it once before, miserably given by Carl Rosa Co. Tonight was a revelation. We had seats in the Dritte Rang & I never heard voices sound so fine. It was spendidly staged, sung & acted & the music was of course magnificent. The orchestra consisted of between 70–80 performers. I hardly ever enjoyed anything so much.

23 'Ein Ideale Gatte' von Oskar Wilde, at Neustadt. Not very well done. None of the men were dressed in English fashion at all.

28 Called on a sister of Tom's who is staying in a pension here. She suffers a good deal from parental displeasure, I believe.

March

7,8, 9 Galleries & exhibitions with Miss Balston. Other visits, & 'Gesellschaft'[12] a combination of ceremonious introductions, theatricals, dancing [*Lore's friends much in evidence*]. The youths finished off all the available beer by about half time & the Lürmans congratulated themselves that there was no more. Certainly some were a bit rowdy at the end but nothing serious. A great success & one of the best evenings I've had.

12   Called on Mr Moore the parson at All Saints here. He showed me his books: he is tremendously keen on Northern saga . . . he showed me a plan of 'Norway & her colonies, England & America'. He taught the Copenhagen princes English & corresponds with Haakon. He was at Worcester Coll. Oxford & then chaplain at Copenhagen for two years.

17   Early Service. Moore kindly invited me to breakfast afterwards. While he was putting things away in the vestry he began an apology for his ritualism as regards wafer bread. It is very difficult to cut up or break foreign bread and he never knows how many there will be: he attaches no 'doctrinal significance' to the use of the wafer. In old days in Dresden there used to be 200 or more at an early celebration & he said the whole words of administration to each though he had no assistant. Now he only says the first part, having obtained his bishop's consent. Moore & Mrs M very kind at breakfast. Tea in the Zoological Gardens where I saw the only Polar Bear reared in captivity. I gather all others have died quite young.

19   In the evening a final game of 'Flinch'.

21   Left Dresden to my great sorrow. Arrived in Hanover about 6. I am staying at an Hotel as the Lahmeyers have no room, but I eat & spend the day with them.

22   Called on Matilda & drank coffee with her. She complimented me on my progress, as the others had done. I do really seem to have to have got on a bit.

25   I dined on the train with the Fergusson-Buchanan girls who have grown older & prettier but not more talkative.

26   Arrived after a good passage & went to 36 Ebury 'Street. Thick fog. At Berners Street found Holmes who showed his recent purchases in Japanese prints. I visited the exhibition of Ruskin drawings at the Fine Art Society Galleries & felt all my old enthusiasm rise again. With Whitty to Savoy for 'Gondoliers'.

30   [*At home again*] Stinchcombe on Outlaw. Maitland Wilson out, rather flourishing. He is less heavy in every way.

April

12   May arrived home from India at mid-day: great rejoicings: she seems fit & well & full of news. I went to the Penleys for a night or two. Reginald . . . arrived home about 10 & we were soon in the midst of Ecclesiastical law. He says that a fair & strict reading of the Ornaments Rubric would result in vestments being pronounced not only legal but obligatory.

14   Reginald & I called on Cousin Annie. She has Ben Browne's children with her: we met them on the road (I never saw her again).

27   Uley on Special. Dr Campbell hinted that Cousin Annie is very bad. Ben's children were at the meet & Lloyd took a great interest in it. They ran from Owlpen to Coaley Wood, then into the Vale: left-handed to Downham & up to the Ridge & lost. The latter part was during a terrific rainstorm from which Uncle H, Mr Tidswell & self sheltered in Powell's farm, near Downham. When we found them again they were

over by Newark: they immediately ran back again towards the Ridge, then turned & crossed the valley once more & ran to ground above Wotton, near Combe. We all took weeping farewells of Thompson (the huntsman: he went to Brandywine Hounds in USA).

May

4 Arrived safely at Paris & proceeded to 174 Rue de la Pompe where I was in September. I shall have it all to myself for a bit, I believe for 4 weeks. I anticipate a few dull moments but it will do my French a world of good.

7 Saw the morgue for the first tme: it is closed now, as a public exhibition that is. Admired Notre Dame more than ever today: it is wonderfully beautiful, inside & out. A few minutes in the Louvre looking at the Chaldean exhibits: some of the early seated figures show marvellous rendering of muscle, especially in the right arms.

11 Concert at the Trocadéro. The first time I had heard Caruso: he has an enormous voice under beautiful control.

12 Broiling hot. American church. By boat to Sèvres: half an hour in the museum, china of all ages & countries, then I walked up the hill into the wood, lay for a while reading 'Figaro' & then on to St Cloud where I arrived just in time to hear the band play La Donna e Mobile. Tea & home by boat.

14 La Dame aux Camélias at Théâtre Sarah Bernhardt. Her voice was extraordinary, soft, gentle & childlike. I thought I had got through without tears but I had to blow my nose very hard during the death scene.

17 The d'Orvals of 61 Rue Borghèse invited me to dinner. They are friends of Father's & stayed at Hardwicke last year when I was away. Monsieur is an invalid: Mdme is a sister of Countess Kolowrat of Teinsitzl. There are two girls. In the middle of dinner Sascha Kolowrat turned up: he is a big jolly person but rather a bounder. We all proceeded together to the Odéon where we saw a rather amusing piece, La Francaise. We were in the Loges. Afterwards Sascha & I called in at Maxim's. It is a curious place & very horrible if one stops to think. What surprised me was the number of quiet, respectable-looking men sitting in twos & threes with their drinks, apparently taking no part in the proceedings. It may have been looker-on's interest, the same as mine, but they were men of forty who would almost have outgrown that.

18 Lunch with the Albert Mettetals [*friends of Father's*]. She is perfectly delightful & he is very nice. I managed to talk French all the time.

21 'Salomé' at the Théâtre de Chatelet. Conducted by Strauss himself [*detailed appraisal*].

26 American Church. Tea, a present from Clare, in memory of last time at Rumpelmeyers.

27 Mabel de Pierredun asked me to dinner. She has grown prettier, I thought but Agnes not quite so pretty as she was 5 years ago. Michel de Pierredun, very nice & kind, & Prince Camille, delightful. I had never seen the Count before; the rest I met whilst visiting Podwein with F in 1902. The théâtre was the Vaudeville where we saw 'Le Ruisseau' . . . beautifully stage-managed & most amusing. The inevitable Englishman was almost more foolish than usual.

28   Bought a plaque for my bike, 3 francs at the tobacconist beyond the Mairie. Then biked to Concorde: the Champs Elysées are full of holes: it is a nerve-wearing business, biking in this place.

29   Bike to Place Bastille. In trying to pass on the wrong side I got my bike tied up in a long cart whip which fortunately broke. A franc satisfied the severe but not unduly excited driver. The Paris streets are really dreadful for riding in: half are cobbles & the other half very holey wooden pavements.

31   Went to see Les Arènes, the amphitheatre in the Rue de Navarre. Only one half is excavated: one can see the seats, restored, the underground cages & prisons. It was built in Hadrian's time: wrecked about 5th century & excavated in 1870.

June

1   Short visit to Luxembourg. [*Amongst many pictures mentioned is 'Pierre et Jean courant au sepulchre'*] In this St Jean has the face of a keen young American & St Peter has a haggard face & his eyes wide open as if he had been crying.

3   Bought a rather nice cloisonné box for Hammy Berners' wedding present at Bon Marché. It was quite a bargain at 6.50 francs.

4   Great excitement! Droghedra Moore is 1st in Foreign Office exam, Ronald Campbell 3rd. Jeanne wild with joy.

5   Read Rasher on the 'New Theology' in 'Contemporary': not very good as he credits his opponents with too extreme views.

9   Russian Church . . . no organ but music which is sweet & plaintive. More men than women, very reverent . . . Antenil steeplechases, especially Grand Steeplechase de Paris. The jumps seemed small compared with what I imagine the Liverpool jumps to be. A motor managed to plunge into the brook another part of which forms the water jump. The crowd most unsympathetic: 'Quel dommage que la machine n'est pas brisée'. It was I think quite sufficiently bashed up.

11   Hammy Berners & his wife passed through Paris but I missed them at their hotel.

13   Madame burst into the room while I was having my lesson today screaming 'Le feu, le feu'. Mdlle & I dashed out & found the little cupboard-pantry place blazing like fun. I must say at first glance I despaired of saving the house, or at least our flat. Mdlle who was quite calm & collected & I hurled water on to the flames & at the end of about 5 minutes it was all over bar the shouting. This latter however occupied some time. First the fire brigade arrived: then an agent & a sergeant-de-ville turned up, rather late. The floor above where the servants sleep was full of smoke so we smashed in a door or two, the doors all being locked, but there was no more fire & the smoke had come from below. The brigade clared off the débris. Two good oriental rugs were burnt otherwise nothing of value. I had my hair, eyebrows & lashes burnt but that was all.

15   'Les Buffons' at Théâtre Sarah Bernhardt. The caste was perfect: everyone looked as if the part was expressly written for them as indeed it may have been. Sarah was even more charming than in 'La Dame aux Camélias'. The acting was brilliant: one was intimately acquainted with each character before he had spoken a dozen lines.

18   Visited Liancourt, (Ecole de l'Ile de France) It is kept by Leplat whose first wife was Miss Brown, an old governess of the Montgomeries. He took me round the place . . .

it is the old chateau of the La Rochfoucaulds . . . ample space for 80 boys and 15 masters . . . splendid grounds. I 'assisted' at a German lesson, had tea with the masters & went round again with Hawkins who was in the Cambridge XI in '96. I began to have palpitations of the heart which increased when he made me a definite offer of a place as master for a year. It was very attractive in many ways but it was rather longer than I wanted to stay in France at the time. I tried to show due gratitude to Hawkins & Leplat.

24 Never walk along the Quais looking at the books for more than ¼ hr! One becomes giddy & I've felt as if I were twisted round ever since. Today Mdlle produced her great exercise in syntax, showing the number of ways in which one can arrange a sentence.

25 Exhibition of plans etc. of Old Paris. It was wonderfully small until the last century: enclosed by a moat, crossed by various bridges leading to the Faubourgs, St Germain, St Honoré etc.

28 The youngest Officier de la Legion d'Honneur honoured us with his presence tonight. He is a cousin of Mdme's. He has been in Egypt for 8 years & is anxious for English & French to unite in preventing the importation of arms from Germany.

July

3 Met Miss Balston in the Metro. Tom had told me that she was in Paris but I didn't know her address. She says Monty is back at the farm but they don't whether he is forgiven by his tyrannical father.

14 . . . rose at 6 o'clock to go & see the Grande Review. Perfect weather. Troops were paraded facing the tribunes, military schools in front, infantry behind, & cavalry & artillery in the third line . . . the captive balloon marched past attached to its carriage. The parade was superintended by General Picquart, the great supporter of Dréfus who is now Minister for War. He has aged very fast: is not over popular sharing much of the dislike commonly felt for the Ministry of Clemenceau. The balon dirigeable 'La Patrie' came flying over the parade ground at Longchamps & wheeled about in the air apparently as it liked. It looked as if it went about 30 miles an hour. Later, fireworks near the Pont-Neuf: about as good as Fourth of June, certainly not better.

15 Miss Balston & I strolled down the Champs Elysées & eventually arrived at Rocher for tea. Monty is probably going to be sent away to seek his fortune: he has been foolish enough not only to quarrel with his father but also to make himself a nuisance on his brother's farm.

18 Left Paris by the 9.30 for Dieppe: beautiful crossing.

20 To Toddy Vaughan at Eton. Prolonged discussion [*8 pages in fact*] with John Christie about his innovative methods by gaining older boys' confidence to improve 'morality', which is not welcomed by older masters. To tea came Robert Bridges[13] who complimented me on my youthful appearance: he was quite amusing & rather wild-looking.

22 Home. Everyone there. Also the new Missioner L. P. Penny of New College: interesting & rather clever: we discussed Christian Science till 12 pm.

28   Flower Service afternoon. Canon Grenside came from Quedgeley: he turns out to be the father of Grenside who was at Malvern Link with me. Read the lesson in the evening: choirboys were rather quick to laugh during service: the vicar gave them a tremendous blowing up afterwards.

August

1   Camp at Beaulieu Park. I shall have the Oxford cyclists under me as well as the Bucks.

28   Picnic at Symonds Yat. Large party of Browne cousins, Grensides & other friends . . .

29   I biked over to the kennels whither Uncle H had preceded me. We looked over all the hounds, new entry & dogs in detail, bitches rather quicker. Mr Legard kept saying 'What a *noble* head'. He was much struck with Gilbert who is to be huntsman now, Thompson having got a place in America.

September

12   Tea at the Palace. The Bishop expressed no opinion as to the Festival but it is generally understood that he approves of it so far. A telegram sent in from home had been pursuing me about the Town. It was from Buddensieg[14] marked urgent & urging me to start at once for my interview. Impossible to pack up for 6 months in two hours so I wired that I would start on Monday if they still wanted. [*There have been no hints about this momentous invitation before this date.*]

13   'Messiah'. Agnes Nichols made a great effort to fill Albani's place: she certainly sang better than Albani has done of late but her voice is on a lower level altogether. Soloman went wrong in the introductory obligato of 'The Trumpet shall sound' but otherwise played excellently.

14   This afternoon I received a telegram 'Duke of Cumberland Gmunden Oberoesterreich expects you Thursday next' & then trains etc. This was my first intimation of the place. I decided to go to Paris first & then on.

16   Met Mouse in Town & had tea & dinner with him: if all goes well he starts for India in November. I said a tender farewell & departed for Newhaven.

17, 18   [*Diarist travels via Rue de la Pompe where he spends the night & no doubt imparts the good news, Munich where he stays at the Bellevue Hotel in Karlplatz & thence to Gmunden.*]

19   Gmunden 3.15. I was met by a short professional sort of man who turned out to be Herr Bibliothekrat Buck. He put me into a smart carriage & pair & another was in attendance for my luggage, & we drove up to the Schloss. Here I changed into frock coat etc. & had tea. Buck showed me over part of the castle including the library & the princes' rooms. The library is a place out of which to take books, not a place in which to read them. Buck apparently orders what he likes from any part of the world. The elder prince has a tame lion; it is 8 months old. Buck advised me to talk much & fluently to the Duke & not to return monosyllabic answers. We went down to the interview. The Duke is an oldish man, bald, ugly: looks a little like a walrus. He was very nice & friendly & we talked for about an hour principally about Oxford. Then I was introduced to the two princes: the elder Georg Wilhelm is tall & pleasant-looking but far from handsome: he has some disease that makes him limp. Both he & the Duke wore some Austrian uniform. The younger prince Ernst August is better

looking, not so tall but straight. We three talked for the best part of two hours till it was time to get ready for dinner. I had an ordinary dress coat with me which the Duke hates. So I wore my frock coat. Buck had distributed my cards right & left so people realised who I was. I was introduced to a mass of people, tutors, doctors, officials of the court & ladies in waiting. Most of them spoke a little English. Just before dinner I was introduced to the Duchess: she is perfectly charming: grey hair, not beautiful but such a quiet shy manner, most fascinating. The two princesses, eldest married to Prince Max of Baden, apparently nice but rather stiff & gauche. We were about 12–15 to supper: very good food but too much of it, ditto drink. The servants wore a gorgeous scarlet livery & are bedecked with medals. I afterwards discovered that these are given by various Dooks etc. who stay here. After supper more talking: we all sat round in a circle, the ladies in waiting knitting: sometimes the conversation was general, sometimes in little groups. About 10.15 the ladies retired & about 11 we all went up. My room was large & comfortable but the window is ridiculously small & the room rather dark.

20   Coffee at 8.30, then got up by degrees. Began writing to Clare. About 11 Buck came in & we sat one each side of the table. He went straight to the point & said that I had made 'a very good impression' on all the family apparently & would 'do well'. They are going to give me board & lodging & 2,000 marks – about £100 – for the 6 months November–April. I shall have to give 2 or 3 lessons a week & spend 2 or 3 afternoons with Ernst August but otherwise I shall have my time to myself. Lunch–Dinner was a gorgeous process. We had to wait for the Royal family for some time: just before they came in I was sent for. The Duke & Duchess professed to be very glad I was going to accept the place & I thanked them as politely as I knew how. They then came in & worked their way round the circle which comprised about 30 people. We had two tables. I sat at the first one with the Duke & Duchess & most of the court: at the second sat Ernst August, a princess & most of the tutors, doctors etc. We ate off silver plates, I don't know how many courses, & towards the end some not over-dry champagne was brought in & we drank the Duke's health, it being the eve of his birthday: he is going away tomorrow so we are keeping it today. At dinner, & at supper last night the Duke drank my health. Today he drank that of von Grote[15] & I observed that I ought to have risen. I hung about after lunch talking etc. & then got off by the afternoon train. It took 2 carriages & pairs to get me & my two small dressing cases to the station. Stayed at the Bellevue again at Munich.

21,   [*Sightseeing in Munich.*] Church, exhibitions, 2 picture galleries, tea in the Hofgarten
22, 23   and two theatres.

24   [*In Paris.*] Found heaps of letters and a telegram of congratulation: Clare, Grace, Mi & Blanchie wrote. Clare writes that Cousin Annie died on Monday.

25   Coleridge Kennard appeared from Hanover.[16] Called on M. le Vicomte de Soissons. He inhabits a tiny room at Rue de Regrattier. The staircase is 400 years old. He was in bed when I arrived. He has just got on to the New York Herald so doesn't get to bed till 4 or 5. He is now rolling in riches, £3 a week, & as he was to be sold up next week this money is very acceptable. He talks with a strong American accent. His sketches look rather nice & he exhibits a certain amount already. He is 22.

26   Dinner with de Soissons at the American Artists Association. A Parisian reputation is worth a great deal in America.

October

11 Clare writes that Arthur Clifford is announced as candidate for the Stroud division.

17 Coleridge Kennard & self to classical matinee of 'Tartuffe' & 'Les Précieuses Ridicules'. We both cried with laugher at the latter, the two Coquelins brilliant esp. l'aîné.

21 'Faust' at Opéra. Csse. Amande de Chabannes had invited me to her box.

22 Bought a new pair of boots at Manfield. I don't think they are very good.

25 I had invited de Soissons to dinner. We had a cocktail – I believe my first – at the Bodega . . . then we walked till he had to go to the Herald office. He showed me the last remains of his family home, a single column built into the Bourse de Commerce. There used to be an observatory on the top where Catherine de Medici observed the stars & amused herself in other ways. The hôtel was destroyed in the Revolution & everything stolen, including solid silver furniture.

31 Off to Gmunden, which is to be my home for six months I hope. I have a different & to my mind much nicer room. It is on the 4th storey, right up in the tower. It has 3 good windows & looks out over the park. At present with glorious autumn tints the view is lovely. Everyone friendly and kind as before. I had a short interview with the Duke & Duchess but did not see the princes till dinner time.

November

1 I gave Ernst August my first lesson. It consisted in his reading 'Pickwick'. He read pretty well but I am not sure how much he understood: he generally asked when he was puzzled . . . In the evening I talked to GW & EA. They are both rather jolly & I believe EA will be great fun when we are less shy & know each other's tongues better.

2 Bought some handerchiefs. The view from the Traum-brucke over the Traum See about 5 in the evening is wonderful. To the left the mountains catch the sun, in front the lake is a soft blue & to the right the mountains are blue & purple with the sun setting in a lemon sky behind them.

3 Tea with Buck who is married to a Frenchwoman. Lutter the mathematics tutor also came in & played the piano for a time.

5 2nd lesson. I had prepared a certain amount of the Pickwick so that I trust EA drew more profit from it. I had a talk with M. Chambille: we are going to exchange lessons. Cinematograph in the evening under Lutter's superintendence.

7 Everyone departed except EA & self & Buck who stays one more night. Getting off was a great process. The Duke went last & didn't appear till 9.15, the 'special' being timed to start at 9.30. He wore a curious hat like a tall bowler with no particualr brim: he had as usual no collar; his clothes except a pair of enormous boots were covered by a yellow Inverness cape: he smoked a large cigar & looked perfectly beastly . . .

10 Sunday EA & I drove down to the Protestant church. We didn't start till 9.30, the advertised time for church. Apparently it is quite correct to come very late. The vicar preached for about ½ an hour without notes & without hesitation or repetition. I understood everything.

16   The weather having cleared up EA decided to take his birthday hunting expedition, lasting till Tuesday. I immediately decided to proceed to Vienna by the afternoon train, arriving at Hotel Wandl at 10 o'clock.

17   Took the tram to Penzing to call on Oberfinanzrat von Kniep. He took me over to the [*Ducal*] Palace where we found Pockels-Sy, the Hofintendant. I went through the Palace but the funiture was all covered up. Pockels-Sy & I then went into the town for lunch at the Opern restaurant. To 'Die Lustige Witwe' which I enjoyed more than at Munich. Short dinner, then to Hofburg theatre to the Duke's box where I found Kniep's daughter & son in law. Afterwards came Finanzrat Andrea. He took me to supper at the Rathaus Keller which was full to overflowing. However we found seats & had a capital time. He is very jolly & we got through a lot of conversation.

18, 19   [*Visits to museums and art galleries, recalling previous occasion with F in 1902. Diarist is particularly captivated by the Velasquez Cabinet this time.*]
The gem is 'The Infant Margareta Theresia'. She has her golden hair nicely brushed & tied. She is laced up in her stiff dress & rests her hands on the crinoline. The colouring is most delightful, the dress being grey slashed with pink: the left hand holds red flowers. I left the hotel at 9.30 pm & had a most uncomfortable journey back to Gmunden which I reached at 6.30 in the morning. It was snowing but they had sent the shut carriage.

28   Tea at Bucks where there was a party with games. There were two very nice Mandelsloh girls. I managed to play 'Consequences' & even 'Telegrams' in German.

29   Hair cut at Knauers. He insisted on curling down the hair that is inclined to turn up at the side of the head, as he said the Prince would say it was not 'schön'.

December

1   EA went to visit Prince Adolphus of Schäumburg Lippe. This was the first railway journey EA had ever made by himself. He carried it out, including one change, quite successfully.

7   Tea at Pockels-Sy. Frau P is a delightful small round creature & they have 3 or 4 jolly girls from 14 downwards. We drank tea out of glasses & ate various Brötchen, eggs, sausage. Then came Torte accompanied by wine. It was an odd meal & the whole party bore a slight resemblance to an Ibsen play.

10   EA took Buck & me for a drive round by Alt Münster. We crossed the railway at a place where Queen Alexandra was once nearly run over.

12   Court returned, apparently all well. The Duke asked me whether 'they had hurt me'. I was able to reassure him. I had my first lesson today with Fräulein Trinks, recommended to me by the Klenck family.[17]

16   Grafin Kielmansegg explained that the reason why the Duke never went to England since his visit with his tutor was because Queen Victoria arranged the marriage of his sister Frederica, a marriage which he did not care about.

18   Talking with Finanzrat Andrea about the Boers, he said his friends had a very poor opinion of the Boer leaders: they were fighting only for power & money . . . Ladysmith might have been taken if the bombardment had been heavier but the Boer commander had property in Ladysmith & would not risk destroying it. Before dinner Wersebe[18] asked me what I wanted for Christmas from the Duke & Duchess. I replied

that I should like to think for a bit. Having seen a nice art-history advertised I meditated that but as it cost about £1 I thought I would ask Buck. Buck & Wersebe came to the conclusion that I could very well ask for 'Paar Hundert Kronen'!! Buck suggested Meyer's 'Konversations Lexikon' which I jumped at.

22 The Grossherzog & Grossherzogin of Mecklenburg-Schwerin arrived. She was Princes Alexandra (died 1963). She is dark & pretty & quite like her sisters. I should fancy she was the prettiest of the three.

24 This is the great day here, or rather the great evening. Festivities did not begin till 5 though the Duchess spent the whole day arranging tables in the Hall. At 5, service, mostly singing, in the Chapel. All the ladies were in white for the first time since I've been here as the Court is still in mourning for the Queen of Hanover. At 8 Bescherung, ie present-giving. At the end of the Hall stood a splendid Christmas tree: all round the walls were tables each with a white cloth: thereon stood the presents. From the Duke & Duchess I received: Meyer's Lexikon. A leather travelling writing case. A leather pocket or handkerchief case. A crocodile & silver purse. A paper cutter with a view of the Castle. A pair of gold links with little stones in them, not to mention a basket of sweets, marzipan etc. & a very pretty English Christmas card. From EA a walking stick (It was carried off from Guys, hairdresser in London on May 20 1908 by F. H. D. Jay of New Coll. He found out his mistake but lost the stick). At dinner & supper we had some excellent cold punch, manufactured by a secret process known only to the Kellermeister.

25 My first Christmas away from home, sad but inevitable. Church in the morning, in the Chapel. In the evening children's service & present-giving. I sat down in the nearest vacant place alongside a row of children. Each child went up & was given its present & then returned to shake hands with the Duchess. The presents were books, clothes etc. Before supper the Duke said to me 'I hear you tried to get a present this afternoon' referring to my sitting with the children. This evening a discussion on orders in Austria & Germany: apparently the former are much more difficult to obtain. Called on the Mandelslohs. I found the Baronin, 4 sons & 2 daughters there. One boy draws excellently (he was killed in 1915) & showed me caricatures of the officers & teachers at Neustadt, the Military Academy. Cinematograph in evening. I presented a box of cigars to my servant & 50 to the man who served me the first week or so. I also gave 5 marks to my housemaid who kissed my hand, slightly to my embarrassment.

29 Expedition to Almsee where the Duke has just built a new shooting box, the Hubertihaus. We drove there in 2 carriages, 4 horses each. Parts of the road were very slippery & EA's horses were not roughed. We changed horses at Grünau & from there it was better. The whole day was good fun but there was too much mist to see much: we went over the old Stifthaus, now an inn. Tea at Grünau on the way back. The Duke was very funny & behaved abominably. The Duchess had to hit him on the arm once, whereupon he turned & hit the Grafin Kanitz saying 'Geben Sie's weeter'.

31 Fitzner of Vienna turned up with his quartet. They played really beautifully & it was a tremendous treat to hear such a concert in comfort & with no applause. We drank the New Year in with some éclat.

1908

January

1   Dr Buddensieg arrived today. He is an oldish man, nice & friendly. We got on excellently together, in German to my surprise & delight. It seems he doesn't care much about talking English. EA told me he could remember the time when he couldn't say his prayers in German: they had an English nurse so that he learnt English really before he learnt German.

3   Buddensieg came into the lesson this morning . . . he seemed pleased, & afterwards advised me to drop grammar & pay particular attention to History of Literature.

5   Sunday. In the evening came extraordinary people called Glockeurs. 35 men dressed in white with bells on their belts. Resting on the shoulders & covering the head was a paper house lighted up from inside: there were houses, castles, churches etc. They danced about for a time & then marched past. No one seems to know the origin.

7   Prince & Princess of Schaumberg Lippe turned up.

8   Grand Duchess of Wurtemberg, mother of Princess of S.L. (above) came today. She is a dear old lady, frightfully keen on soldiers.

9   The Duke was very amusing tonight about his visit to the Shah at Vienna. The Shah was wearing a wonderful coat, the front entirely covered with pearls: & the trousers of an Austrian field marshal! A few days afterwards he came to shoot with the Emperor. His carriage was driven by postillions: he sat in front & his brother held a red umbrella over his head. It was the depth of winter. He was received & then drove on to his stand: the carriage stopped in the middle of the field, sank into the mud & had to be pushed out by six men. As it jerked free of the mud the Shah toppled over, red umbrella & all, into the body of the carriage! He was placed to shoot near an opening in a wood fence: the game was driven out straight at him. He shot a right & a left & then refused to take any further notice of the mass of deer pouring round him. The Duke thought the better of him for refusing to shoot in such an unsporting way.

14   EA, Princess Olga & self to Wiedman's Ruh for tobogganing, a big toboggan with brakes.

22   This evening Pockels-Sy asked me 'Does the air here make you tiresome in the evening?' EA roared with laughter.

February

3   Another new game. Mary Klenck had offered to teach me ski-running & then Graf Pachta offered to lend me his skis. So we had our first try on Tastelberg. I fell a lot but ran & slid enough to realise what a grand sport it is.

7   The Duchess showed me her room: it is full of books & photographs: some lovely china & miniatures.

10   Today arrived Florizel von Reuter & his mother. He is 15½: born in America, his father German, his mother's father English, & her mother French so he has a fair mixture of blood in him. He played after dinner, very wonderful technique & a Strad, but not desperately inspiring.

13   Cloudless sunshine on the snow. Large party to Aussee then walk about 3 hours then toboggan some 2 miles to Steg. The mountains were white & grey & blue against a deep blue sky. Tobogganing at the end went well especially the last bit where there are jumps.

17   Tobogganed in the garden with Reuter who is quite human at times. He left today.

24   Great excitement: the Prüfung[19] began. Today EA did a German essay. We took turns to sit by & watch, also encourage but of course not help. Buddensieg doesn't come till the oral.

25   English in the afternoon. I had sent in three themes for Buddensieg to choose from ie Story of Quentin Durward, or Merchant of Venice or Diary of a Shooting Expedition. Without supplying him with word for word essays I had stuffed him full of subject matter as the point was that he should show knowledge of the language rather than brilliance of ideas.

26–29   Prüfung continued. EA fairly tired by now.

March

2   The Duke & Graf von der Deckern-Adendorf talked among other matters of Munchhausen, the Hanoverian minister. He challeneged Bismarck to a duel but B wouldn't fight & simply sent his adjutant to be rude to M: M however refused to be drawn into a fight with *him*. When M was arrested he was treated with every indignity & put into a 3rd class carriage: he threatened to show his Red Eagle at the window & so obtained his transfer to a 2nd class.

8   Buddensieg arrived from Dresden to conduct the oral Prüfung.

9   The Duke & Wense attended & all teachers were present. Mathematics, Chemistry & Physics went very well. Religion most trying: old Koch asked questions & couldn't hear the answers. Each tutor examined in his own subject. In the evening the Duchess told me I was to come back whenever I liked: she told me I was a 'good boy' & seemed generally satisfied with me.

10   . . . Last of all, English. Poor EA was absolutely tired out & made some very wild shots. I asked him the story of The Merchant of Venice, one of the themes we had prepared. He broke down utterly, turned round to the 'assistants' saying he knew the story well enough but he could not explain it. However they gave him quite a good mark even on his actual performance. Buck thought he ought to have A as he is notoriously better at English than at French, but Buddensieg said quite rightly that they could only go by the actual performance. After the examination was all over & we had discussed the marks the Duke & Wense & EA came back & Buddensieg made a rather impressive address. He told EA to give thanks first to God & then to thank his parents & teachers. The Duke spoke & almost broke down, thinking of Prince Christian I expect. He thanked us all very much & shook hands with us. It was really quite touching.

11   Left Gmunden for Vienna. The parting was a very real wrench for me. I have been so happy there. The whole family travelled by 'special', very comfortable. The Palais is most beautifully furnished with the Hanover furniture. There are several wonderful silver tables & excellent Gobelins. EA & Buck left for Egypt. We took a touching farewell. I was very sorry to see the last of him.

[The diarist stays at the Ducal Palace in Vienna until well into April but follows his own pursuits now that tutoring is over though still seeing a good deal of the Duke & Duchess. He writes perceptive notes about the family with whom he has been so happy.]

The Duke Born 1845. Ernst August Adolphus Georg Frederik. Duke of Cumberland. Duke of Brunswick Luneberg. Succeeded to British titles of his father in 1878. In same year he married Princess Thyra of Denmark. He is tall, close cropped white hair on a nearly bald head: dark moustache: small nose, hooked keen eyes: slightly pugnacious expression. Intelligent & well-educated, asks thousands of questions & wants to get to the bottom of everything. Good company: full of good stories & appreciates other peoples'. His behaviour at meals is remarkable: he will suddenly turn & kiss the Duchess & strike the lady on the other side. He is fond of giving horse-bites to his neighbours. He gave the Duchess of Würtemberg quite a sharp one & she leapt with a cry. At dinner he takes biscuits for the family & throws them to the various members. His favourite expression of disgust is 'Es ist wirklich zu dumm!' the accent increasing on each word.[20]

The Duchess b. Princess Thyra, youngest daughter of Christian IX of Denmark. Medium height: plenty of grey, almost white hair which became much whiter during the illness of Prince Christian: small rather upturned nose, large grey eyes: sweet & charming expression. Her manner is simple & graceful: sometimes rather shy, sometimes emphatic & decided: she has quite her own ideas about how things should be done: she is an extremely orthodox Lutheran & heard with marked disgust of the honour conferred on Strauss. Devoted to the Duke & to her family, as they all are to each other.

Prinz Georg Wilhelm b. 1880. Tall, a little like his mother: suffers from hip disease & is lame & altogether delicate.

Prinz Ernst August b. 1887. Extremely nice & open-hearted. A born sportsman. Not literary at all but works conscientiously: memory not nearly so bad as he makes out: spontaneous intellectual thought is beyond him.

Other children

Pz Christian Frederik b. 1885. Died young

Pss Marie Louse b. 1879

Pss Alexandra b.1882

Pss Olga b. 1884

March continued

12 The Duchess gave me EA's photo, signed. She also introduced me to the old nurse who has been there 25 years. Walk with Lutter to the Zoo where we saw the lion 'Willy'.

15 Sunday. English church at the Embassy. Left cards at the Embassy in the afternoon & coming away met Palairet[21] whom I had not seen since Eton.

16 Walk in Schönbrunn. English Embassy to dinner ie Sir Edward & Lady Goschen[22] Carnegie: Gregory & Mrs G., Bruce[23] & Palairet. Bruce was my fagmaster at Eton & is as delightful as then: we had a most amusing time together.

24   Concert at the Embassy. Mrs Gregory, a granddaughter of Jenny Lind, sang very nicely.

27   The Duchess gave me a ticket for 'Wintermärchen'.

28   A party for the Schatzkammer.[24] The jewels are wonderfully fine & there are 'relics' usually inaccessible. Box for 'John Gabriel Borkman'.

30   Box with Wense & Lutter, 'Husaarenfieber'. Supper in Löwenbräu, just outside Burg theatre. I drank 2½ pots of beer, about 2½ pints: Lutter drank 3 & Wense 5 of course without turning a hair. We had some Liptauer cheese. The waiter told me that I could get it in a place in Leicester Square.

31   Dinner with Palairet & then to the Duse[25] in 'Rosmersholm'. Her extreme naturalness is most attractive.

April

2   Count William Akleveldt to dinner. The Kellermeister produced some 1783 Rheinwein: it was brought out of the Rathaus cellars of Bremen & lay in the Hanover cellars for about 100 years. It was quite bitter but when one added sugar it was good: no-one would prefer it to 20 or 30 yr old Rheinwein.

3   I am 25. Dinner with Palairet. To the Duse in d'Annuzio's 'La Gioconda'.

5   Tea with Palairet. F writes from Egypt: he has met Prinz Georg Wilhelm at Assuan, was invited to dinner: they seem to have got on splendidly. This evening the Duchess read extracts from GW's letters: he complained of the complicated nature of the English service at Khartoum: the Duke sympathised & expatiated on the difficulties of following: the Duchess merely remarked 'It is so simple'.

7   Yesterday I asked Lutter to suggest that I should retire on Wednesday. He had not found an opportunity to do so & the Duchess first heard of my intention from the Goschens. This was extraordinarily awkward & this evening I was on tenterhooks all the time.

8   Left Vienna. Before dinner I was summoned to the Duke's study. I expressed my sorrow that the news of my going should have got round in that way but he made nothing of that at all. He & the Duchess said most awfully nice things, & gave me their photographs, also Olga's. The Duchess gave me a beautiful monogram pin, EA & T intertwined with a crown above. I wore it after dinner. The Duke forgot to drink my health till dessert but then thanked me for what I had done & invited me to return whenever I liked. I said goodbye to the Duke after dinner. The Duchess sent for me in the evening & said goodbye. Lutter was with me to the last moment. I went by the 9.50 for Hanover.

[So ended a most extraordinary six months. News from Gmunden filters through into the diaries: EA's successful military career and his marriage to the Kaiser's daughter: the birth of another Ernst August who was to continue the warm friendship over the years, into the diarist's 93rd year when he made his final visit: the last of many he made in response to the Duke's hospitable invitation.]

9   My fellow passengers were excited in various degrees by the Duke's label on my boxes, the remains of my Gmunden–Vienna journey.

13, 14	Left Hanover, arrived Victoria. Tom Balston met me on the platform: we hadn't met since we went down in 1906. He is living with Page at 107 Eaton Terrace. Lunched at the Mess of the Inns of Court Rifles with Ben Cotton, Tom & Fitzgerald.
15	... lunch whither came Tom & Whitty who pretends to be complete master of the novel department at Chatto & Windus. With Tom to see Maud Allen who has arranged dances to pieces of classical music: she dances barefoot ...
16	Assisted Tom into his uniform: he is going to camp. Then home, after much the longest absence I have ever endured: 7 months.
17	Good Friday. We have a new curate.

May

8	About 4 o'clock telephone goes. I dash out & Ketha tells me from Cottage that Blanchie is ill: doctor & nurse there & all well. About 7 we heard that a girl was born. Audrey Pamela. Dr Knight reported to have remarked 'D.n'. Mi & Bl have always professed not to mind but the rest of us rather bored.
15	... I went to tea with H. H. Hardy who was up with me & is now a beak at Rugby. He invited me to stay the night & I, though luggageless accepted. He showed me over the Close, the Armoury & the Chapel: this is Butterworth of Keble, & apart from its streakiness, is good.
20	Town for the day. Travelled up with Linda Birchall who looked beautiful in purple. Hair cut at Guy's where Jay of New Coll. carried off the stick EA gave me. *see* above. Measured by Davies & Son for evening suit. Photographed by Beresford of Brompton. He took 16 positions, talking almost incessantly.
23	Up to stay with Butler at New Coll. Nothing would satisfy Joseph but that I must talk German with Zimmern.
25	Went to see Waterfield, Oxford Appointments Committee, & put my name down there.
26	To Eton to stay with Vaughan. John Christie took me to his digs in the High. H says he is getting on excellently with little friction. I should fancy he has slightly modified his methods.
27	Chapel. Shakespeare Society: they read Faustus. Birrell, son of Augustus Birrell, entirely broke down while reading 'Gluttony', from excessive sense of humour. I heard Toddy take his division which he did on the lawn. I sat on the terrace reading Bernard Shaw. He referred to me as a 'distinguished French professor'! ... the delinquents took their *poenas* with the most charming grace.

June

4	(At Rue de la Pompe for a month). Changed my room as Mdlle's cats are so strong in this weather. Met Tom ... & Laura Balston at the station: introduced me to Bob, a pretty younger sister.
6	... nice letter from EA thanking me for mine. English shaky at times but sentiment very pleasing!
	At this time I was much richer than ever before. I had come down from Oxford owing about £70. F continued my £300 a year & paid for my lessons. I had paid off a good

deal before Gmunden. Then 'I earned' £120, plus princely board & lodging, in 6 months.

13   Versailles with Fitzgerald. A fine day & we saw everything, Trianons, l'Hameau, & the Salle du Jeu de Paume . . . Moulin Rouge. Max Dearly gave us some good fun: the best bit was his dance with Mdlle Mistinguette, an apache dancing with his love, passionate violence combined with a sort of Whitechapel slouch. Several hitches occurred: it was the première. On to Bal Tabarin where we talked to two girls who were jolly but lamented that we were so 'méchants'. As I got home there was a full moon at one end of Rue de la Pompe & the dawn just beginning at the other.

20   Duncan of Hare's & Balliol has turned up, in for Foreign Office this time. He has just finished History Schools & is burning with admiration of Napoleon & Hal Fisher.

30   Liancourt. *see* June 1907. Lunched with Leplats & supper with Hawkins.

July

2   Arrived at Ebury Street where F & two girls are. Spent the day with various tailors. [*Account of the Balston–Page ménage which is not at all serene. Faults on both sides summarised by diarist who hopes there will be a happy outcome.*]

9   May & I to Harrow, my first visit. I was favourably impressed with the place but thought the boys' garb atrocious. We visited Uncle Brian who has just got into a delightful house with a gorgeous view. Drill at Slough in the evening.

15   I gave Tom & Whitty a dinner at the Dieudonné: then to Isadora Duncan: she is a greater artist than Maud Allen. Gibby . . . is in great spirits about his singing: he meditates Italy in the spring & perhaps Covent Garden in the summer.

19   Sunday. St John's Westminster to hear Wilberforce[26]: excellent in a vague sort of way. St Margaret's Westminster: Henson[27] gave us an excellent sermon, very little abuse or bitterness: his voice not pleasant & appearance worm-like.

21   Lunch with Belhavens. Ralph & Lady Grisel there. Ralph is fatter, not so good-looking & far saner than of yore. Lady Grisel is rather pretty, smart & extravagant: quite cheerful & amusing.

August

1   To camp at Swanage. Glosters under old Sturmy-Cave again: Johnson is Brigade Major.

9   Church Parade. In the afternoon a great party went off to visit the 'Black Prince', a cruiser at Portland. The Captain is a Bucks man & invited any Bucks who liked to come over. We chartered a steamer, glorious voyage there & back with our band playing. Officers & men took parties all over the ship. I've seldom enjoyed an afternoon more. We went fairly deep down into the engine room but not to the stoke hold. Tea in Captain's room, & the men also had a glorious tea. We steamed away with the band playing 'Old Lang Syne'.

14   Field Day near Tidworth House . . . Vivian & I were with the rear guard & we had a difficult job to check the men when they were retiring & to make them turn & fire. Some of them were as frightened as if it had been the real thing.

18   Uncle H told me that Ketha has written to say she has accepted Wilfrid Browne! We are all immensely pleased.

25   Garden party: great success though there was hardly a flower to be seen in the garden. About 250 all told. Rowlands band played very well a programme arranged by myself. Vivian, experiencing his first garden party, was much struck by the beauty of Gloucestershire girls: Mab Calvert, Mrs Billy Darell – a real cat but very pretty – Violet Birchall, Cecily Barnet etc.

31   Town, to go through a Maxim course at Vickers Sons & Maxim at Erith, Kent. Staying at 107 Eaton Terrace in Page's room. To Erith in afternoon: met by Ratcliff, introduced to my instructor Histed a naval gunner. Spent 3 hrs learning to strip gun.

September

1   Good day at Erith: learnt a lot. Lunch with men in the works.

2   Bad day at Erith: stupid & clumsy: couldn't remember things.

3   Did some firing in the tunnel: everything better than yesterday. Histed showed me the new gun which has been adopted by everyone except England. It is simpler, more compact & more accurate.

4   Examination by Ratcliff. Written exam, consisted of about 56 questions almost all answered in a line: included the principal 'stops'. I made one mistake & one in the practical, letting the lock go home before closing the cover. Ratcliff seemed rather pleased, Histed also.

7   . . . Telegram from Cousin Effie inviting me for Festival.

8   Worcester for 2nd half of 'Elijah'. Ben Browne, Ordes are here & Barwick at home.

11   . . . 'Messiah'. Clara Butt resisted the temptation to be dramatic & sang with great feeling.

25, 26,   [*Various meets*] I have never had Outlaw go kinder, not hanging on the bit or playing
28, 29   any of his old tricks.

October

1   In Town. Called on the Battines, saw Nigel.[28] He thought I ought to have tea in the drawing room but I protested & had it with him, the Fräulein & Oswald James who is a duck. Talked a little German with the very nice Fräulein.

2   Looked in at V & A & at Nat Gall. to see the new Franz Hals, certainly very fine. 'Faust' at His Majesty's. Tree was superb. Marie Löhr hardly as good as I expected, & Ainly a trifle insignificant when rejuvenated.

4   Powell arrived[29] at Rue de la Pompe. He seems a very good sort, modest, intelligent & cheerful without excess. We went to Eglise Evangelique, a very moderate sermon.

8, 16   'Expeditions' to Chantilly & Versailles with Charlie & Valentine Orde, seeing the chateau at Chantilly and Charlie's pension & French coach, Mdme. Léonard at Rue de Solferino, Versailles. 'She is singularly charming & well-educated'.

24   Duncan[30] is reposing with his people in Paris after being fourth in FO exam. They've only given one place so far. 'Israel' at Théâtre Réjane. This is the most delightful theatre I've ever been in. Not large but comfortable. Everything pink & white without gilt or fuss. Large foyer with band between the acts. Good attendants in place of the usual harpies.

28   Letter from Orderly Room requesting to know 'for the information of the GOC' why I have come abroad without sanction.

31 Called on Ctsse. Récopé, Ave d'Iena. Mi had met her at Kineton [*Blanchie's home*]. She is said to have been the mistress of Henri d'Orléans. She & her daughter quite charming & didn't hesitate to give me a sort of lesson as we went along: very useful & just what French people won't do.

November

4 Letter from Buck Telling me that Buddensieg had a stroke a few days ago & died suddenly. After lunch met Father, Nelly & Gracie at Gare de Lyon returning from Italy. F had to go straight on: took N & G to GFS where they are to stay. Champs Elysées: Opéra: tea at Rochers.

5, 6 [*Diarist escorts his sister to Notre Dame, Sainte Chapèlle, Invalides, Louvre & Cluny. Also to 'Israel' where the girls were enchanted with the theatre as well as with the acting'.*]

8 [A rare person interpolation] Sunday. The love for my family, always so strong that it can be taken for granted, occasionally makes itself felt with almost oppressive vehemence: it was so on Friday night after leaving N & G.

10 Lord Eustace Percy turned up. Quiet & clever. Jeanne had prepared us for a brilliant French talker which he is very far from being.

11 Walked in Bois: warm enough to sit about which I did reading 'Contes Choisis de Voltaire'. Just before tea time Marie announced 'Un Monsieur qui demande de vous voir' & in walked a pleasant looking youth with an OE tie. He was Jasper Lee of Churchill's & he wanted me to coach him for Smalls at Easter.

14 Powell & I had long discussions. It came out that his father has been clergyman at Escrick for about 5 years, so must have been there when I went. At Eton Powell got a division prize his first six halves, working like a nigger. We discussed the Christie problem & are both largely on John's side, though I hardly think that P realises how mortifying it is for a beak to know that another beak knows all the goings-on in his house.

15 Tea at Récopés. Talked principally to the young Comtesse & a man called Florian. We discussed marriage, engagement etc. They complain of the English coldness towards a wife, eg going to play golf on a Sunday, also letting the ladies go after dinner. The young Comtesse said she would never marry an Englishman as they are not 'tender' enough.

22 Meals have cheered up immensely since Percy came: he chaffs Jeanne well & we all brisk up.

24 Dinner wtih M. le révérend Cremer, Protestant Pasteur. He is uncle of Frau Buck of Gmunden. I asked him what translation of the Bible he used: he immediately gave me a copy of the Traduction Synodiale of the NT. It seems very clear & readable.

25 Mdlle in ecstasies over my 'extempory' this morning. A piece of 'Rasselas'. She thinks I've made tremendous progress this time.

29 Dinner at the Récopés. We were 16. The dinner very good. People keep the same knife & fork for all the meats, & a free use is made of tooth picks during dessert by both sexes.

December

10 Tea with de Soissons: in bed as usual when I arrived. We talked some time but somehow I didn't seem to get on so well with him as before. He has got a trifle stiffer & more aggressive I think owing to his rise in life.

15 Conversation turned tonight on the Comte Wydrange whose pedigree goes back according to Jeanne 400 years before Charlemagne. He is the last of the direct line & lives 'en grand seigneur' on his estate, king of the village with one servant.

17 Arrived in early morning after a not too peaceful crossing. Clive Bowman[31] to dinner; he is just off to Beaulieu to do land agency.

18 Met Tyrwhitt in the street: he asked me to lunch with him at 28 Egerton Gardens. He is going to Constantinople as Honorary Attaché. During the afternoon talked to Gibby who is going to Berlin for a year.

19 Tom & I to Tower to see the Cullinan diamond. I disliked the way one is ordered about everywhere. Dinner at Inns of Court Hotel as Gibby's guest. We made up a hilarious table. The point of the gathering was that Gibby was going to sing at the after-dinner concert, which he did, very well. Few were unbiassed but everyone admired his voice.

25 Last year I was away & the year before May was in India but we were all together again this year with the addition of Wilfrid & Audrey Pamela.

26 Special at Woodford. During the day both my leathers broke. My proper saddle is still in Gloucester & this was an exercising saddle. Uncle H was very much annoyed about it & muttered something about getting a new groom.

1909

January

20 <u>Ketha's Wedding</u>. A fine frosty day, clear & sunshiny. Everything went off without a hitch chiefly owing to Michael outside & Clare inside. Uncle H. & I went down to the Church in the motor about 1.15: Mi & I did pew-opening, we reserved the front 8 pews on each side for relations of whom a few more turned up than we had reckoned on: however with a bit of squashing everyone got in. I stood by the pillar nearest the door when the procession came in. K looked lovely. About 200 came up to the Court afterwards. The presents made a very fine show. Aunt Nelly Montgomerie had supervised their arrangement. Ketha & Wilfrid went off to Lampern in the old Clarence. Everyone very cheerful this evening: no weeping. Edgar Sebright [*Ketha's godfather*] loud in praise of the general success.

26 Oxford Appointments Committee sent me notice of Temporary Assistant Master wanted at Radley. Hunting at Woodchester [*met*] Robeson, staying with Montefiore:[32] he strongly advised me to apply which I have done.

February

2 Cambridge on Slide . . . pecked in a field, cantering, & I came right over her head: according to Willie Canning she stood on her head for a moment & then luckily fell back on her feet. I managed to come off once again, & Slide refused Frocester brook: water is decidedly her weak spot.

3   Am bored at hearing nothing from Radley.

9   Lily & Hans met me [*at Hanover*] Nicholson[33] whose brother was in Hanover in 1906 & Sullivan are here: nice rather quiet people.

15   Marktkirche for some church music, principally Mendelssohn's 'If with all your hearts' on the oboe. Sounds splendid. Started Vieter's 'Kleine Phonetik' recommended to me by Charlie Orde.

17   Walter Batten-Pooll has turned up to do some more German. He has not improved with time.

27   Called on Fräulein Wenzel, sister of Emma at Gmunden whence several interesting pieces of news (a) Graf Grote has married a Dame Countess of Holstein whom he met in Egypt. (b) When the Duchess of Anhalt & her daughter were staying at Gmunden recently the rumour of the latter's engagement to Pz Georg Wilhelm was circulated without a word of truth in it. The poor princess soon left with red eyes & tear-stained face. (She married Fred Schaumberg-Lippe in May 1909) (c) EA loves soldiering & is very attentive to his duties: he went on the Alsace–Lorraine manoeuvres & specially asked to be treated as a simple Lieutenant: he thus escaped being introduced to his eventual overlord the Kaiser: a pity I think.

March

1   Lord Colan Stewart has come from Jeanne's.

11   Read Dr. Downes' pamphlet on Poor Law Commission. 'Fliegender Holländer' for the first time: much of it is splendid, the spinning wheel song delightful & the chorus of the Dutchman's sailors most ghostly.

13   Walk with Nicholson when as usual we discussed people. Sir Coleridge Kennard is apparently unhappy at the FO. He comes in every day & walks straight to his desk, much too frightened to join the group round the fire. Artistic & eccentric, he is very sensitive to chaff & has no idea of making the best of anyone who comes along.

16   Adam a distant cousin of Nicholson arrived from Rue de la Pompe. Studied the first letter of Toussaint Langenscheidt's 'Französich': interesting & good.

19   Berlin, to stay with Gibby in Passauer Street. Gibby engaged so I went to the Wintergarten: one wants a good seat, it is hard to hear the singing.

20   With G looked into the Kaiser Friederich Museum: chiefly the Botticellis. Met Conrad Kardoff, an artist who took us to a dealer where we saw several good modern pictures . . . Van Gogh, something like Segantini but not nearly so beautiful, very strong outlines sometimes enclosed in dark lines.

21   Sunday. Altes Museum: Greek sculpture good. To Strauss 'Elektra'.

24   After lunch left for Hanover. I have enjoyed my first visit to Berlin enormously.

27   First performance of Strauss' 'Elektra' in Hanover. Great enthusiasm. The women's parts were taken quite as well as in Berlin, the men were not remarkable. The orchestra only numbers about 70 but sounded well.

29   Lily & I to Herrenhausen[34] for my first time, I'm ashamed to say. It looked desolate today, the yellow castle with its blue blinds seemed terribly uninhabited. The Familien Museum had all sorts of uniforms etc. & children's clothes: many pictures including a fine drawing of Ernst. August: & many Hanoverians including the forefathers of both Grotes: the Hausmarschall is ridiculously like his ancestor.

31 'Elektra' again: it is so dramatic, every minute full of meaning . . . Lahmeyers asked me to stay over Easter as guest: I can't see my way to it unfortunately.

April

5 Abgereist. Very sorry to leave: this is probably my last long visit. Met Miss Cotton on the boat, on her way from Dresden: she was with an uncle who was a Harrow master & in digs with Uncle Brian for a long time.

6 At 107 Eaton Terrace Tom calmly announced that Whitty was engaged! To a sister of Keble Howard. They are engaged more or less privately for six months & if by the end of that time they haven't got up the energy to marry it is to be off: a curious arrangement. 'Penelope' by W. Somerset Maugham at the Comedy . . . beautiful clothes but somewhat threadbare wit. Marie Tempest her inimitable self.

10 Nibley on Special. The Grevs out ie Grev, Mary & Jack[35] whom I haven't seen since Mi's wedding. He has turned out a nice boy, talkative but not obnoxious.

17 Nigel Battine to stay for a week: a jolly boy, just been to school: inclined to be cheeky.

21 Bazaar for St. Mary de Crypt at the Guildhall: as usual everyone who ought to have been buying was selling: the best feature was the Tableaux Vivants: also a nigger duet by Cecil Elwes[36] just promoted to MFH, & Lady Agnes Howard.[37]

26 National Service League meeting in Gloucester. Vassar Smith in the chair: speaking of May he said 'You may take it from me that she has done all the work'. Meeting enthusiastic but proportion of members large, hence few converts.

27 Letter from Jelf.[38] Harping on Maths, especially Geometry.

May

1 Letter from Jelf. He hopes to see some 'possible men' on Monday & is still agitated about Maths but he says 'It is only this which makes me hesitate to offer you the post'.

3 'Superintending Officer' for the Yeomanry class-firing at Sneedham's Green. In the middle Father rang me up & announced that Jelf had wired 'Glad to offer you the post for one term anyhow'. Which is good.

4 Stopped to talk to Nana on my way back from Gloucester: she took me over the Lodge which I never remember examining before. It is a large cottage & has nice rooms & a fine oven.

7 Set off to The Grange, Folkestone 'for one term anyhow'. [He stayed there for 5 years!] The masters live in a separate house, the Little Grange. The first person I met was Wodeman[39], an old hand at the game but new here. Saw the boys at tea, a nice looking lot. After tea to see Jelf: he is extremely nice & we had a delightful talk.

8 Chapel. 1st hour with the 2nd Maths, my first real school hour: quite a success. Found I could do the Maths at sight quite satisfactorily. Off for 2nd hour: 3rd hour was Dictation to the Upper 4th. Rather good fun. Golf with Wodeman.

10 Got to know my real division at last. I asked one Hutton[40] whether he lived in Gloucestershire: he said no, but he often stayed there with his aunts at Harescombe. Had he ever been to a place called Hardwicke? No, but a Mr Baker rode over from there to help start the rifle club at Harescombe. This was Mi who has been helping

Caroline Hutton! Rather curious: the boy who is clever & industrious is quaintly like Caroline in some ways.

14   Sports. Henderson walked away with every event & won the Challenge Cup with maximum points. He could only take 3 prizes so 2 of his went to Morkil who also won one on his own account. Prizegiving: quite a ceremony, Jelf rather amusing. Darby returned today. He is Chaplain here, nominally curate of Canon Gardiner's at Holy Trinity.[41]

16   Sunday. Supper with the Gardiners: he is very friendly & Daisy[42] is delightful.

20   Ascension Day. At cricket a ball of mine bumped up & hit Elim on the mouth. It broke two front teeth, one short off & one slantwise! He bore it awfully well. Jelf took him to the dentist who promises a perfect renewal by means of crowns. I went to apologise to Jelf who said 'Why, it wasn't your fault old man'. The boy also shows no disposition to blame me. Apparently neither the breakage nor the dentist hurt him much.

22   Up to Town. Ebury Street, only May & Gracie up. Saw Tom Balston & Paul Methuen. Gracie & I to 'School for Scandal'. Tree not quite perfect, but most brilliant cast especially Marie Löhr, Robert Lorraine, Charles Quartermaine & James Hearn.

23   Church at St Peter's. Called on Helen Lascelles who is librarian–companion to Lady Lovelace at Wentworth House, Swan Walk, Chelsea. We talked over Ruskin, Wilde, Shaw: we are both older than we were & have settled down to fairly sane, not to say commonplace views on art & morality. To the Park for ¼ hour where I only saw John Christie to speak to.

30   Sunday. My turn of duty began. It is not very arduous in itself but is rather a worry on the whole, like being subaltern for the day. Tea at the Vicarage.

June

2   The afternoon being wet I had taken the boys for a walk about 4 o'clock, a most wearisome business: Morkill, Hadow & Herring raced on & left us, lying in ambush somewhere: they afterwards did impositions. On the other hand Keble, Capper & some of the little ones were difficult to keep moving.

3   OAC sent me Repton for which I applied.

18   My first experience of 'sending in' a boy. Buss ma. already loaded with impositions ragged in prep: so I suggested a hiding to clear the slate. Jelf took him into the study whence he issued, literally howling. I had a very bad moment, but I firmly believe that licking is the best & most efficacious remedy in a case like that.

19   Father's match. 6 turned up: Stamford Hutton[43] captain: Morkill, a Yorkshire squire, very nice took things easy: Selby, very tall, doctor, goodish player: Forster, rather'sidey', solicitor . . . Darby & I & 3 boys played for the fathers.

20   Mid-term reports. [*Example from a complete list: 'Hutton age 10. Has worked well & conscientiously & takes a good deal of interest in his work: his writing is generally dreadful even when he tries hard' (like his father's)*]

July

3   With Darby to dance at the Metropole: very well done at 3/–. Quite good fun & good dancing.

10   Town. Got to Lords just as they decided not to play. Saw the Wynter boys, Trittons et al . . . Gracie & I to 'A merry Devil' at the Playhouse. Found Percy & Violet Birchall & Edith Alhusen. Play would hardly stand a second visit.

11   . . . National Gallery to see the Holbein my guinea had helped to buy. National Portrait has just got two fine Watts of Swinburne & Meredith.

21   Town. Saw Whitty whose engagement is apparently still on. Went to 'The Arcadians'.

28   Supervised last exam, then hastily corrected papers, added up marks, made out lists etc. in time for the concert: altogether rather a rush. Met Eustace Knollys whose father used to be at Quedgeley & Hardwicke.

29   Travelled up by the Pullman with Morkill & Busk. To Great Central Hotel to interview Waterfield of Cheltenham[44] *see* 25.5.08. I talked a bit of French, & we discussed volunteering: he gave me to understand that I should probaby not be wanted, but he asked me to propose myself for lunch anytime!

August

4   [In camp at Beaulieu Park] This evening I led a certain number of 'C' company in a night reconnaissance . . . by a piece of stupidity almost incredible I led my lot a long way towards Brockenhurst . . . The moment I realised my mistake was one of the most awful of my life.

5   Brigade Day. Towards the end we got the order to crawl . . . doing so we offered a much better mark target to a rifleman looking down on us: & we moved very slowly: the only point urged in favour of crawling was the psychological effect: it is contended that a man crawling towards you has a much more disconcerting effect than a man running & dropping.

13   After seeing the first contingent off Vivian Birchall motored me home. First to Milford on Sea where he bathed & I paddled – delicious! tea at hotel. Then started home about 4.45. We went via Brockenhurst, Lyndhurst, Salisbury where we visited the Close, Warminster, Chippenham – supper at the Angel – Malmesbury, Tetbury, Avening Hill, Stonehouse & Standish. A perfectly lovely drive although there was no moon.

27   Tennis Club tournament . . . Michael & Miss Danks played Di Guise & myself. We won after a play-off, best of five. The first time I've ever got a prize in a tennis tournament. Di Guise played awfully well.

September

13   Cubbing at Frampton. I rode The Nun for the first time: very nice & strong.

15   Uncle H, Mi, Wilfrid & self trained to Stow to watch manoeuvres. We went to the Maugersbury Tower near Wick Hill. The Grenadiers were in position, & Irish Guards, Dublin Fusiliers & Scottish Rifles attacked desperately. With the Irish I met Hammy Berners, very fit & cheery: he is scouting officer. I walked down into Icomb where there was a great fight going on round the church & a beautiful Perpendicular

house . . . We heard afterwards that several authorities called it the most realisitic field-day ever seen. I was surprised & in one way disappointed to find the difference between Regulars & Terriers not so very great.

17 Back to school We have 7 new boys. I lose my top 4 boys & get 4 from below: scholarship will be remarkable by its absence.

28 Played football for the first time for about 3 years. Contrary to my expectation I enjoyed it immensely. Some of the boys play quite well.

October

2   Town for weekend. Found Tom just home from Constantinople. To 'John Bull's Other Island', though not perfectly acted was excellent fun. Met Geoffrey Scott.[45]

3   St Margaret's, Westminster: Henson on the signs of a Christian.

19 Fearful news from Whitminster: Kathleen Teesdale fell dead at a meet of the beagles.

23 Up for one night with K & W. K is getting on well.

24 Albert Hall concert to hear Sammcero, Gibby's admiration.

25 About 3.30 I got a telegram 'Uncle Henry died quietly out hunting this morning. Clare'. I went to see Jelf at once who was most kind & told me to do just what I liked: then I walked about the field, the boys having gone for a walk, & tried to realise all it meant. I had always thought of Uncle H hunting on till he was 80 like Mr Garth.

26 Saw the notices of Uncle H in 'Mail' & 'Express' also letter in 'Times'. At midday a letter from Clare giving more details but it was not till I got home on the Wednesday that I discovered that death was almost certainly caused by the fall on the kerb & not by any fit. All the staff here very kind & offered to do any work for me.

27 Home. The family were settling down fairly well. F had been very bad at first I believe. Letters pouring in. I went for a last look before going to bed: the face was bruised but there was nothing unpleasant. F, Clare & I put in the coffin some lilies sent by AG [*Lascelles*] for this purpose.

28 HC in the morning to which all went. At 2.30 the procession started from the Court. Amongst others were Will Rawle, Gilbert, 2 whips, Travers, Charlie Beecham.[46] A few people came to tea including Uncle Brian. In the morning Haines [*solicitor*] came out to talk over matters. I am executor & heir to whatever is left after the girls have had £10,000 between them: this may be betwen £400–500 a year.

29 Rode with Mi to see the place & track the horses back to the Matson Lane. I rode Spirit. I am keeping Spirit & May Queen but shall dispose of Special & Sappho as soon as possible.

30 Searching & putting in order. Everything is very tidy but there is a good deal of hunting up & ticketing to be done. Bussage[47] & hunt matters take a certain amount of settling.

31 Left by the 12.2. F was much better & brighter. Had tea with Ketha. She says AG who was with her when the news came told her that Uncle H's letters were full of references to K & myself: he mentioned us oftener than the others.

November

1   All Saints. The lesson was 'The Souls of the Righteous'. The boys know nothing I believe, with perhaps one or two exceptions: Keeble asked me if I had been on holiday

& Julius took him away & seemed to be explaining something: Hutton may possibly know too.

4   Dined with Gardiners. Mountjoy Upton [*later 5th Lord Templeton*] was there, invalided from Eton: nice boy, enormous for his age. Canon G showed me a nice obituary in the 'M/c Guardian' by Cousin Charlie.

19 Ketha, a son: 'Billy'.[48]

21 Supper with Captain A. A. Carter of Hill House, Hythe, a friend of Mi's. Has no great opinion of the Territorials: is desperately keen on cyclists & machine guns. He told me of Marindin's range finder & how mean the government have been.

27 Up to 117 Beaufort Mansions, Chelsea, a delightful little flat which Tom & Page have taken. Very comfy, nice furniture, crockery all leadless glaze. Page is going to give up John Lane. Dined at Simpsons then on to the Empire.

28 Finished Tom's MSS novel 'Chiefly Jack': much of it is excellent but it is doubtless more amusing to his friends than to others. In the afternoon to Moscow Court where I saw K & William Granville. He is a very quiet, well-behaved person with darkish hair, & is not very beautiful yet. K seemed extremely flourishing & Wilfrid triumphant.

December

2   In Geography gave a lecture on the war [*the South African war*].

4   Margaret Cooper & company gave an entertainment. MC sang with good expression.

18 Moore gave a tea to 12 boys. [*Names supplied*]. Great sport: they enjoyed themselves immensely & were very quaint. Concert: Darby had great success with topical verses of 'A Policeman's Lot'.

21 Usual rush to get Geography corrected. My top boy was Broughton[49] whose work has been so notoriously bad that Jelf witheld the prize. He is frightfully idle & about 2 years older than Buss mi, the 2nd.

22 Home. K & WG have come.

25 Christmas: quite cheery though we all get the dumps now & again.

27 Christening of WG. He was very good. Cousin Charlie read the service & plenty of people came. Mi, Granville[50] & Consie How[51] were godparents.

29 Professedly children's party at Northgate Mansions. My partners included Hylda who goes fairly: Olive went before my dance.

1910

January

5   To Bitterne for Southampton Hospital ball. Brydone much as usual except that the adored Koko has died: at midnight with the whole family at the bedside! I wore my new hunt coat for the first time although Davies had stupidly omitted the velvet collar. However it was a tremendous success, Mrs Cotton being especially enraptured.

19 The great day. I got down to the school where I was first. Mi just looked in, had a squabble with the deputy assistant Liberal & passed on. On the whole we had a

successful day: we polled everyone whom we believed to be on our side. We had the following motors: Miss Curtis-Hayward, Davy, Horlick, Borrer & one or two others . . . my trap had to take the Reformatory master to Berkeley: the brougham had two journeys, the pony-cart was working all day & Michael's gig brought our last man to the polls 4 minutes before closing time. Mickey [*Beach*] came round, but neither Lister nor Fox . . . I was on my legs from 7.30 to 8.30: I think my volunteering experience pulled me through.

20   Declaration of Poll: Hicks Beach, 6050; Lister, 5088; Fox, 238. Conservative victory over Liberal 962, over Liberal & Labour 724. Not such wild excitement as last time but plenty of enthusiasm.

21   Back to Folkestone. Only one new boy, Kempe.[52]

February

6   Sunday. Supper at Vicarage. Also there Paget of Stepney, brother of Oxford.[53] He told us a story of Father Waggett. W was looking into a shop window when a small boy came along selling papers: catching sight of W he broke off his cry of 'Winner, Winner' & shouted 'Awful fire in Jerusalem'!

23   Half day excursion to Town, 3/6 return. Attended my 'First night' at the Repertory Theatre: 'Misalliance'. In spite of clever acting it was not a patch on 'Getting Married': a collection of nasty people instead of nice ones.

27   Sunday. Canon G talked aobut the school & remarked 'Jelf thinks you are all rather slack' . . . he advised me to study discipline: he opined that the power of maintaining it could be cultivated to a very great extent.
     [*Diarist evidently took Canon Gardiner's words to heart. He wrote at length on the subject on facing pages of the diary: but it appears that discipline was a continuing problem even at Cheltenham College in the 1920s & 1930s.*]

March

9   The boys are doing entrance papers so I got a night off. First met Page & fed at Gourmets, then to pit for another 'first night' at the Repertory. 'The Madras House'. Among the audience Page pointed out Max Beerbohm & Galsworthy, the last is a fine-looking man, very neat & upright. Outside I saw a figure in a cap & waterproof: Page said it was GBS: my first sight of him: except for being whiter than I expected he is quite like his portraits.

April

1   Having hinted that April-fooling was a punishable offence I remained unmolested. At the last Geography lesson I wound up the term's course on the Empire by reading 'The Flag of England' with very fair effect.

3   Sunday. Took 'Booney' & Robert Hutton for a walk on the hills beyond the waterworks: the object was lizard-hunting & we captured several. I improved with practice though I could not see & seize them with the boys' rapidity.

7   Dinner to Whitty as 'farewell' before his marriage. Tom, Page, Ben, Smith, self & Whitty dined at the 'Good Intent' on the Embankment. We dined well & cheaply & then adjourned to Beaufort Mansions where Tom & Page were uneasily sharing a flat.

12 Whitty married to Phyllis Grace Bell at Henley in Arden. Whitworth family there, quite cheerful. Bell family also cheerful & average nice with the exception of 'Keble Howard' who is a bounder.

18 To Aylesbury for a regimental tour. Met by Crouch who took me to a skating rink: it is much easier than ice. We met Mrs Lepper whose boy[54] is coming to Jelf's. I made the acquaintance of our new Adjutant, Mitchell[55], who seems a great improvement on the late unlamented Henley.

19 Town. Tried on clothes, bought bike. To 'Trelawney of the Wells', one of the best I've seen for a long time. Staying with Page & Tom: the flat is now cut in half, metaphorically: each lives & feeds separately.

28 [*At Hardwicke*] Robert Hutton came for a night: he was very jolly & amuses himself excellently, catching a lot of sticklebacks & an eel in the Fishpond[56] & therewith stocking our new basin, the converted centre bed.

30 Sir Athelstan & Lady Baines came.[57] He is an old ICS man, pleasant & talkative with a fund of knowledge & interests. Lady B is another good talker, keen on education: sisters say she has only taken up social work since leaving India.

May

3 Father, Clare & self to Malvern Conference.[58] After dinner the Boards of Guardians presented F with a very fine silver rose bowl & 3 gold plated dessert dishes in honour of his 25 years as Hon. Sec. to the Conference. Sir William Chance & others spoke & said lots of nice things about Grandpapa, F & Mi. There was the greatest enthusiasm, people standing on the chairs & singing 'For he's a jolly good fellow'.

4 Blanchie took Audrey who has been ailing ever since Christmas to a London specialist. He believes it is a form of blood poisoning. She is to go into a home for a month to be 'watched'.

6 Serious news of the King's illness, the first intimation to the general public. Back to Folkestone. We have lost Bland (to Osborne). Herbert (training ship). Coote (Radley) & Gollan (Eton) & have 5 new boys in return.

7 The King died at 11.45 last night. I saw our flag in the field at half-mast about 8.30 am & went to ask Moore if it was confirmed: he had a 'Telegraph' so there was no more doubt possible. It comes as a stunning shock, at the very worst moment. It will, I imagine rally everyone round the Throne: my gravest anxieties are for Foreign Affairs after a year or two: one can't help feeling that everything will depend on King George. We know little about him, but that little is good, except that he is supposed to be rather gauche.

9 This evening a discussion of curriculum with Jelf leading on to a general confab on discipline. Moore, I gather, rather hints that he is left alone to bear the odium of severity. This is, as I have myself suspected, to some extent true but it arises largely from the fact that the members of the staff in perfect good faith take different views of certain offences. However I expect we must tighten up.

20 King's funeral to which Cruse & White mi. went. We had a memorial service

June

8   Up by special excursion. Tried on clothes at Martin & Thorneley. Martin had been my cutter at Davies' *see* 5.1.10. Visited NPG & found Page & Holmes almost more frivolous than usual. To Olympia for Horse Show, my first visit.

11 Fathers' match. Dr Selby (captain) Hutton, Dr Lewis, & Morkill's big brother. The boys played up well as a team: they are far more interesting than last year.

20 F came down: much pleased with the place, & place with him.

25 'Cruise of the Constance' by Cyril Stacey with Violet S née Gibbons. Less vulgar than most musical comedies & the music quite tuneful. I fancied I saw the youngest Gibbons sister in the stalls & went up to speak but it wasn't & the man sitting next to her was furious. He met me afterwards in the lobby & said 'What was your point?' I explained: he said he was angry because he knew people here had 'habits'. We parted friends & I spent the rest of the evening conjecturing on his precise relationship to the girl.

29 Nelly & Grace down. We watched the cricket & they were introduced to the staff, whom they liked, though Moore was an easy favourite. Everybody came to tea including Mrs Jelf & Daisy Gardiner. The girls much pleased.

July

9   A day of days! I got off by the 10.45 to Town & got to Lords by the luncheon interval [*there follows a 3-page ball-by-ball account of exciting play ending with an unexpected Eton victory*]. We all yelled ourselves hoarse in front of the Pavilion & Fowler was carried round the ground. There was a little ragging but almost all was got up for the benefit of the police & subsided directly an inspector took control. 'The Importance of being Earnest', with Nelly & Grace. Met Mat Hill of Eton: he tells me that one has to scrape & scratch to get a house full at Eton, Wellington having competed very successfully of late.

10 Sunday. St Margaret's, Westminster. Henson gave us a good sermon, contrasting 'God moved David', 2 Sam.24:1 with 'Satan provoked David' 1Chron. 21:1. Lunched with Page, also there Loch Ellis, a minor poet. Called on Mary Klenck: she tells me EA is having a riotous time in Munich, a rather big change for him. Grote's wife, a Dane, holds strong Evangelistic views & has Bible meetings which she compels her husband to attend. To supper came Ketha & Wilfrid. Down by the boat train after a most thrilling weekend.

17 Mitchell, new adjutant, & Hugh Wethered lunched with me at Hunderts. At supper at Gardiners I found a Miss Morrell of Dorchester, Oxon: rather a handsome woman. [*Possibly Lady Ottoline Morrell, diarist suggests*]

28 Forster mi. badly bullied, principally by Herring & Lewis, for no particular reason. As usual the real 'licking' was done by people who had no object but brutality. F mi. was knocked almost silly, chiefly by having his head banged against a wall & then left. Gilbertson found him & carried him to Miss Edwardes. The offenders were well thrashed.

August

2   Concert & prize-giving successful but rather a sad day: so many of our nicest boys leaving. Morkill was crying before lunch: Hutton was weeptious after his talk with Jelf & after prayers I found Frampton sobbing, incapable of speech.

12   Stamford & Robert Hutton came to cricket . . . 'Froggie' Mackenzie introduced me to H. V. Page at his request.[59] She had previously informed him that I would like a place at the College! He promised to do his best for me.

17   Down to the cricket at Bourton, then back to Rissington with the Pratts. He & she are delightful & the girls have grown up very jolly & less plain than they started. I chaperoned the girls to a dance at Burford given by a collection of hostesses. I danced every dance except 2.

18   Mrs P. & the daughters rose at 7 & proceeded to Ilfracombe. Pratt showed me all over the church which he has restored: it was left in a very bad state by Henry Rice, uncle of Uncle Dynevor who died in 1896.

24   Battine family & Cousin Bevil staying.

25   Garden Party: rain in the morning, fair in the afternoon: a great success.

27   Tennis at Elmore: bad tennis but good fun. Anselm & I, Old Etonians, beat Kit & Newton, present Etonians.

September

3   Violet, Valentine & Jack Orde came for Festival. Jack I had seen years ago when staying at Nunneykirk. He has grown up a smart Gunner but is a bad talker when not on his own subjects, I gather from our girls. Went to help with Field Firing at Sneedham's Green.

4   Whitminster, where Flos asked me to recommend 'serious' books.

    [*A large named house party assembles at Hardwicke for the Music Festival, but strangely there are no entries describing the event. Several pages are blank.*]

10   Camp at the Bustard, Amesbury. We greatly miss the Colonel who is ill, & Vivian Birchall, visiting Percy in Canada.

11   Wore full dress for the first time, having always paraded as a cyclist recently.

15   Adjutant's parade. Afterwards the men had dinner which had been taken in our travelling cooker, a one-horse contrivance which will cook a half ration for the whole battalion. The idea is that we may get another next year & that two little ones are better than one big one, having regard to the battn. being split up.

October

2   About 6.15 Selby came over shouting for Darby: he & I came over to the Grange as 'Mr Moore was sick' [*Moore had had a stroke & died almost at once: diarist writes at great length about the incident & is obviously very deeply upset*]. Poor Selby had a frightful shock. Jelf arranged a very good service on the spur of the moment: we managed to sing & the whole thing was soothing.

3   Yesterday's tragedy turns out to be even worse than we thought. It turns out that Moore was engaged to Miss Chase. The post mortem called the cause of death apoplexy

4   The wreath from the Little Grange came today. We wrote on it 'In loving remembrance from his colleagues at the Little Grange'. We had a short service including the marriage psalm, chosen I presume by Miss Chase.

5   Early service. Work as usual. Funeral 1.15. Many parents came. Darby did the service in Chapel then we all walked down to the Cemetery. We sang 'Oh God our help' & then home, very sorrowful. The flowers were lovely: the boys gave a splendid wreath of white flowers & violets tied with the school colours.

28   Anniversary of Uncle H's death: another bright clear day.

29   Town. With Whitty & Page to 'Pains & Penalties' read by Lawrence Housman. He read beautifully & the play was interesting. One would harldy want it at the moment of the coronation but otherwise there could be no harm in it.

November

17   Darby's mother is very ill: he had to go off.

20   Queen's Hall where 'Tannhäuser' was as magnificent as ever: and 'Don Juan' interesting.

December

11   Bishop of Croydon at supper at Gardiners. G & he talked a lot about the Bensons[60] especially Mrs B who is apparently the confidante & critic of all her very different sons. G recalled an incident: Mrs B was seeing Robert Hugh Benson off to Rome, well knowing that it would be his last journey as an Anglican. Just as the train was starting Bishop Wilkinson came up & said to her 'If on earth he wished his sons to follow their own conscience how much more must he wish it now'. Croydon once asked Temple if he didn't find teaching boys trying work now and again. T replied gruffly 'I love boys'.

14   Home for election. Travelled down with Jack Birchall. He is greatly inflamed against Percival Hughes & the Central Office who are apparently very inaccessible & cliquey.

15   Polling-day. We did pretty well, polling all except 4 Unionists. Floods accounted for one or two. We only had two motors, Horlick & Curtis-Hayward.

16   Back to Folkestone. Called at Nat Portrait Gallery whither they had sent a telegram 'c/o Director, Mickey in by 432'. Arrived at Folkestone I settled down to hardish work, I have to make up for my 'leave'.

20   Finished off exams. Jimmy Sparks had extremely bad luck: he missed the Classical prize after being top on the term, and my maths prize by 3. I gave him a consolation prize on my own as he had worked splendidly in both subjects.

31   Hussey's car took me to Gloucester Midland whence I trained to Berkeley Road. The first time I have trained to hunt with the Berkeley. Near the end we ran from Bowcot to Newark: it was pretty to watch & provided plenty of hill-climbing. Talked with Chetwode Green who is now at Eton.

THE GRANGE, FOLKESTONE

School Roll for Autumn Term, 1910.

The numbers denote the Mathematical & French divisions. No. 5.

* Prefect.   † Captain of Games.
Boys marked *N.G.* take extra Mathematics instead of Greek.

	FIRST CLASS.		
M	F		12.	10
1	1	D.G. Chandor * †	13	2
1	1	H. G. Elphinstone	11	10
1	1	L.A. Keeble	13	4
2	1	H.A.B. Donkin *	13	0

	SECOND CLASS.		12	6
1	1	C.W.P. Selby *	12	8
1	1	H.A. Price *N.G.*	12	11
2	1	R.L. Sparks *N.G.*	12	3
1	2	J.E.S. Thompson	11	10
2	2	G.G. Finn	11	8
2	2	D.H.S. Gilbertson *N.G.*	13	8

	UPPER THIRD CLASS.		12	6
1	2	F.D.V. Thursby *N.G.*	13	3
1	2	C.M.F. White	13	2
2	2	S.A. Forster *ma.*	11	2
2	1	A.L. di Balme	12	2
2	2	P.H. Lewis *N.G*	12	8

	LOWER THIRD CLASS.		12	0
1	2	F.H. Plummer	12	5
2	2	C.W. Busk *N.G.*	12	7
3	2	H.K. Capper *N.G.*	11	11
2	1	F.R. Forster *mi*	12	3
2	3	G.D.L. Nicholson *ma. N.G.*	13	0
2	3	G.D. Elin *N.G.*	13	4
3	2	R.A. Buss *ma.*	11	8
3	3	I.R.A.B. Bradley *N.G.*	10	8
3	3	S.A. Buss *mi.*	10	7

	UPPER FOURTH CLASS.		10	10
3	3	J.H.T.C. Butler	11	6
3	3	B.E.D. Broughton	12	6
4	4	L.C.L. Nicholson *mi.*	12	5
3	3	D. Cruse	10	11
3	3	A.B.F. Painter	9	11
4		W.W. Briscoe	9	9
3	4	D.H. Secker *mi*	8	6
3	4	R. F. Bernal	11	2

	LOWER FOURTH CLASS.		9	11
4	3	A.H.M. Kempe	9	10
3	3	A. Lepper	10	2
3	4	C.M.V. Macdowell	13	3
4	4	G.O. Secker *ma*	10	5
4	4	W.F. Godden	8	10
4	4	W.E.G. Young	9	9
4	4	F.W. Holdgate	9	8
4	4	H.W. Bredin	9	8
4	4	H.B. Dous	7	8

Boys at the Grange preparatory school, 1910

1911

January

7　Florence mounted me on Esau: she didn't hunt herself. It was the first time I had ridden him: he went perfectly.

12　Mi lent me his big mare. Florence & I trained to Yate for a hunt at Rangeworthy, my first. Rode through Iron Acton & saw the lovely church & house.

18　Cuthbert advised me to have varicose veins out.

February

6　Father is 70. Uncle H's death last year pulled him down but last holidays he was as jolly & healthy as I've ever seen him.

11　To stay with Tom Balston who has moved to 110 Elm Park Mansions. I sleep in a room let by his landlady & feed in his flat. Tom has written a rather amusing story of a young engineer & an old maid who married & quarrelled. The engineer is of course himself & the old maid, Page.

12　Sunday. T & I to Hampstead Heath & had a look at the Garden City. Saw the crematorium, the first I've seen. Lunch with Ketha & Wilfrid, William flourishing.

18　To Eton. Got there just in time to change – I am staying with Robeson – & run with the beagles.

19　Upper Chapel where Tucker of Uganda preached. Afterwards, at 1 to be precise, went for my first interview with Lyttelton. Tucker was there & recognised my name, F having sent him something for his cathedral. L & self had a long talk: the practical upshot is, there is no vacancy now. Lunch with Toddy Vaughan. His head boy is Wedderburn, Ruskin's executor's son. After lunch I went round to Byrne to talk things over. He said he was quite satisfied as to my languages & that J. de Hénault had spoken very well of me. But he almost urged me not to take a post if offered . . . 'at 45 you are a discontented man'. He said he had been much struck by one or two refusals from men who did not consider the prospects good enough . . . & he remained mildly discouraging.

March

14　Heard from McDowall of King's School to whom I applied for a berth.

15　Half day in Town. 'Preserving Mr Panmure' was an amusing farce. Page tells me that the impossible little girl was founded on Elizabeth Asquith.

22　To King's School Canterbury to see McDowall. Mrs M. received me & I had lunch with her: also there two boys & the M little girl. Mc came in afterwards & we talked business: then he took me round the town to see one Rigden, a doctor & head of all the OKS. After a talk with him we came back, had some more 'shop' & then I departed. I read Willie Temple's 'The meaning of Personality' in the train: good as always.

25　Sleet & rain effectively disposed of sports. Watched hockey, England v. France. This was the first first-rate game I had seen.

28　With Woodman's elder brother & others to 'Marriage of Kitty' with Marie Tempest. There met Mitchell, adjutant, Mason of the Berks, Guy Campbell formerly of

RWW-T [*Housemaster at Eton*] & Tritton, another Eton man, cousin of Oswald & co.

29   Sports. Few parents

April

5   For the first time I 'took the School Train', ie. superintended the saloon: it was rather fun.

6   To Spaldings, High Holborn, to help boys select bats. Sparks was brought by his grandfather, a fine Old Etonian & great believer in the 'stick' as he remarked with one hand on the boy's shoulder. After about 1½ hours of choosing bats we adjourned to the Matinée Tea Rooms & had a splendid lunch, boy-fashion, ie. what one chose all chose. Afterwards I went with Cruse & Nicky to the Brit. Mus. to see the Tercentenary Bible exhibition. With Tom & Bailey to the Working Mens' College, many mementoes of Ruskin, Kingsley Furnivall & others.

7   Round to the new V & A. The arrangements show off the objects to great advantage though one misses the excitement of the search in overpacked rooms. Salting collection very fine especially the miniatures.

9   To Wotton Lodge where I am to have varicose veins out. Saw Cuthbert who marked the veins. I have a nice nurse.

10   About 10 o'clock Cuthbert prepared me. I had previously shaved my legs with a Gillette, without soap, most successfully. C cleaned me very carefully, rubbed me with ether & bound me up. About 3 o'clock I was put under ether & choloroform in my room: I came to about 5, I think. I was sleepy but not uncomfortable. I had a nasty taste in my mouth.

11   Didn't sleep much last night. Some tea & toast 'paid me a short visit' & it was not until 3 in the afternoon that I could take & retain some Bovril.

16   Easter Sunday. May is in the Home doing a rest cure. We have a telephone rigged up & converse frequently.

20   Canon Nash came in to celebrate for me. Clare came, also my nurse.

25   Robert Hutton called & Stamford came along later with the news that Burge (HM Winchester) had been made Bishop of Southwark. Much excitement.

26   Arm chair. Was carried down to tea with May, Ketha & William.

May

2   Home. Very shaky on legs. Florence came to tea.

5   Back to Folkestone. I am wobbly but quite sound enough. The new master is N. G. Deed, late of Emmanuel, Cambridge. President of Lawn Tennis there.

13   Cricket in full swing. Deed & I supposed to exercise a sort of consulship: Jelf was anxious that I shouldn't think Deed had been put in over my head. I take the first net & naturally arrange most things as Deed doesn't know the boys.

21   Sunday. Tea with Ketha & Wilfrid. William in great form. Heard interesting announcement. *see* Nov.16. Old EM Grace died yesterday. He used to hunt with the Berkeley. Went to Tate Gallery: my first visit to Duveen's Turner Wing. What between the new rooms at Trafalgar Square & this wing Turner has really come into his own at last.

June

5   Whit Monday. With Charlie [*Orde, staying at the Gardiners*] walked to Dover & back. Lunch at Hotel de Paris. Very hot as it has been all this term. We did each way in about 2½ hours. Dined at the Gardiners, then Daisy, C & I to 'Brewster's Millions'.

9   We hear that poor Bland has died, from illness, at Dartmouth. He was a red-headed person, rather bumptious but jolly: the only son of his mother & she is a widow.

17   Daisy had another theatre party consisting of Percy Orde, Standfast (Secretary of East London Church Fund) & self. Bishop Paget is staying at the Grange.

18   Sunday. At supper we started on F. Temple stories. T once got into a train with a curate of Evelyn Gardiner's whom he knew: his sole remark was 'Where do you get out?' King Edward was very unwilling to make his communion at his coronation: he hadn't been for years & apparently both he & Queen A wished to have that part omitted: T's only comment was 'Then yer can't be crowned'.

22   Coronation Day. Whole holiday. I was on duty & had rather hard work keeping the boys amused. Tip & run lasted several hours in the morning & regular cricket in the afternoon.

July

1   By Pullman to Town, thence to Slough. I found the Bucks practising lining the streets. I was told off for the Guard of Honour which consisted of Slough Coy under Barrett, self & Guy Crouch . . . I saw Fred Cripps, Dalmeny Rothschild & others. The King arrived about 4.30. We gave him a salute when he first appeared & then ordered, while he received addresses etc. . . . I had to squint round as the cheering prevented my hearing any orders. As the King approached us Leslie Barrett prepared to salute again but the King said 'No-no-no-please: slope arms'. Leslie at once gave the order: not for the King will we slope arms on ceremonial parade! The King walked down the ranks passing behind the subalterns, so I saw nothing of him. The Prince of W. came & sat in the carriage just opposite me: he looks intelligent & moderately pleasant. We marched back to camp: very hot but the full dress was not so terrible as might have been expected.

2   Sunday Church Parade: then battalion drill, then to Slough then back to Folkestone where I found a telegram saying that EA, GW & Grote would like to see me at the harbour on Monday, time to be wired later. [*Postponed for a day*].

4   Went to morning boat & found the party travelling in strict incognito. They were all cheery & friendly though slightly unshorn. EA was very much the same: says he works very hard at soldiering at Munich: looked extremely healthy but says the Coronation was hard work. GW has smartened up a lot: he asked after Father whom he met in Egypt.

31   Father came to stay with Johnson. I dine, Also Miss Gye, Maid of Honour, & Rose Hubbard of whom I had just bought lace for Blanche Langton, née Murray-Browne.

August

1   Johnson took F & self for a motor drive to Tenterden-Rye-Old Romney-home. We only had about 15 minutes at Rye, beautiful old church in which is a memorial to Meryon who was killed in the Alps. (a boy I much disliked at Malvern Link).

2   Concert to which F came. Sparks kept my prize, beating Selby chiefly owing to the latter's absence at the Naval Review.

6   Sunday. Vivian Birchall motored me to camp at West Lulworth. Two new men, P. A. Hall, Malvern & Cambridge, & Guy Crouch [*see* July 1 above]. Williams is Colonel & we have a new brigadier McClintock who is dead nuts on lectures.

13   The Brigade had organised a party to go & see the Fleet at Weymouth. My lot went to the 'Bellerophon' where we were shown round by Hallett, a brother of Mouse. I had met him years ago with his wife, having tea at Fullers.

19   We went to bed in great agitation: ever since Wednesday the railway strike had been growing & we looked like being left high & dry at Lulworth. Our last orders were that no horses or baggage were to be taken.

20   The strike was settled – temporarily – yesterday night. After seeing the Battn. off Vivian motored me home.

September

5   Versailles, 12 Rue Maurepas, Charlie Orde's place with the Léonards. I am going to be en pension with them for about 3 weeks.

7   Expedition to St. Germain-en-Laye whither I had somehow never been. Church with monument to James II, restored by Qu. Victoria. Chateau is lovely & is, I am told, very like the Loire style.

8   Louvre. Saw the nails where the Joconde used to hang.[61] Every species of canard is flying about over that business: largely anti-semitic.

9   Called on Agnes de Crequi-Montfort who received me very graciously in her new house at Neuilly.

11   Lunch with Agnes C-M. Also there her husband, Mabel & Miss Barnett a clever girl whom I met with Mabel 3 years ago. She is a daughter of ex-MP for Torquay & is learning recitation.

13   Woodman arrived from England. We lunched at Zucco, Bd. des Italiens: good. He is going to stay with the Count di Balme (father of a Grange pupil).

15   Summoned up my courage to call on Jeanne. By representing the Léonards as friends, which they are, I staved off any inconvenient questions. Madame received me, looked as old & dirty as ever. She couldn't remember me until Jeanne recalled the famous fire. Jeanne herself was in a nightgown & kimono. She had meditated dressing till she heard me say my name, when she concluded there was no need for ceremony. She was extremely agreeable & complimentary: much regretted that I was not at Eton. Altogether we had a charming talk. Her French is certainly more beautiful than that of Mme Léonard.

16   To Melun to visit di Balme with whom Woodman is staying. The Count is a good-looking smart man who after 16 years in the Italian cavalry lost most of his money in the Whitaker-Wright business. This plus interminable lawsuits have reduced his income considerably. He now lives in a little comfortable house in Melun & does a little journalistic work. We had lunch, then a row on the river, very jolly, then dinner & so home.

19   To Pere Lachaise to seek O. W. 's grave which I did not find. Noticed the fine busts of Corot, Alphonse Daudet & the fox on La Fontaine's tomb.

25 Left Versailles which I have enjoyed mightily. To Amiens where the Cathedral impressed me more than Chartres. I found myself going round with Ruskin 'Our Fathers have told us' picked up second hand. I saw the choir stalls in a hurry, but a good look at 3 or 4 pays better than glancing at all.

26 For the day to Rouen. First to St Ouen: lovely inside & out. The wall round the triforium & round the outside is not to be missed. St. Maclou is fine if barbaric.

29 Back to Folkestone. For the first time since Jelf has had the school he has no new boys: we lost several last term, so numbers are down to 36.

October

20 A very unpleasant incident. Painter, reported for talking in prep, entangled himself in a very obvious lie. Nothing is so trying as punishing a boy who sturdily denies the charge.

29 Took Deed to supper at the Gardiners. Pereira, Bp. of Croydon, was there: nice but a trifle oily.

30 Continued my study of Military Law which I am doing for Certificate B

November

16 Ketha has a daughter! Kitty [*Catherine Clare*]

19 Whitty came to lunch: very cheerful: took me round to see Mrs W & the baby: the latter has an intelligent but ugly face. Gave Tom & FitzGerald tea at the Piccadilly Hotel.

?   Town. Saw Ketha who looked well & so pretty, & baby who looked well but hardly beautiful.

December

5-7 Staying in Town for 2 nights with Tom to do Certificate B at Imperial Institute. Met several Eton friends including Delves-Broughton whose brother at the Grange has just got into Eton.

10 Called on Broke-Hunts . . . he is infirm but quite cheerful. They have got a beautiful Greek head, which Mrs B-H could remember all her life at their home. It is said to have come from Rome. It looks to me to be somewhat Pheidian, not unlike the Furtwängler's Lemnian Athena.

21 Milbury Heath on May Queen. A moderate day round Tortworth, Tytherington etc. Tea at Eastwood House where Sir George [*Jenkinson*] was in great form. On arriving home I found the Coronation Medal waiting for me 'His Majesty's private gift' as a reward for my labours at Slough. *see* July 1 above.

26 Christening of Catherine Clare at Hardwicke Church.

1912

January

2 To Huttons to lunch. Mrs H., Robert & Cecil Julius there. I stayed to tea. Julius is at Burge's at Westgate where he is kept hard at the Classics.

4   Meet here as usual. I rode May Queen who went fairly but refused once or twice. Ball: our party included Mrs & Margaret Chester-Master, Robeson, George Witts, FitzGerald & Cotton. The ball universally voted the best of recent years: this was largely due to Michael . . . We left soon after 3 when the programme was finished but I believe they went on till nearly 4.

5   Robeson & Gerald expressed a desire to go up Haresfield Hill. All the men turned out but Gerald & I outwalked them with ease. Mrs Penrose-Thackwell gave a dance at the Winstones. Rather a crowd but quite good fun. Molly P-T is a delightful girl, red-haired, interested in Germany.

?   To Southam for a half & half dance. Mrs Ratcliff, Sylvia & Phyllis the two brightest of the girls, also Jack & Dolly R, née Gladwin, Farrars cousins of the Arbuthnots, Miss Russell-Kerr, rather pretty. It was excellent fun.

9   Hunted with the Cotteswold at Stoke Orchard. My mare refused to jump even the smallest places though she galloped like fun. I discovered afterwards that she had a sort of gout which made her giddy when she tried to jump: it probably arose from over-feeding.

10 Fancy dress & 'Book' party given by the Witts at Leckhampton Parish Room. Blanchie motored the children, Clare & myself over. Olive looked sweet as a Bavarian peasant of which there were about 10!

11 Journeyed down to Portsmouth where we are going to be shown over our exact positions on mobilisation. Stayed at Pier Hotel. 16 of the Bucks turned up. Major Jordan of the Gloucesters came over to see me later. I hadn't realised how long he had been out of the country: things like Ketha's wedding, & Toffee Darell's to John Hill were quite news to him. In the evening we had a 'rapid solution' scheme. Mitchell took Christie-Miller, Guy Crouch & myself.

17 The Bush's late of Standish gave a housewarming ball at Eastington Park, late the Leaze. They have built a fine ball-room, plastered with the most miserable pictures, & knocked the hall into another room so that the whole makes 2 fine dancing rooms. Excellent White Viennese band. The whole was very well done except that the champagne ran out which perhaps saved me from proposing to KG [*Katharine Green?*]

19 Folkestone. We have acquired O. Warner (Maritime Historian) W. Copeman (an authority on rheumatism) & Shipley.

24 Town. To Warrends (solicitors) where I signed about 40 conveyances of Dynevor property.

31 Town. Follies at the Empire, where Fay Compton, sister of Compton Mackenzie & wife of Pélissier, is new. Tea with Page, then to an excellent seat for 'Oedipus Rex'. The first hour I thought most impressive, the second however I got tired of the performance. Martin Hervey was excellent in parts: Lillah Macarthy looked very fine & spoke beautifully. The staging was by Reinhardt.

February

21 Ash Wednesday. Attended a meeting of the Constitutional League. Lady Meyer spoke well on various points of Suffragism. Then Chapman of the Savoy Chapel spoke earnestly: he looked on the suffrage movement as a real rising for the sake of

liberty: essentially Christian. On the whole I incline to giving women the vote but there is the immense difficulty of the numbers. I confess I don't want to be ruled by a majority of women.

24 To Oxford for a bgde tour. Saw Magdalen bump New Coll in Toggers. Saw the Warden, & Joseph. Tea at the Grid. To Randolph to dress. 'Rapid solution' scheme: thoroughly practical & interesting.

25 Motored out to Brill, continued 'rapid solution' scheme. En route through Town I went to Evensong at St. Paul's: Willie Temple preached. I could only stay for about half: mainly historical on the idea of the Messiah. He has a fine voice & talks sense.

March

4 Great coal strike started.

9 Bought & read 'Emma.' While I can entirely imagine people being captivated by it I find much of it very thin.

10 Hartshill, Archbishop's chaplain, tells me that Denton Jenner-Fust of Hill got to know his girl when she was about 13, went to Pelham to be near her & proposed when she was 17. This is a very thorough wooing.

April

3–26 Bristol for musketry course: stayed at Queen's Hotel, Clifton. Instruction took place in 4th Battn Drill Hall: Office & Instructor: Capt. R. G. Clarke. There seems to have been plenty of free time.

5 Service in the Cathedral: rather dull. Home.

6 Hunt at Stinchcombe on Esau. At Piers Court ran into Hereward & Winnie plus Cherry & Barbara.[62] They were motoring round, inspecting Winchester, Marlborough etc. Cousin Charlie too, delighted at staying at Piers Court rather than the Gables.

8 Gracie & I helped Eliza Eagles to make her will: everything to Lucy Dallas.[63] Daisy & Dill Crewdson to lunch & old Mr Crewdson, much pleased with their new car, of the Ford type which is becoming so popular.

9 Another luncheon party. Sir Stafford & Lady Howard & Lady Stepney: the Dean & Mrs Spence-Jones. The Dean in tremendous form.[64]

10 To Bowden to coach Jack & Vivian Birchall for Certificate B. They know a fair amount but won't read their books.

14 Sunday. At Bristol Stn I ran into Ben Browne, to our mutual intense surprise. We travelled as far as Gloucester together. His family are here for a bit.

15 First news of the 'Titanic' disaster. I got the Citizen at Gloucester which said that all were saved but at Bristol the rumours were very bad.

17 Amusing practice on 30 yd range near Clifton Suspension Bridge. I was made 'fire controller' & got through a fairly easy piece of 'indication' with credit. Home. Cousin Bevil there, also Ketha with William who is talking fluently if incorrectly.

19 Primrose Day, but very few wore them. Miniature range. To 20 Sion Hill in the evening where the Warwickshire Yeomanry are living [*Thumb nail descriptions given of all officers there, including Wheatley who had been fag to Birchall at Eton.*]

20   Had a long talk with the Dorset Yeoman Jordan: he stays with the Gibbons & with Charlie Barnet & knows the Fred Lascelles well.

21   Sunday. Home taking Wheatley who is going to stay with Michael. Cousin Bevil preached in the evening.

24   Written exam in the evening. Clarke read through the questions to us very carefully & gave us hints on the answers!

25   Heard I had passed 3rd, 137 marks out of 160. Clarke said he had spotted me for 2nd: however I am very well pleased.

May

21   Appalling news of the death of Georg Wilhelm. Motoring to his uncle's funeral (the King of Denmark) he drove against a big stone & ran into a tree. He & his servant Grebe were killed instantly.

23   Took Page to Annual Meeting of National Art Collection Fund. Balfour spoke: charming in manner but not very fluent & his subject matter bothered him a bit. Balcarres presided very nicely though he is not a great speaker.

24   Violet & Valentine staying at the Vicarage. Daisy & the girls sang us all their nursery songs & Evelyn played Chopin. I had never heard him before.

25   To Beaconsfield for a weekend camp with E Coy. I saw Chesterton who has a house here: he is no thinner than he was 8 years ago.

26   Church Parade conducted by Comeline. Before evening church we went into the beautiful Jacobean vicarage to meet Mr & Mrs Comeline. He comes of an old Hugenot family who lived for about 300 years in Gloucester.

28   Wrote a letter of condolence to Grote, the Hofmarschall.

June

7   The last 2 volumes of my big Ruskin turned up. Nine years ago I started buying them: much water has flowed under Magdalen Bridge since then: but I don't regret a penny of the money or an instant of the time spent on them.

11   Voted for Sir Philip Sassoon who has been shoved into his father's shoes. Jelf & some others abstained as a protest against the mixture of nepotism & semitism.

13   To Wellington, to interview Vaughan with regard to a vacancy in September. Walking in the drive I met Gilbertson in the nets [*former Grange boy*] & talked to him a bit. Then to Vaughan. He is a nice man, thoroughly competent, though he looks harassed. We went out to watch the cricket & I met Stansfield whom I met at Liancourt. After tea I roamed about by myself & found Frampton & Sparks [*ex-Grange*]. Both seemed flourishing. Vaughan reports well on all our boys, especially on Dyer who has come out as a boxer. Went in to see Vaughan again & then back.

July

8   Clare down for the day from Town. She enjoyed herself muchly. Lunch at Gironimos, then she sat in my room during school, then we watched cricket until 8 pm.

27   Jelf came into my room & remarked 'Have you ever thought of taking this place on?' I stammered that I had thought of it but had rather rejected the idea. He went on: 'Because I've got a job'. I was dumbfounded. He explained that he had been

appointed head of Kings College Choir School, Cambridge: this for next term! We hummed & hawed in half sentences to each other, I completely boulversé, he frightfully cut up at the thought of going, & then he departed to tell the others. Wodeman suggested we should take it in partnership: I was rather lukewarm, but ready to consider the proposition.

28 Supper with Gardiners. On getting home I found a scheme afoot for the whole staff, later reduced to Wodeman, Deed & self, taking on the school.

30 The mixture of exams & schemes is very wearing. Wodeman would rather go in with me alone than me & Deed. None of us inclined to take it single handed. I don't much care for Deed alone. Dr Lewis prophesies success for two & certain failure for three. Meanwhile Jelf wants something like £10,000, some on mortgage. It seems to me a biggish price.

31 Concert. The great 'turn' was of course Jelf's farewell speech. He spoke very well & everyone was touched. Parents all much concerned, asking whether we are stopping on. The scheme at present is that the assistant masters shall carry it on till Christmas under Jelf's direction unless a purchaser appears.

August

1 Home, after a very sad leave-taking from Jelf. Family full of curiosity. The idea of my taking the school even in partnership is not enthusiastically received, but the family seem inclined to consider it.

3 Today read in the Times that I am promoted to Captain. It has taken just 10 years & I have never been superseded.

4 Sunday. Vivan motored me to camp at the Bustard where we were in 1910.

7 Went over to Larkhill to see aeroplanes. We saw 3 good flights: almost all the machines are French. I had seen aeroplanes in the distance in 1910.

9 Aeroplanes buzzing over camp between 5–8 in the morning & 4–6 in the afternoon. I counted 8 in the air at once.

10 Lord & Lady Addington[65] & their girl came down. He is nice but not talkative: he is very jolly. Dined with the Gloucesters as guest of Helm. Very cheery evening, we cock-fought, high cockalorum etc etc.

22 Violet rang me this morning to ask, from Vivian, whether I would come on a motor tour to France with them . . . accepted joyously the invitation.

26 Up to Town to buy a motor-coat & to see Wodeman. We discussed possibilities but I take a gloomy view of prospects especially after seeing the list of fees actually paid by our boys – one pays £51 a year! Bought a nice coat at the Stores (strong cord outside a fleece lining: very long & full, wrapped over knees: all this was considered necessary for motoring in September).

30 Started on the great motor tour. Violet & I motored to Southampton & there awaited Vivian's arrival. He came & made arrangements for the motor. Ernest Davis the chauffeur has never been abroad before but seemed quite keen.

31 Got to Le Havre after a good, slightly rough voyage. Violet & I who had partaken of Mothersills had a splendid night. We drove through Caudabec to Rouen, turning aside to visit Jumièges which Vivian thought the best thing we saw on the tour. At

Rouen Violet & I did the Cathedral, Mclou & St Ouen: when I saw them last year I felt it would be years before I saw them again.

[The round trip took the travellers ten days. From Rouen they went to Chartres, Chateaudun & Tours: thence along the Loire valley to Nantes, & back through Brittany via St Nazaire, Rennes, Fougères, Bayeux & Caen to Le Havre where they parted, the Birchalls returning home & the diarist going on to Hanover. Their aim was comfortable, informed sightseeing; this is reflected in the details of places visited – & there are some surprising omissions – the hotels deemed satisfactory or otherwise, & the predictably English attitude shown by the party in certain situations. Only a few extracts are chosen from this densely written account to give some idea of the French experience.

September

1   Sunday. Violet & I to a quaint & very ugly English chapel south of the river at Rouen. Then Louviers . . . Chartres full of soldiers preparing for manoeuvres. My crushed cane portmanteau, bought for my first tour in 1902 with Father has been resting on a grid just over the exhaust. Although the portmanteau itself is not burnt through one pair of drawers & a shirt have large black marks! Vivian is having a plate made to go over the exhaust.

3   Amboise. St. Hubert's chapel: guide all talk about 'dentelles en pierre'. Blois, having seen Chaumont in the distance. Long discussion as to Chambord. Everyone had ragged the B's for not going there before: contrariwise it made rather a long extra bit if we didn't like it. I said 'Let's do it, then we shan't have to come here again!' We did it. I was quite delighted with it. The B's somewhat less enthusiastic. We did not enter. Back to Chenonceaux. There we all agreed the chateau was as beautiful as could be: we didn't go in, preferring to spend all our time in the garden.

4   At Azay-le-Rideau met the Bishop & Mrs Gibson. The chateau almost as beautiful as Chenonceaux with interesting things inside. We had to give up Chinon: went on to Langeais, then Luynes: it looks fine & imposing but we didn't go in. Mosquitoes a nuisance the last day or two.

7   . . . Bayeux, where we only stayed long enough to see the tapestry which is delightfully vivid & quaint & well displayed. The Cathedral we didn't give enough time to which was a mistake. To Caen. Hotel Angleterre, pretentious & dirty & bad.

8   Sunday. Violet & I saw the 2 Abbayes & the Lycée. The inside of Abbaye aux Hommes & outside of Abbaye aux Dames pleased me best. Lisieux for lunch. I examined the south door of the west end with all the attention due to Ruskin.

9   I left the B's at Le Havre after one of the best weeks of my life.

10 Arrived at Hanover: have not been there for 4 years. At home were Mama, well & cheery, Hermine, & the Engländer consisting of Herbert (Eton & Balliol) Bulkley-Johnson, (ditto) Barnes (Eton & New Coll) & de Salis (University). I went to meet Hans as he came from his business: he is taller, much fatter & typically German.

13 Called on Fräulein Mathilde. She thought I had preserved my German very well. I feel myself quite at home in it but my vocabulary has fallen away very much.

15 Sunday. Called on Fräulein Wenzel. We talked about everything in Gmunden. She said the Kaiser was very nice to EA & she has hopes that some marriage may be brewing.

16   Dinner party at Abbentherns [*Long guest list supplied*]. Last but not least Greta Frost, a rather delightful Swede, not pretty but having lovely eyes of which she well understood the use. Hans & I had great fun with her.

18   Crossed Flushing - Folkestone: for 5/– extra you get a nice large cabin to yourself. To the Empire in the evening where I met Vivian. 'Everybody's doing it' was good. Robert Hale worked hard with great success. I rather regret that they've adopted the Parisian habit of singing only one verse of each song.

20   Folkestone. We find things just settled up, viz. the school etc. is sold to de Winton & Shaw of Gore Court [*a local preparatory school*].

21   Discussed scheme of work. We have to get along with 4 masters as Jelf goes at once. No early school!

22   Shaw departed saying to me something about 'hoping I should be able to stay on'. Wodeman is head pro tem: they mean to keep myself & either Darby or Deed.

28   de Winton & Mrs Shaw came down. S had warned us that de W would seem a trifle 'sidey' but we can't see any trace of this. Mrs Shaw is extremely nervous.

October

[*Entries this month are scrappy and consist mainly of descriptions of the boys' rides with the diarist, his frequent theatre visits & a conjunctivitis outbreak at the Grange*]

November

7   Bernal came out with conjunctivitis several days after we thought we were safe.

13   Came back from Gardiners to find Hill-Wakefield of the Irish Fusiliers visiting Deed. They were enjoying my newly-acquired gramophone!

20   Town to talk to Algy Mansel about stocks & shares. He more or less convinced me that his advice was sound.

21   Shaw came. We are all doing the Common Entrance exam so as to be able to compare Gore Court & ourselves.

27   Up to Oxford to take MA. Dined with Barnes whom I met in Hanover.

28   Took my MA. We assembled, paid our fees, & were introduced by our deans. Henderson presented us, holding my hand. Then the Proctors walked: then we said 'Do fidem' to the oath: after that we were blessed by the Vice-Chancellor, kneeling before him in threes. We then went & changed our robes, came back in threes & bowed to the Vice-Chancellor.

December

8   At Gardiners Mrs & Miss Brackenbury to supper. After they left Evelyn remarked 'What a nice feeling it is when something you have been looking forward to for a long time really happens: there is all the Brackenbury family gone!'
       [*Diary for 1912 ends on December 14.*].

1913

January

1   Gloucester Ball party arrived. Lady Raglan, Freda Somerset, Mrs Charlie Llewellin & Barbara. N. G. Deed.

2   Ball excellent though rather marred by Ly. Raglan & Mrs Ll. deciding to go home about 1.30 leaving me to collect their unwilling daughters.

4–5   Regimental tour at Aylesbury

6   Stag-hunting with Evelyn Rothschild in command.

7   Tom Lepper mounted me on a hireling for the Whaddon Chase . . . I rode up to look at the pack & observed the second whip taking off his cap to me. It turned out to be Joe Lawrence who left us to go to the South Oxfordshire. Dalmeny & Primrose out.[66] We went to Mentmore: it was interesting to see the place (contents were sold in 1977).

8   Proceeded to Risby.[67]

11   On to Garboldisham.[68] My first visit to this far-famed house.

13   Mary Montgomerie took me to Ferryside but Aunt Nelly away. I understand she always keeps it very cold but the two girls had heated it up well.

16   Gracie, F & I to stay with Mrs Wilfred Cripps for Bathurst's ball. Mrs C. knew Deed's brother when he was at Cirencester Grammar School. Ball very select & no 'bunny-hugs'. Ben Bathurst appeared about 1 o'clock, having left the House after the Home Rule division.

17   Heard of poor Mildmay's death: jumping a stile at Cam he fell under his horse.

21   Folkestone. de W & Mrs Shaw haven't managed to get married yet owing to her illness.

February

11   Received wire from Cecil Battine asking for some account of EA whose engagement to Princess Victoria Louise, daughter of the Kaiser, has just been announced. I sent him a fairly intelligent & not too fulsome wire.

12   Town. My Telegraph account is inserted as from 'a well-informed source'. (After long delay I received a guinea from the Daily Telegraph).

March

2   James [*a pupil*] was taken ill last night with acute indigestion: we had to get Dr Lewis who poured boiling water into him [*metaphorically it is hoped*]. He brought up many undigested & indeed unbitten currants! Mr & Mrs Woodroffe to lunch: she was a Broom Witts[69]

15   Made the acquaintance of Bartlett, our new Adjutant.

29   Oxford for Brigade tour

April

4   Gerald Fitzgerald & I to Liverpool for the Grand National. Fairly comfortable journey by L & NW, 1st class: breakfast, dinner & tea good but carriage much overheated. Went to top of stand, very crowded, & saw well. Extraordinary race: only

3 finished & one of those lost his jockey: horses & jockeys fell at every fence. The most trying to watch was the water-jump as one could see directly the horse rose that he wasn't going to clear. Jockeys used short stirrups & seemed to come off pretty easily. Met Harry Lascelles & Tom Rawle.

6   Went round to see Douglas Chandor. He is wild on drawing & wants to take it up professionally: it sounds to me rather venturous, as his drawings can't bring him in much for years to come.

7   Took Douglas' drawings to Holmes at Nat. Port. Gallery. He thinks D has got 'fingers' but says his drawings don't show enough invention to base much opinion on yet. I am trying to persuade Douglas to go into the Civil Service or something in order to have a profession to fall back on. Gerald Fitzg. started work today with the Public Trustee: he means to take a house in the Newbury district.

10   To Bodingtons at Calne[70] for the Spicers' ball at Spye. The eldest son is coming of age & the daughter came out last summer in London.

12   Nelly & I dined at Saintbridge. Vivian suddenly suggested that we should go to Canada in the autumn: must think.

16   Funeral of Allen Allen, carpenter at Hardwicke. He was aged 90. Gracie & self went.

17   Eleanor Adlard[71] came. Nelly, Gracie, & self to Northgate Mansions dance. Lord Alfred Douglas is summoning Ransome for libel: the chief result is that large portions of the unpublished part of 'De Profundis' are read out.

22   To the Audley Neelds at Grittleton. Lady Neeld entertained us. The house is very fine & the pictures magnificent: the pick of all is a really beautiful Constable. We had luncheon then went over the house & gardens: the latter extraordinary from an expert point of view but most of the chief glories are under glass. The stables are beautifully kept & every detail studied: the stable forks are stained & provided with brass rings on brass holders. A fine array of carriages but curiously enough we saw no motors. Lady N told us the whole place took £7000 a year beyond what the estate brought in!

28   Heard that Helen Lascelles is engaged to Eric MacLagan, son of the late Archbishop of York.

29   Walked & talked with Helen in the Park & afterwards at Max Beerbohm's exhibition. She seems very happy.

May

23   Dined at the Burlington with Leo Amery.[72] He is a Fellow of All Souls, editor of Times 'History of the War', MP, etc.: very clever-looking, cheery & amusing but might be a dangerous enemy. He has travelled a lot. His wife is May's friend.

24   EA was married to the Kaiser's daughter in Berlin. I am delighted but the old Welfer-Anhanger have had to swallow something.

June

12   Town to meet Vivian. American trip is in full swing, but many details have to be arranged.

21   Fathers' Match. Everyone cheery & no contretemps. Col. Nicholls struck us as particularly nice. (He was killed at Loos in 1915).

30   Mi sent tickets for the Horse Show so Deed & self went up. We saw a Musical Ride by the Hussars, the Arab display & the jumping for the Connaught Cup.

July

6   Tea with the Broke-Hunts. Mrs B-H has just had their beautiful Greek head photographed for the BM. I guess the date at 350 BC. Arthur decided that it was in fact an ancient copy of Furtwangler's Athene Lemnia head.

7   Nelly came down: not much doing but we spent a jolly time: bought from Miss Hubbard a piece of old English embroidery on fine muslin, bordered with Bucks lace for Helen Lascelles.

21   Waterfield of Cheltenham had written a few days before to suggest my being candidate for a job there. I replied that I was booked for America. He now suggests an interview.

22   To Cheltenham. Principal announced that he was willing to wait till January. Took me over to Thornton who explained the supervision work. Met Basil Bowers.[73] Home for the night: everyone seems keen on my taking the job if offered.

25   Waterfield made offer which I accepted.

28   Everyone is being most awfully nice to me these last days: if I was sorry to miss the Michaelmas term before, I'm broken-hearted now.

29   A thoroughly successful concert. Many parents down: people very nice indeed to me: we were pretty near breaking down.

30   Travelled up in school train.

August

3   Camp on St. Martin's Plain, Shorncliffe

20   Tennis Club Tournament. Edith Bazeley & self won the whole. Edith hit well & I patted with considerable cunning. I chose 2 vols of Gibbon as prize.

The American Tour

[*We have by now had considerable experience of the diarist's enthusiastic approach to new ventures. His account of the 14-week North American tour occupies pages of the 1913 diary with numerous extra facing-page comments on the people he meets, hotels good, bad & indifferent & so on. This section could well stand alone for it gives a fascinating picture of fairly luxurious travel in Canada & the United States of America just before the 1914–18 war overtook Europe & stopped such exploits for several years. We get a really fresh look at such wonders as Niagara Falls, the Yosemite Valley & the Grand Canyon: and we traverse the Civil War battlefields in the company of men who fought there. It is impossible to do more than sample the diarist's experiences whilst hoping that the flavour will not be lost in the process*].

23   Sent our luggage off by Morris the butler. Vivian motored Gracie, Violet Birchall & self to Avonmouth where we mounted (sic) the 'Royal Edward'. She used to be the 'Cairo' but has been adapted by the Canadian Northern Railway. We have a nice outside cabin, £25 each.

24   Sunday. A day of ups & downs! I was well & cheerful till sometime after lunch & faced service read by the Doctor with complete equanimity. About 4 I was unhappy

& followed V's example in taking Mothersills . . . We have a nice port-hole table in the saloon shared with 2 excellent fellows . . .

27   Mudie, an old pupil of Pretoria's [*prep school cricket rival team of the Grange*] gave a rather good lecture on Esperanto.

28   I had my hair cut, the sea being smooth. Concert.

30   Reached Quebec about 10. Up to Frontenac Hotel where we found a telegram from Violet. Admired views of the river, then rejoined boat & on to Montreal.

31   Arrived Montreal about 8 am. A long wait at Customs, the officer being slow & disobliging. Caught the 9.45 to Toronto stopping at 72 places. The nigger porter was a graduate of Pittsburg University & spoke French & German.
      [*An example of the notes on hotels is that for the Queen's Hotel, Toronto. 'A' '$5 Good all through. Large & excellent menu. Poor band. Quiet & respectable. The barber told E that an important part of a hotel clerk's business is to pick out people who turn up with different wives & refuse them rooms*]

September

1   Left Toronto. Met at Mushoko Wharf by Percy Birchall & Maud Denison[74] who conveyed us to Col. Septimus Denison's holiday shack Agiochook, meaning 'spirit of the pines', by motor boat. Lake very beautiful with grand islands dotted about.
     [*Here the diarist & Edward, no longer called Vivian, join a large & convivial house party for a week of bathing & games, expeditions by motor boat, informal picnics. The diarist remarks 'We wear the same clothes all day long with exceptions for bathing'*]

9   Left Agiochook after one of the happiest weeks I remember.

10   Sightseeing in Toronto. Drove round in an observation car. Much struck by the pretty houses in Rosedale & by the Provincial Parliament. The whole town gives a pleasant impression though directly the main streets are left one can see wooden shanties.

11   To Niagara. Started 7.30 by P & O steamer for Yonge St. Wharf. Day sunshiny & a trifle misty. At Lewiston changed on to Belt Line & proceeded up gorge: it was quite beautiful: the sun shone on the opposite bank where the autumn tints were beginning: the waters foamed & swirled a few feet below the car. This part of the expedition should certainly not be missed. Arrived at Niagara Falls NY: walked to Prospect Park where you can stand within a few feet of the top of the American fall. The water goes over with a smooth motion & then breaks into white bands like wool: from below the spray rises in a regular smoke which is sometimes almost black. Down the lift to the 'Maid of the Mist'. Very enjoyable voyage all around the Falls, water wonderful in the sunlight. Up to lunch at the Clifton Restaurant on the American side: cheap & fairly good. Goat Island gives another fine view. We decided to do the Cave of the Waters which necessitates taking off all clothing & assuming a picturesque & effective garb, flannel inside & yellow oilskin out, with half sandally shoes. The walk over the wooden bridges is delightful & quite easy: little rainbows lay about casually on the rocks as if they had been thrown there. When the actual cave is reached you join hands, turn your faces to the rocks & sidle along with the fall (a small branch of the American one) thundering at your back. There is no question of seeing the water, all you see is the rock in front & beneath you: the water is blown in lashing streams on to your back: I don't think there is really any danger but you might have an anxious

moment if you slipped. I visited the 3 sisters, E took a rest. It is quite worth seeing the rapids above the Falls. We drove across the Upper Bridge & to a Power House, a large white building on the Canadian side; this was quite interesting to E. Back to Table Rock: went down the passage behind Horseshoe Fall. This is a badly organised show with long waiting & casual attendants: after the Cave of the Waters it is certainly not worth doing. Tea at the big new Clifton, not to be confounded [sic] with the place where we had lunch. The Belt Line again to Queenston: this side is very attractive though not as good as the other: pleasant voyage back with excellent dinner. Arrived about 9.15 (scheduled 8.35) after a brilliantly successful day

12 To Ottawa. Travelled by CPR with parlorcar & observation platform in rear, new to me. Staying at Château Laurier, very luxurious & huge. We have 2 single rooms with one bath between, $3 each.

13 To Archives chiefly to use our letter of introduction to Dr Doughty. He was much excited to learn that we had a portrait of Joseph Brandt & talks of having it copied full-length. Tram to Chaudière Falls: Parliament Buildings very fine.

14 [*At Montreal*] Early service at Trinity in Place Viger. Up the Mount Royal, beautiful view in danger of being spoilt by ugly buildings: a few more loopholes through the trees would be an improvement. The hill is full of chipmunks. Called on Henry Drummond & Professor Leacock [*Stephen*].

15 Château de Ramezay: interesting relics of old Canada, well worth a visit: engraving of Joseph Brandt quite unlike our portrait. Met Rashdall & wife, who both pretended to know me: he was hot & flustered as usual. Lunch with Col. Denison at the Mount Royal Club, jolly & hospitable as usual.

20–21 Arrived Quebec early. We went a round tour on an observation car. Dined at the Garrison Club as guests of several RCR men: one of whom, Willoughby, comes from Cheltenham & knew the Arbuthnots.
[*Escorted by various new military friends visits are made to Fort Levis, the Plains of Abraham with the controversial English & French positions where E propounds a new explanatory theory, the Citadel, the Arsenal, the Ile d'Orleans & the Montmorency Falls. Having expressed boxes to England containing spare clothing the journey westwards starts in earnest.*]

22 Snow in places lying on the shocks of wheat. Lake Superior looked very bleak & cold. Arrived at Winnipeg. Met by Percy Birchall. Drove to St. Regis Hotel. E Paid $3, I $2. Dark & not too clean. Town very new with few fine buildings except for banks. Lunch with P at the Country Club. He instructs NCO's of RCR & others including Strathcona's Horse. We watched him at work. Dinner at the Manitoba Club with P & Col. Steel, a pioneer of the NW Mounted Police. He was a great raconteur: and an admirer of Wolseley with whom he went on the 1870 Red River expedition [*a very full account of this stirring event is given separately*].

25, 26, 27 Across Saskatchewan & Alberta: rolling plains, very few trees, occasional shallow lakes. I read ¼ of 'The Wrecker' which I started in 1896! Woke up just before the Rockies: entered the Gap & passed an endless succession of beautiful scenes. Reached Banff Springs Hotel: we walked up Mount Tunnel. Early service at St. George's: about 18 there. Visited a buffalo park & saw a herd quite close: then to Minnewanka Lake.

30   To Laggan by train . . . I rode a pony up to the 'Lakes in the Clouds', & back by the Glacier trail.

October

1–2   Train to Glacier. This is a gorgeous journey & must be done by day. Scenery through Kicking Horse Pass the finest we've seen. Then the Rockies give place to the less savage Selkirks. Got to Glacier late. Walked to Illicewact Glacier. It has a beautiful blue underneath it with brilliant crevasses.

3   Mounted Imperial Limited for Vancouver. I dropped off at Sycamore whither I had invited Orde Murray-Browne[75] for a dine & sleep at the CPR hotel. Orde very cheery, talkative & Canadian: 'Gee whiz' 'you bet' 'dandy' & 'guess' formed the major part of his conversation.

4   To Vancouver by the Toronto–Vancouver express. Along the Thomson River & canyon there are enormous bare mountians, all browny-yellow clay & green tree-clumps, rather like the Nativity of Piero della Francesca.

5   I had called for a Benedictine about 9.45: the waiter brought it but another waiter hastily snatched it away. As at Banff, in Alberta & BC you can't get a drink between 6.0 pm Saturday & 8.0 am Monday except with a full ordinary meal, ie not bacon & eggs.

6   To dinner came Gore[76] & his pretty & piquante wife. The first time our dress clothes had seen the light since the Royal Edward.

7–9   At Victoria Esquimault, and an Indian reservation: then back to Vancouver & on to Seattle by the night boat.

11   Custom House people nice & quick when they arrived. E declared a large quantity of tobacco: they let him off that but proceeded to rummage his boxes very thoroughly. Boarded a compartment on the Shasta Limited. The train kept stopping owing to a fault in the oil-pipe. We are on an oil engine for the first time.

12   Beautiful journey through California. Mt. Shasta rose very clear on our left. At Shasta Springs I drank the rather Hunyadi-like water, E abstaining. At Red Bluff a dark Italian looking boy was selling very good grapes . . . At Oaklands took ferry & approached San Francisco by moonlight.

13–14   Messed about the city separately. It climbs up & down hills . . . the more modern the buildings the bigger & uglier they are. Traces of the fire are not obvious. At the Presidio some of the 16th Cavalry were playing games with their horses: one of them got his horse to lie down for my benefit. Golden Gate Park trip in a 'rubber neck'. The Pacific pleasant to look on but no seals on Seal Island.

15   Went to call on the Lockes. Miss L a great friend of Eleanor Adlard. She met us in an electric automobile: she was pretty & well-dressed (rather diaphanous for motor-ing) with bare arms & head. A perfect drive round Berkeley & Oakland, the University & Greek theatre. Curiously enough Rashdall was lecturing in the Univer-sity that evening.

16–17   El Portal: Merced: Sentinel, 2 hour dusty trip. Driver Henry Hedges drove the old stage from Wawona 40 years ago. Then entered the real Yosemite valley quite one of the most glorious sights I've seen: El Capitan: walked to Mirror Lake, surface gently ruffled. Tall white shining cliffs give an impression of unreality: they look like some gigantic stage scenery made luminous & translucent. Only drawbacks are the Falls are very empty & the dust is atrocious.

18   An unforgettable day. We took the Glacier trail, E riding for the first time for 15 years. Vernal & Nevada Falls. Gradually as one climbs Half Dome changes its shape: at last it stands out splendidly clear-cut, almost as steep behind as in front. Lyrical description of Views over Yosemite valley, very green with toy trees & houses, horses & carts: feeling of unreality again. Trail coming down a little trying: the mules have a regular game: they walk along the outside edge & when they come to a corner they walk right on & stick their heads over: then they suddenly swing round under one, & one realises that one is not dead after all.

20   It became obvious about a week ago that I wanted more of the West while E was in a hurry to get to the eastern battlefields. So we agreed to part till about 3rd November.

21–28 [*Diarist enjoys exploring Del Monte, The Santa Clara Valley, Monterey with its Mexican population, old Spanish missions, bizarre Monterey pine trees. He books his berth home on the Lusitania then takes tickets for St. Louis via Los Angeles & the Grand Canyon aboard the 'Angel' train. Breaking his journey at LA he visits Pasadena, has chop suey at a Chinese restaurant & continues through Arizona's wild & strange country on the 'California Ltd'.*]

28   Arrived Grand Canyon 8.10 am. The canyon itself very strange & perplexing. First impression is depressing. It looks as if the arch sinner of America had been engulfed here & the earth had never quite closed, while the curse had smitten the ground with barrenness. Later in the day the colours begin to distinguish themselves. I drove to the head of Hermit Trail & saw the sunset from Hopi Point. Early morning & evening are the best times for the Canyon. Received money wired me by E. Glad to have spare money to spend on rugs etc.

29   Bright Angel Trail. Went with 3 Yankees, rather objectionable. Mules were good: the guide Fred half French. The riding however almost more terrifying than in the Yosemite. I followed the guide's example in hanging my reins on the pommel. Another time I should only go as far as the plateau: from here you see all the best colours & shadows. To Navajos Indian dance at the Hopi House, built by Fred Harvey.

30   To Grand View, well worth the trouble. One looks more lengthwise down the Canyon. From 3 pm the blue shadows grow deeper & deeper & lovely pinks & crimsons appear.

31   Bought Navajos rugs & spoons at the Independent Store.

November

1   'California Ltd' through weird scenery, bits that looked stolen from the Grand Canyon. Fred Harvey gave us an excellent 5-course dinner for $1. Albuquerque: Kansas City: St. Louis, where drew a fresh letter of credit & money from Mercantile Trust: also collected washing from Vancouver at Adams Express Co. Day hot & muggy, streets filthy, so decided to push on: bought a drawing room to Charleston on the 'Dixie Flyer'.

4   Time to wait at Nashville: took tram out a little way: saw families of real Darkies for the first time. At Atlanta drank Coco Cola, the staple product: not very nice.

5   Arr. Charleston S.C. E met me. I had read Wister's 'Lady Baltimore' in preparation & found the town accurately described. We called on Mrs Drayton-Grimke who lives in Legare Street, one of the real old ladies of Charleston. She took us to the Country Club, a fine old Colonial house. Our equipage consisted of a landau & pair of fine white horses steered by a big negro in livery. We stopped at the Confederate cemetery. Down here their great hero is Lee, the 'cavalier': Jackson the 'puritan' though much admired is a bad second to Lee.

> [*From 5–19 November when Edward leaves for home on the 'Cedric' the programme leans heavily towards Civil War sites, museums & battlefield visits all described clearly & interestingly. Amongst these are Fort Sumter, Richmond Va., Fredericksburg & Chancellorsville, Harper's Ferry & Bull Run with Jackson's 'Stone Wall' shown by the best of the many guides they encountered, & Gettysburg with guns still in situ in the Confederate emplacements. Other places visited include Williamsburg with its links with Bruton, Somerset; the William & Mary College. At Washington D.C. they see the Capital, Arlington Cemetery & Mount Vernon: meet Eustace Percy at the Embassy & hear of Mme. de Hénaut's death: present their letter of introduction from their table companion aboard the Royal Edward to Senator Gallinger of New Hampshire who arranges for them to attend a meeting of Congress & to see the War, Navy & State Departments. Alone once more the diarist's interests widen: galleries & sport reappear.*]

26   Philadelphia . . . Academy: Stuart's portraits of the Presidents are exceptionally fine: he has Van Dyck's trick of ennobling everybody.

27   Saw Cornell beat Pennsylvania 21 to 0. Cornell's first victory over P for 11 years. P lost 2 good men knocked out, but the game was not otherwise unduly bloody. To a stranger the 'dressings' were as amusing as the game itself . . . the cheer-leaders who controlled the shouting of the college cries etc. They would announce what cry they wanted through megaphones, then conduct with vigorous gestures of both arms. When anyone scored they hurled megaphones into the air, turned somersaults etc. At the end of the game the Cornell band marched over the field, the supporters forming in serried ranks. As they marched under the goal posts they threw their hats over the bar, some catching, some failing to catch them on the other side.

28   Explored New York: Broadway: trammed right down Wall Street. The most curious feature is the churches which seem like bits of Old Times left by mistake. The skyscrapers are wonderfully effective, making a sort of Yosemite of every street. George Cruse [*father of Donald, a Grange pupil*] arranged for me to have a room at the Calumet Club, 267 Fifth Avenue. A quaint old-fashioned house, no elevator, winding wooden staircases & big light rooms: service is good & the whole comfortable. Quite a relic, in 5th Avenue.

29   Metropolitan Museum, seeing fine Praxitelan head . . . Astor Theatre: President Woodrow Wilson there. Great enthusiasm when he arrived, band playing & everyone standing up.

30   Tried to go to St. Mary the Virgin but it was hermetically sealed. Visited Brooklyn Bridge, the aquarium and walked down Fifth Avenue to the Waldorf Astoria. This street is as top-hatty as any London street on Sunday. Saw Ellis Island.

December

2   About 8 I took my big trunk to the Pier, & about 10 I went on board the Lusitania. Stateroom A14, an inside single cabin with an electric fan, very well ventilated, £25. On board is Evelyn Rothschild who superintended the stag hunt *see* January 6 above.

7   Sunday. Nice service taken by the Purser. Ship's band played.

8   Landed by tender at Fishguard. Long wearisome wait . . . home at 6.45.
[*After this long period of constant travel and change it is remarkable to see how quickly the diarist settles down; making plans for his new post at Cheltenham in January, paying a nostalgic visit to the Grange and revelling in a Hardwicke Christmas. His remarks on the latter make a happy ending to a year which in other respects had been frustrating.*]

12   [At Cheltenham] Lunched with the Principal. They have staying with them the three sons of Yuan Shi Kai, the President (77)

23   Ketha & children came. Billy is cheery & talkative, Kitty a darling chatterbox

25   A very happy Chirstmas. I got many nice presents & gave away American trophies. The house ringing with children

1914

January

7-8   Ball party includes Hall of the Bucks, Robin Hale son of Tom Hale of Alderley, Laurence Godman & N. G. Deed.

12   I went to Hucclecote where Billy is ill. Talked with Cousin Charlie about Orde whom I met in Canada. He is worred about Orde's farming: however Orde has just become postmaster so that sounds better *see* October 3, 1913.

13   Rode a big brown of Cox's. The animal was pulling considerably & my hands were cold, & soon after Coaley station he took control. He ran away, not going very fast but so persistently that I could not stop him. I turned him up Cam Pitch but that didn't blow him: we went all along to Dursley, through the town, fortunately not crowded, & out the other side, up Whiteway. At the foot of the hill he stopped. It was one of the worst experiences of my life.

15   Began wrestling with the 14 Tate sugar cases which have arrived from Folkestone containing my books: stowed all away in bedroom, gunroom etc.

17   To Cambridge to stay with Jelf. Both he & Mrs are cheerful & happy. Kings College school is a pretty building standing in fine grounds: the house in accordance with tradition is kept at freezing point. Only a few choristers there.

18   Sunday. Chapel at Kings. The singing was good but not superlative. The chapel I admired quite as much as I anticipated . . . In the afternoon I called on the Edward Brownes. I found E alone & when he had realised who I was he was delightful. Lally came in later, & two jolly boys, Patrick & Michael were brought down. Edward grouses a lot about the teaching of modern languages.

21   To Cheltenham to start my new job, living in the Junior school. Boys not back. Made the acquaintance of the inhabitants, ie Miss Wolf who manages the house, & the new staff, consisting of G. M. Paterson, Clifton & Trinity, Oxford, J. S. Bond, Chelten-

ham & Emmanuel, Cambridge where he knew Deed, a fine mathematician, & Crump, very young & enthusiastic, a humorist, has been with Lyttelton.

22 Examined our one new boy, Darbishire: he is backward.

23 Began my work in the Senior. The sets were pretty well full. Boys seem very good, good-mannered & quite amenable. The first man I met over the way was Nestor-Schnurman: he took me up to Scot-Skirving's room where I had to take over supervision while SS went to the 'Promotion' meeting. Everybody was mouse-like.

24 The Junior boys seem nice but are not forthcoming: they were considerably sat on by the last set of men: they have little liberty & the prefect system is non-existant.

30 Dinner with the Principal. I sat next Mrs W who is cheerful, homely & pleasant. After dinner Miss W (sister) Paterson & self played inferior billiards.

February

1 Chapel in morning. A pleasant building but suffers from complete absence of stained glass. I was on duty in the afternoon ie from 1.30–10 pm. Afternoon chapel. Then we walked up Leckhampton Hill to the Devil's Chimney, quite a good walk which the boys much enjoyed.

7 Johnson, Adjutant 5th Gloucesters, motored elder Collett & self to Oxford for a Bgde tour. Also there Guy Crouch, Hall, Leslie Barrett & some 16 others.

19 Nelly over for a music lesson. Went over the Junior – she seemed much pleased.

20 Slight rows with IIIi, my most troublesome set.

28 Tea with Butler[78] who is the best man intellectually on the staff. The Junior elected Prefects tonight. Fairly successful. It is supposed to be a step towards the self-government they so sorely need.

March

7 Train to Broadway: met by Sylvia Percival's[79] motor. We went to Chipping Campden where May was lunching with Mrs Ashbee. Their house is an old monastery. Everything beautiful & not too Morrisy. To Kingham to meet Meiklejohn, formerly private secretary to Asquith. Agreeable but rather frigid. Back to Burford to stay with Syliva Percival. She lives in the Old Greyhound which she has made into a delightful house. I made the acquaintance of David & Alicia.[79a] Country dancing in the parish room: my first taste & great fun . . . among the dancers Mr & Mrs Gretton. He is a writer for Liberal journals & she has just written a masterly work 'A Corner of the Cotswolds'.

8 Sunday. Service in the beautiful church. Only about 100 people which struck me as rather few. After tea called on the Grettons who live almost next door. Another splendid house. Their courtyard is the frontispiece of Mrs. G's book.

9 Sylvia's motor brought me in just in time for school.

10 Junior Masters' dinner. Everybody concerned in the Junior except Luckham & Page. We took a long time to do a very little business. It was especially galling for me as I had had to refuse an invitation to Cecil Elwes' small dance.

11 I got off at 11 having no last hour & proceeded on a bike to the Races. Bill Playne vouched for me. The National Hunt Cup had attracted an enormous crowd. All the usual people plus Harry Lascelles, Sir George Jenkinson, Lionel Montagu & Nunn.

Lunched with the Adelards. To the Race Ball . . . well done but I was rather bored on the whole in spite of cinematograph & oyster bars.

21 Folkestone for the weekend. Things are again in the melting pot! Shaw is going to do stockbroking & wants to get rid of his share of the school. Incidentally it has come to light that they got the school for about £6000, much less than any of Jelf's offers to us. Afterwards talked to Deed: he has thoughts of trying to buy Shaw's share.

22 Sunday. Early chapel. Breakfast at Grange: chapel again, then lunch at Vicarage. Tea at Grange: off by 5.7. Dinner at Club, caught 9.10 at Paddington, arrived Gloucester 12 midnight & taxied to Cheltenham. It was goodbye to some of the best of them: Donald Cruse is going to America, Drew Lepper to Haileybury, Gerald Secker to Radley.

April

12 Easter Sunday. Johnny Godman at the Cottage: he is going to be looked at by Bill Playne with a view to Yeomanry Adjutancy.

16 To Paris, then Bourg-la-Reine, to find Mdlle Lund who is going to give me phonetic lessons at Grande Rue 27, a large house owned by a painter Henri Motte. I was ushered in to a rather tremendous lady with embroidered robe & white poudré wig. She is I fancy Mdme Motte . . . My first lesson with Mdlle Lund was devoted to i, e, & E. Though she taught me very little theory that I did not know it was invaluable to have the practice. Called on Michael Palairet at the Embassy. They are up to their eyes with the King's visit.

18 Called on Agnès Crequi-Montfort who has just had a little girl (Camille: she was to marry the Marquis de Lillers).

19 Sunday. Church at St. Georges. Called on Récopés whose 'At home' day it is.

20 Lesson: chiefly oe & o

21 The King & Queen arrived: they had a wonderful reception by all accounts.

22 Off to Versailles. Visited my favourite rooms in the château. Then to the Léonards to lunch. They have just got a new house, rather larger & with no concierge. They have a Bodington there: they were enchanted with Kit Guise whom I sent to them. He & Madame apparently became great friends. When Kit was killed in 1915 a letter to Mdme was in his pocket.

25 Lunched with M. Philippe & Mdme de Vilmorin. He is grandson of the great gardner & keeps on the business. She is handsome & clever but slightly alarming. Vilmorin means to send all his boys for 3 or 4 years to English schools.

26 To Malmaison by tram. My first visit. The rooms are very pretty, mostly furnished in Empire style. The gardens are being laid out by the generosity of great florists, among them Mme. Vilmorin.

28 Dinner with the Pierredons. The only visitors were M. Massabaun, the just-defeated Député of Aveyron Espalion, & his son. M. has sat as 'Action Libérale' for about 17 years & has now lost his seat for supporting the 3 year military service which is unpopular in the unthreatened south. He talked southern French which caused me some difficulty.

May

8   Had a bad hour with I2. We have received one Moor, of Boyne House[80] who gave me so much trouble that I turned him out of the room.

9   Sports. The day fine but cold. Clare & Nelly came over.

18   Masters' meeting to try to adopt a candidate for our representative on the Council.

30   Weekend camp at Wycombe. Found Josh Reynolds comfortably ensconced in a nice little house. Mrs J. not in. Marched from Wycombe to Beaconsfield: hot but everyone got along well including the recruits.

31   Sunday. Drilled on till about 1. Then I left for Town. Officers in camp were Josh, self & Hall who has just got a place as Vice Consul at Dunkerque.

June

6   Sybil Witts had a birthday party consisting chiefly of Ratcliffs, Gems & Cardews. We had tea in a field opposite Southam. Then we walked all the way up over Cleeve & over the top. I walked with Mr Gem, a very good sort. The boy is up to H V Page & G complains of the amount of prep that P sets the boy.

13   Folkestone for the weekend. Shaw no longer teaches & is not much in the place. Deed cuffed Neill mi on the head: great fuss from Captain N. Deed sent in his resignation but has withdrawn it again. De Winton is quite keen for him to stay on but is naturally upset at similar incidents.

20   Juniors cricket v. Malvern Link school [*diarist's prep school*] I went over with Thornton after lunch. The first time for about 18 years. The cafe where we used to buy Nelson buns is gone: also the paper shop on the corner where we got Tit Bits . . . I went to look at the school: on the whole few changes: conspicuous is the big swimming bath down by the nets.

21   Sunday . . . evening rather spoilt by discovery of unpleasant similarities between the work of two Newick boys. I rang up Shaw Page & we are to discuss it tomorrow.

22   Div I set troublesome. Handed out 3 impositions. Shaw Page has satisfied himself that there is nothing wrong. I take his word for it gladly. I talked to the two boys who I thought seemed a trifle sheepish (I am sure they were guilty, S.P. conducted the enquiry in the most haphazard way).

26   Speech Day. Speeches from the Principal, ditto from James, prize-giving & French & Greek playlets. James' most interesting remark was that the school was perhaps the hardest-working school in England.

27   Motored to weekend camp . . . Buckingham & Wolverton where we found the army just preparing a battle . . . I umpired.

July

2   Principal's Garden Party. They were expecting 1200 but I can't believe they had half that number. Jack Birchall came with the Scobells.[81]

4   Picnic. Motor char-a-banc to Tewkesbury, then by steamer up the Avon, then tea, then cricket, then home.

5   Sunday. On duty in the afternoon. All went well till prep when they were very troublesome.

10–11 Cheltenham v. Clifton. Beat Clifton by 25. I didn't see much as I went home to play v. Tuffley. The ground has not been mown for 5 weeks & is like a hayfield.

[*Diary breaks off at this point & is not re-started till December 6th, according to a subsequent note. Included then are detailed notes on each boy in all the sets taught by the diarist.*]

29 Much excitement about war & rumours of war

31 Much talk about possible mobilization.

August

1 Town, for Cheltenham v. Haileybury. We were doing very well when rain stopped play. Rather pleasant roaming about the Pavilion which I had never entered before.

2 Sunday. To camp at Marlow. Several new officers including Viney-Green, my new subaltern for 'A'. Bartlett warned me that if we were mobilised I should be Staff Captain to the Brigade.

3 At 3.30 we were wakened by the bugles playing 'Orders'. The Orders were in fact to pack up & go home. The Bucks were the last to go, & 'A' Coy naturally the last of the Bucks to leave. We had to strike the whole camp: then down to Marlow to load the trains, stopping on the way to get rid of kit & to give instructions re mobilisation. We left the station at 7.30 pm. I went to stay with Frank Wethered.

Notes for Transition Section.

1. Byrne, L. S. R. Assistant master at Eton. Taught German.
2. Oliphant, General Sir Laurence James.
3. Hénaut, Mdlle Jeanne de, Directress of prestigious language coaching establishment at 174 Rue de la Pompe, Paris, described by Harold Nicolson in 'Some People' pp. 76–91 (1927).
4. Batten-Pooll, Walter Stewart. Eton & R. de la Pompe. Gave up Diplomatic corps aspirations for an Army career. *N. Somerset Yeomanry, 1909–22*.
4a. Campbell, Ronald, Haileybury & R. de la Pompe. Came 3rd in FO exam, *British Ambassador in Paris, 1940*.
5. St. Aldwyn, Lady Catherine Lucy, daughter of 3rd Earl Fortescue & wife of 1st Earl St. Aldwyn.
6. Beach, Margaret Agnes 'Daisy'. 2nd dau. of W. F. Hicks Beach of Witcombe.
7. Lascelles, Richard. 1st cousin. 5th son of Walter Richard Lascelles, eldest brother of diarist's mother.
8. Berkeley, Charles Paget Fitzhardinge. 3rd Baron Fitzhardinge. m. Louisa Elizabeth Lindon-Lindow. succ. 1896.
9. Somerville, Annesley Ainsworth. Housemaster at Eton. Taught French and Maths.
10. Hardy, Gathorne. 4th Royal Berks regt. *Awarded MC at Hébuterne*.
11. Chute, Charles Leonard. Eton & Magdalen. Gave his home The Vyne to the National Trust.
12. Gesellschaft – a party, sociable occasion.
13. Bridges, Robert, *Poet Laureate, 1913*.
14. Buddensieg, Dr. Director of the princes' education at Gmunden.
14a Buck, Herr, Librarian at Gmunden.
15. von Grote, Graf. Court Chamberlain at Gmunden.
16. Kennard, Sir Arthur Fitzroy Coleridge, 1st Baronet. Diplomatic Corps. Attaché 1908–10. *1st Secretary 1919, Chargé d'affaires Helsingfors 1919*.
17. Klenck, Baron. Master of the Horse and Court official at Gmunden. His daughter Mary Klenck taught diarist the sport of snow-running (skiing?).
18. Wersebe, Ludwig, Imperial & Royal Riding Master at Gmunden.
19. *Prüfung* – examination.
20. '*Es ist wirklich zu dumm*' 'It is really stupid'.
21. Palairet, Charles, M., Eton. Diplomatic Corps. Attaché Vienna 1908. Last British Minister to Vienna, *Ambassador to the Greek government in London 1942. Assist. undersec. of State, FO, 1943–35. Kt. 1938*.
22. Goschen, Sir Edward Henry & Lady, Ambassador to Austria-Hungary 1905–08; to Germany 1908–14.
23. Bruce, Henry James. Eton (RWT-T) Diplomatic Corps. 3rd secretary Vienna 1906–08; *1st secretary 1918; retired 1920*.
24. *Schatzkammer* – literally 'treasure house': repository of the Hanoverian jewels.
25. Duse, Eleonora. Italian actress who excelled in Ibsen parts: she was noted for her expressive capabilities. GBS greatly admired her acting.
26. Wilberforce, Ven. A. B. O. Archdeacon of Westminster and Rector of St. John's .
27. Henson, Rev. Herbert Hensley, Rector of St. Margarets, Westminster. *Rt. Rev. Bishop of Durham, 1929*.
28. Battine, Nigel & Oswald James, sons of Cecil & Daisy Battine.
29. Powell, Captain of the Boats at Eton: President of the Union at Cambridge. R. de la Pompe.
30. Duncan, Eton & Balliol. Came 4th in FO exam.
31. Bowman, Clive, Oxford friend.

32. Montefiore – There are 3 contenders for this note: in the absence of more information it is likely to be Rev. E. B. S. Montefiore of Kelmscott.

33. Nicolson, Hon. Harold George. Wellington & Oxford. Held appointments in FO and Diplomatic Corps, 1909–20. Author & critic, *see* note 3 above. *MP & League of Nations.*

34. Herrenhausen: palace of former Kings of Hanover, forbears of Duke Ernst at Gmunden.

35. 'Jack' John Henry Peyto Verney. Blanchie's nephew. *20th Baron Willoughby de Broke.*

36. Elwes, Lt. Col. Henry Cecil of Colesbourne Park.

37. Howard, Lady Mary Agnes. daughter of 18th Earl of Suffolk. m. Hon. Henry Westwood of Jamaica. Lived at Petty France, Didmarton.

38. Jelf, Charles. son of Sir Arthur Jelf (Judge Jelf). HM Grange school Folkestone: later HM King's College Choir school, Cambridge.

39. Woodman, also Wodeman. Assistant master at Grange school.

40. Hutton, Robert. Pupil at Grange school: son of Stamford Hutton, q.v. *Chairman of Glos. Quarter Sessions.* Lived at Harescombe Grange.

41. Gardiner, Canon Evelyn. Holy Trinity, Folkestone. m. 'Daisy' Orde.

42. Gardiner, Daisy née Maria Frances Orde daughter of Charles Orde of Nunneykirk.

43. Hutton, Stamford: only son of Crompton Hutton of Harescombe Grange. He was Recorder of Lichfield.

44. Waterfield, Rev. Reginald. Principal of Cheltenham College 1899–1919. *Very Rev. Dean of Hereford 1920.*

45. Scott, Geoffrey: son of Scott, Editor of the *Manchester Guardian.*

46. Mourners included Berkeley Hunt servants: Will Rawle, Gilbert, 2 whips.

47. Bussage. A House of Mercy was founded here in 1851. Uncle H took over the interest which his philanthropist father had kept in it.

48. Murray-Browne, William Granville 'Billy.' Ketha & Wilfrid's first child, and F's only grandson.

49. Delves-Broughton, Brian, 4th son of 10th Baronet. Pupil at the Grange school.

50. Murray-Browne, Granville. 2nd cousin, brother of Wilfrid M-B. Went down with his ship in 1916.

51. How, Constance, née Murray-Browne. Sister of Granville, above. m. Sidney How.

52. Kempe, Humphrey, s. of Sir Arthur Kempe, Treasurer of the Royal Society.

53. Paget, Rt. Rev. Henry Luke. 4th Bishop of Stepney, from 1911.

53a. Paget, Rt. Rev. Francis. 34th Bishop of Oxford, 1901–11.

54. Lepper, Drew, Pupil at the Grange school with whom diarist kept in touch.

55. Mitchell, Charles. Adjutant, Bucks regt. *Staff Captain to 144 Brigade in 1914; Brigade Major to 5th Corps.*

56. The Fishpond appears to be part of the medieval moat associated with an earlier building on the Hardwicke site.

57. Baines, Sir Athelstan & Lady Baines. Formerly of ICS. Parents of Sylvia Percival.

58. The West Midland Poor Law annual conference was held at Malvern, established by T. B. Lloyd Baker who acted as secretary until 1885 when G. E. Lloyd Baker, 'F', took over the duties. F had served for 25 years in 1910.

59. Page, Herbert Vivian. Old Cheltonian & Assistant Master at Cheltenham College. Housemaster of West Day Boys' house until 1923 when the diarist succeeded him.

60. Benson, Most Rev. Edward White. Archbishop of Canterbury. One of his four sons was A. C. Benson, *see* Eton List note 41.

61. Joconde – La Giaconda – Mona Lisa. It has not been possible to explain 'that business' satisfactorily.

62. Browne, Winifred & Maud, sisters, married Hereward & Cyril Brackenbury, brothers. The sisters were 2nd cousins of the diarist & lived in Northumberland.

63. Eliza and Lucy were old Hardwicke servants.

64. Spence-Jones, Very Rev. Dr. H. D. M. and Mrs. author of 'The Dean's Handbook to Gloucester Cathedral'.

65. Addington, Lord and Lady, 2nd Baron. Parents of J. G. Hubbard, *see* Oxford List note 23.

66. Primrose, 5th Earl of Rosebery: created Viscount Mentmore 1911.

67. Risby, Norfolk. Home of the Burrell cousins. Kitty Burrell was a granddaughter of Aunt Nelly Montgomerie, sister of the diarist's mother. *See* Eton list note 20.

68. Garboldisham. Formerly the home of Aunt Nelly but now that of her son, George, and his wife Sybil née Somerset.

69. Woodroffe, Mrs. Daughter of Rev. Francis Edward Broome Witts and thus a great granddaughter of Rev. Francis Edward Witts of Upper Slaughter, the 'Cotswold Parson' of the diaries edited by David Verey.

70. Bodington, Ven. Eric James. Archdeacon of Wiltshire from 1913.

71. Adlard, Eleanor. Lived at Postlip Hall near Winchcombe.

72. Amery, Leo. Statesman and journalist. *Intelligence service during 1914–18 war. See also* entry for May 23, 1913.

73. Bowers, Basil Alcot, son of Canon Bowers, College Green. An Old Cheltonian. Assistant master at Cheltenham College.

74. Denison, Col. Septimus J. A. of Toronto Canada, and his daughter Maud. There must be a link between Col. Denison & S. C. Denison of New College, contemporary with the diarist, but no such link has been found as yet.

75. Murray-Browne Orde, 2nd cousin. Brother of Wilfrid, Granville, Constance and others. Lived in Canada at the time of the diarist's extended visit. K. in 1914–18 war.

76. Gore, Charles. Brother of John Gore who wrote the official Life of King George V.

77. Shih-Kai, Yuan (1859–1916). Chinese politician. Elected President of the Chinese Republic in 1913: arranged for his own coronation in 1916 thus proving himself a traitor. Forced to abdicate, and disappeared.

78. Butler, Leonard Gray. Rugby & New College. Assistant master at Cheltenham College. K. in France 1916.

79. Percival, Sylvia née Baines. A long-standing friendship.

79a. Percival, David and Alicia. Children of the above. David a pupil at Cheltenham College.

80. Moor, G. Troublesome schoolboy of Boyne House, Cheltenham College. He later won the VC at Krithia, Dardanelles, on 5 June 1915 at the age of 18. K. 1918.

81. Scobell, Ven. Edward Chessall, Archdeacon of Gloucester from 1903

The War Years

1914 (August) – 1919

Until July the diary for 1914 followed the usual pattern of winter balls, meets of foxhounds, theatre visits, cricket & tennis matches but with the important addition of the diarist's new appointment to the staff at Cheltenham College where he was to teach a range of subjects. His comments and comparisons with preparatory school teaching experiences at The Grange are revealing. Not until 29 July is there any real hint of coming events: the diary had been broken off on 12 July and copied up in December, starting with 'Much excitement about war and rumours of war'.

Entries concerned with the outbreak of war seem casual in the extreme. Though the diarist was engaged in the usual summer Territorial camp from 2 August the order to mobilise on the 4th was conveyed by means of notices in the local post office. Thereafter the diarist was involved in some bizarre incidents worthy of an Ealing studio film, before settling into his new role of Staff Captain to the South Midlands Brigade.

Whilst still in England eagerness for an overseas posting simmered constantly but the new job was exacting, requiring both energy and tact. Possession of these attributes enabled the diarist to enjoy his successful handling of difficult situations. At the same time a curious subculture developed, a reflection of normal home life. Relatives & friends rented houses in the vicinity and dispensed hospitality, organised sporting events and invited visitors to stay: the diarist's sisters came by turns to be entertained. When the overseas posting eventually materialised on 30 March 1915 it is followed by almost a year of silence.

Diaries for 1916. 1917 & 1918 are in small pocket books, written for the most part in pencil, and in the field. It seems likely that the intention was to write up these years more fully: indeed this may have been done (*see* October 1917) but no trace of any Army Books have come to light so far. The content of entries is often of compelling interest though written tersely and evidently with much left unsaid. The Somme offensive starting on July 1916 affords just such a sequence. Cryptic sentences make poignant reading: 'Drenching rain last night. To trenches'. 'Men very hard worked & progress slow'. After four days they are relieved & move out to dirty billets: 'Quiet. Hot. Picked raspberries'. Next day, Sunday, he attended Holy Communion as was his custom whenever possible.

During 1916 his brother Michael was killed: and also his great friend Edward Birchall with whom he had been at Eton and Oxford, and shared the French & American holidays described in these diaries. There were many, many more losses among his friends in Gloucestershire and elsewhere. Temperamentally the diarist was equipped to cope with these grievous events and the painful stresses of war, as well as with its tedium & discomfort. His religious convictions were strong & unfaltering: he was brave, and inspired his men in turn to bravery & to stalwart stoicism. He was unmarried, which must have relieved him of the anxiety arising from having close dependents. He was able to accept the years of service with dispassionate though not phlegmatic calm, making the best of the interludes which came his way: the periods of leave; the Etonian 4th of June celebrations held in most unlikely circumstances when magically

Etonians from considerable distances foregathered; and the equestrian competitions held when the Brigade was being 'rested' and in which he revelled.

After a three months Senior Officers course early in 1917 the diarist returned to France in time for the Arras offensive, followed later by the Ypres onslaught in which the Brigade achieved great distinction and many individual awards: the diarist received the DSO. There were appalling losses, however, & the list of friends' names in Killed, Wounded & Missing became ever longer. As the year wore on another leave was followed by action at Vimy Ridge in November, but by the thirteenth of that month we read 'The air is full of Italy', & the long journey thither starts a week later. The fragmentary entries make this campaign even more difficult to follow than the foregoing French sequence: the diarist does not mention the award to him of the Italian Croce di Guerra: nor does he explain the controversial affair of Major General Fanshawe's return home which caused great indignation in the Division which was devoted to him. Other similar problems persist.

At the end of August 1918 a home posting for six months was proposed & although the GOC said the diarist could not be spared he was home by mid-September. More leave, a posting to Ireland in November, followed by attempts to get another overseas posting, then a variety of splendid-sounding but nominal appointments with no less than five more periods of leave in three months made the diarist at last eager for demobilisation. The final series of excerpts show the diarist returning to Cheltenham College & the extended range of civilian activities which he now saw as his way forward, serving the County rather than the Country but with equal resolution & taking on ever more commitments as the years passed.

War Service

1914 (August) – 1919

[*It is hard to believe, as the diarist tells us on August 5th 'things were not in a whirl at all' for there is considerable confusion & incoherence in the early days & we are not given much reliable information. Presumably the diarist has been promoted to Staff Captain: certainly he is in charge of billeting & seems to be in perpetual motion, dealing with officers, men & horses, over a wide area. It is evident that he has powers of persuasion together with an uncanny knack of finding old friends who are useful & making new ones, which goes far to account for the General's refusal to release him on his senior officer's request.*

The diaries, written in the field in France & Italy would surely be much more rewarding if handled by an authority on the 1914–18 war. Constantly changing place-names makes the action hard to follow: and the reason for transfer to Italy in 1918 is obscure. It would be illuminating to discover when & in what action the DSO & mentions in despatches were awarded: the diarist's niece says that he never would talk about it & there for the present it rests.]

August

4   Frank told me that we were going to be mobilised so I got into my uniform straight away. As a matter of fact the order didn't come till about 7 pm. The first news we had was through the Post Office displaying the posters. I made an effort to mobilise the Company for the 9.22 train but it couldn't be done so I handed over to Colour

Sergeant Sellman & started for Oxford. Arrived at Bourne End I found that my sword must have been left in the Tilecotes carriage. At Maidenhead I had a long wait so motored back to Marlow and got the sword. Arrived Oxford 2.30 am, was told to go to the Randolph and get a bed which I did.

5   Contrary to my expectations things were not in a whirl at all. Nunn is very calm, deliberate & efficient. We were medically examined by old Sankey . . . Walked through New College & Balliol, both full of soldiery. Met Joseph, Butler etc. Started for Cosham . . . arrived at the Railway Inn. Not very high class. They wanted the General & Nunn to sleep in one rather narrow bed! Eventually Nunn slept in the Commerical Room, Forshaw in a bed but took out more than he put in: while I was quite happy in my valise on the floor.

7   Oxford. Office work. F, Nelly & Grace motored over. Mrs Tock & Mrs Nunn also came.

8   To Swindon to take up billets for Hd. Qrs. Dined at Ry. Inn where I met Savage, late of New College: he is a doctor in Egypt but now in RAMC. Slept in the office with one or two secret documents: had my revolver loaded by my side, mercifully did not shoot myself.

9   Sunday. Brigade transport arrived: 2 two-horse wagons of Hall's Brewery, 4 horses, a Lce Corpl & 2 men from ASC. We have put the horses in Victoria Park.

12   Wandered about Swindon for some two hours trying to find 7th Warwicks from whom I had been told to draw all the ammunition they could spare. We loaded up 18000 rounds. I thought that must be enough & at last got Nunn on the telephone. He said they wanted 2000 only! So we unloaded again. A dismal affair & a lesson on indefinite orders.

13   We have been asked to volunteer for service abroad. Response was disappointing, not much more than 65% from 3 battalions & the Oxfords had hardly 200 volunteers. The men were extremely suspicious of going in 'composite battalions' or with any other unit than their own. Almost all the officers volunteered.

16   Sunday. Trained to Leighton Buzzard, then rode to Dunstable where we are billeted in Sugar Loaf Hotel.

18   Met Nicholls of the Howitzers: their Colonel Moellock has just gone off his head after ordering silver-plated harness for the battery.

19   We are to move to the East. I was sent on to Hitchin . . . I made the Sun Inn Hd. Qrs. then called on the police who were helpful & efficient . . .

20   To Ware, billeting

21   To Waltham, billeting. I fixed Hd. Qrs. at King's Head Hotel, High Beech: the manager, Gumfrecht, is much upset by accusations of disloyalty: his father was a naturalised German. I was sent to scout the residence of Horace Baring, who asked if he could do anything. I suggested very tentatively a billet for the GOC: he was delighted: I continued à la Abraham & eventually got all 5 in. The house is comfortable & roomy & the feeding superb: I have seldom consumed so many varieties of liquor in two days. By the time one meal was really over it was nearly time for the preliminary cocktail for the next.

27   Mrs McClintock down. She & Tock are going to take a house here. He has now moved to Chelmsford.

28   Clare came down: great fun. But news bad, talk of heavy losses. Welcome letter from Charlie Bodington [*ex-Grange pupil, son of Archdeacon Bodington*]

30   Sunday. Church at the new Cathedral Chelmsford. Times correspondent sends a terrible account of the army broken up after Mons: in the evening the Press Bureau issued a reassuring statement. Frank came up & asked to have me back. The General said he couldn't let me go then & shelved the question. I was much torn between the two ideas but now I've got sufficiently into my work to find it interesting. To tea with the Trotters, brothers of Mowbray, Canon of Gloucester.

September

2   Billeting in Colchester. Met L. E. Jones of the Bedfordshire Yeomanry. He was Captain of the Boats at Eton, & then Balliol where I knew him slightly.

9   Rode with Jones to Hatfield Peverel & dined with John Gore[1] *see* October 6, 1913, & Tommy Lascelles.

21   May came down, full of news from Leo Amery who is on Rawlinson's staff.

22   Sunday. Hall had told me that his billeters were old friends of Hardwicke, so I went to tea. They were Capt. Showers Chief Constable of Essex, Mrs Showers better known as Comtesse d'Epineul[2] & an adopted daughter Pansy Somerville.

30   Glosters sports. Leave which has been very sparingly granted, a little easier from now on.

October

2   Clare down

8   Col. Dickenson, an amiable old man, appeared from the WO as 'billeting expert'. I took him round the Bucks with Guy Crouch, & The Glosters with Little. He was fairly well satisfied but agreed the place was about as full as it could go.

10   The Nunns dined. The General has now got his wife here in rooms at 109 London Rd.

13   We were violently rung up & told the King was coming on Friday. Great fuss & excitement.

14   King's review at Hylands. We marched past in fours & I fell out to hold the General's horse. From about 20 yds in the rear I had a very good view of the King's back, & a better one of the Brigade who went past quite well. The spectators were not properly kept back off the road, with the result that the troops were pushed over to their right, bringing them to the edge of the road nearest the King. Bower of the Bucks wandered so far across that he stubbed his toe on an edge & went on his nose. His Majesty was much amused & remarked 'You had better look out else they will all be doing it!'. Directly it happened Crawshay, Heath & Tock rushed to the road & stretching out their arms stood the soldiery to the other side of the road as if they were protecting HM from a herd of cows . . . Tock, not being dismissed stayed with HM while the Engineers, RAMC etc went past. He told me the King lamented much the dissolution of the MI companies & thought they would have been very useful on the retreat from Mons. This was a nasty one for French! The King was accompanied by Wigram[3] father of the boy at the Grange. Tock declined to ride off till the last motor had gone, so we did not get home very early.

16   Father down: seems very well: had tea with the Showers. Livesay told me that in South Africa he had sometimes taken 50 or more pairs of boots off dead men, persuaded his sergeants to carry them to another place & then induced his men to put them on.

17   Entraining practice carried out by Oxford (fair) & Bucks (good). A rehearsal to see how the proposed move to Colchester would go off – one sees what a lot might be made of transport work.

November

6   Up to Ketha on leave. K, W & self dined with May at Coburg Court Hotel. I put on mufti to May's great disgust.

7   Home with May. The house is full of Belgians (friends of Father's). They had a fearful time getting through Holland, most concerned that the Dutch were going to join in.

9   Back to Town with Nelly, then on to Chelmsford. The Bucks have been ordered to Great Totham to dig trenches.

10   Tea with Countess to meet Mrs George Hopkinson (her sister).

11   Charlie Orde married

18   Great excitement at the arrival of a flight of the RFC. I had to billet them in a row of houses near the Constabulary. Clare & Violet Birchall came to stay with the Grippers in Springfield Road as PG's.

21   Percy Birchall down. He has more or less recovered from his appendicitis operation & is instructing Canadians on Salisbury Plain, waiting for a staff job with the contingent.

28   Motored over to Haileybury to see a party of Grange boys organised by Drew Lepper. I was met by Drew & Buss mi, later there arrived Buss ma, Finn & Gray. The whole place impressed me favourably . . . the boys are allowed anywhere in the country outside. We went to tea in the 'Parents' Room' an arrangement that might well be initiated elsewhere. The boys . . . were all wonderfully unchanged, Buss ma having grown up more than the rest: there was certainly room for it in his case.

December

1   The story is that 12 of Kitchener's battalions have been sent out: if this is so it is very annoying. We are given to believe that as we really *are* some use we shall probably never leave these shores.

6   Sunday. Percy Birchall here again. He is now a major.

9   Conference at Saracen's Head about leave. All generals & heads of departments. A good deal of gas which ended in 5% being given leave for 5 days at a time. I fancy Heath[4] misunderstood the 'Secret' letter.

11   Ride with Pansy Somerville. We only went a short way but managed to meet all the Gloucesters & Berks. Nelly arrived to stay with Violet Birchall. Our newly gotten Xmas leave all stopped.

12   Town, on an excursion train, with the 5th Glosters. Lunched with Helen [*MacLagan*] at the Public School Club. To Queen's Club to see the Glosters play the 5th Canadian Cavalry. On to Carlton Club where I met Gilbey, our old Colonel, who was very

friendly. Glosters dinner at the Princes. Met Lloyd, 18th Hussars, home on leave from the trenches. He says the post arrives every day with extraordinary regularity & the men grouse like fun if it is an hour late. Cheery dinner then on to Alhambra. A large number of the Division were up [*Names supplied*]. I also met Shaw of the Grange who is in the 5th Royal Fusiliers. His brother in the Regular regiment has just been killed.

16   Xmas leave, removed on the 11th, is now restored.

23   I had arranged to go on leave today. At about 10.30 Reilly rang up to tell us to cancel all leave till further notice! A great deal of disappointment but on the whole they took it well. Apparently the Huns had been seen to board the transports.

25   7 o'clock service fairly full. Lunch at Bellefield. Fairly jolly but Nunn is not a great Christmasser. Dinner with the Birchalls: altogether a very good Christmas under the circumstances.

27   Sunday. 7 o'clock service produced a congregation of 4 of which I was the only soldier. Tea with Birchalls. Christmas leave restored.

1915

January

3   Rode out with Nunn to battlefield for tomorrow: brigade training is commencing.

4   I commanded a skeleton force, 2 coys of the Berks . . . these days are designed to teach Bn. commanders to stick to one place & to keep in touch . . . this day brought out the old points, importance of intercommunication & danger of verbal messages.

5   Rode out with the General, an unusual performance, to meet the route march coming back.

9   Started on my five days' leave. Met Edgar Sebright & Stuart Johnson in the Club. Travelled home with Lord Bathurst. At Stroud I met Percy Marling who is on French's staff. I said I supposed we were getting on gradually and he paused & said 'Well anyway *they* are not getting on. Didn't sound too cheerful. Mi seems well & happy but evidently thinks Hunstanton is a long way from the front. The Glos Yeo got very near to going out & then were suddenly switched to the East Coast.

11   Biked to Gloucester. Tea with the Bishop & party, including a Belgian lady with two pretty daughters. They had been with Vaughan at Eton.

12   Hunt at Down House. F the only person in pink. 30 out, reckoned a large field.

15   Brigade attack . . . 3-point conclusion drawn

16   Inspection of Bucks in billets. Chief defect was the long hair which the General greatly objects to.

18   Battle at Boreham . . . the pièce de résistance was to be the bridge built by the RE's over the canal. I acted as Staff Officer at the bridge. The RE's were very disappointing. They got the near trestle up & then managed to let a lot of it drop into the water: half an hour later a rope broke & destroyed the new effort: eventually the bridge took 4 hours to build instead of one. The four officers all gave directions at once which mattered little as nobody obeyed any of them.

22   Heavy snow. Gracie came down to stay in the house which the Birchalls have, the B's having gone on leave.

29   Gracie went. Violet B is going to join Percy who is to start to the front shortly.

February

2   The work is pretty hard now & I get little time off. Talked with Teddy King, interpreter & intelligence officer. Billeting is as difficult in France as in England. German prisoners all expect to be shot & are full of information about their units, second lines etc.

6   Nunn for 10 days sick leave, General went on leave, Sergt. Mayne went for one night, so I was left to keep house till Tuesday.

13   Conference at Corn Exchange. Everyone down to double company commanders. Heath spoke extraordinarily finely, chiefly on discipline: a well-disciplined regiment has small crime sheets: punishment the last resort but must be used sometimes: officers must be ready to do all they ask the men to do: punishment in France very severe & leniency here may lead to severity later. Heath is really a leader himself.

14   Sunday. Early service not overcrowded. Worst news of the week is the increase of cerebro spinal meningitis. Our brigade has had one death, 2 or 3 others among the soldiers & several among the civilians.

20   May came to stay with the Birchalls. I dined there, also Toddy Wright & his jolly wife. We are much excited by the news that the North Midland are really under orders for next week: it has always been understood that we go next.

25   Frank's board vet him as permanently unfit for foreign service: Heath is recommending him for a reserve unit. I posted the documents to Frank at Marlow.

March

1   Revolver shooting at Berks miniature range. My gun has too short a barrel & kicks fearfully. I scored 52 out of 96.

5   I had Fortescue as 'flagged enemy': agreeable & pretty efficient but a poor horseman.
     [*This is the last entry for 1915 apart from the following –*]

30   Crossed to Boulogne

1916

[*Entries for this year are made in a small 3 in. x 2 in. Walker's pocket diary and are written in pencil with rare annotations in ink. Curt & cryptic, the material contrasts strongly with that of earlier years & probably the diarist's intention was to write up an expanded version using the 1916–18 diaries as rough notes. No such version has yet been discovered. Great attention is paid to the weather especially during periods in the front line where bad conditions were much aggravated by snow & rain. Place-names abound & an informed reconstruction of the diarist's travels would be of interest to a 1914–18 war specialist. Personal names outnumber place-names; some 142 at a low estimate are given over the three years*]

Feburary

[*Diarist is returning home on leave*]

7   Amiens: good look at Cathedral. Arr. Boulogne, Louvre hotel.

8   Crossed at 12. Stayed with Ketha.

9   Home.

11   Bournemouth with N: Blanchie better than might be expected. Children very well. Talked with Bl about Hylda's illness.

12–15 [*Church, hunting, London with F, Grange school, lunch with Daisy Battine.*]

16   Amiens. Pelting rain. Letter from Division saying that I was to be relieved by Maude.

17   Maude arrived. 10th ? Lancs. Very nice.

19   Talk with Josh Reynolds about coming back to Bucks.

20   Talk with Edward. Fanshawe[5] told me not to be 'downhearted' as not everyone had the same qualities.

23   Bitter cold snow.

26   Up to line with Aldworth & Challon for their instructions.

March

1   HC. Rode with E to Souastre-Couin

2   Up to Hébuterne. Shell cottage. Reserve coy, Gloster HQ dugout.

3   Relieved Lionel Crouch on R.

4   Snow.

5   Glorious sunshine but trenches very wet, little mud, all water.

12   Sunday. DC. Only Durrant & self. Moved to another billet, very nice room with one wall blown away, at Sailly: dear old lady.

13   J. Rollestone came in.[6]

19   Sunday. Up to Guindry: shrapnel, minnies: I wounded. Heavy firing for one hour. All men cheery & happy & bloodthirsty.

28   Sunshine & rain. Shell on shelter, 3 killed, 5 wounded.

29   MG & shelling. Funeral: on our faces, very cold snow.

April

9   New trench dug by 5 Glosters (in front of front line: Fanshawe's idea)

25   Out of trenches very late. No guides. E much upset.

28   Yeomanry engaged. <u>Mickey</u> [*Michael Hicks Beach killed*]

30   Sunday. HC in tent.

Amiens Cathedral before bombing

May

3   <u>Mi</u>. (reported missing)

12   Fine day: very quiet. Clanricarde[7] leaves money to Harry Lascelles.

31   Good march to Neuville. Only one fell out. Nice billets.

June

1   Training attack on Agenvilliers. E in trouble with Gen. (E & Done differed on tactical points & Done got very ratty).

3   CO bad. I act 2nd in command. Leahy has a fall. Attack from Yvrench follows. Our rt out of place, rather poor.

4   OE dinner at Godbert. [*9 names of Old Etonians listed; Ted Trotter is the only one to have been mentioned in the diaries already.*]

7   Horse show. Bucks did well. Heard first bad rumours of Jutland.

10   Started 7.30 am from Candas, arr. Havre 11.0 pm! Lunch basket at Amiens. Long wait outside Rouen. On to boat 'Mona'.

11–18   [*Usual leave activities: visits Blanchie, has tea with Birchalls, takes May & Gracie to 'The Bing Boys are Here' in Town & has lunch with Leo & Florence Amery.*]

18   Sunday. HC. Started at 12.2 from Gloucester. London, Waterloo. On to 'Copenhagen'.

19   Long tedious journey to Belle Eglise, then to tent at Couin.

23   Drew my certificate for War Loan from Precepteur of Doullens, also half year's interest.

July

1   Marched off 8.30 to Mailly Martel bivouacs, impossible to get news (first day of SOMME offensive).

2   Long hot wait. Other 3 battns marched off to show, afterwards washed out.

3   Not quite so hot. Waited all day, then marched back to huts.

4   Hot & stuffy in huts, very little news.

5, 6, 7   To bivouacs. Weather fine. Army Corps Commanders passed towards Sailly.

8   Drenching rain last night. To trenches. Oxfords had done O to trenches.

11   We again provided covering party to wiring: no casualties.

12   Out of trenches to bivouacs

13   Motor buses to Bouzincourt. Walk to Senlis. Billets mostly very dirty.

15   Quiet. Hot . . . picked raspberries.

16   Sunday. Still at Senlis. Service & HC by Moreton of Corps.

17   Rode with Hales & Viney to La Boiselle. Met Dundas of Luxmore's.[8] Trenches & corpses. Bn to dump on Bapaume road & 2 coys, A & D, reconnoitred trenches. Rigden v. successful, rest did their job. Norwood missing, Hall very bad.

21   Brought up 5% & officers. Last night Bn attacked without success. Josh & others very sick. Lionel Crouch killed, also Trimmer & Chapman. Jackson missing. Mason wounded. Harry Lawton killed, also Munday.

22   Rigden wounded, came in last night, also Molloy & Young. Godfrey wounded. Up to support Glosters attack. Moved out of bivouacs 9.45. Long wait in trenches SW of Ovillers. Tremendous gunning everywhere.

23   5 am returned to bivouacs. 6.30 Bn attacked. Magnificent. Took 2 lines, held them. Edward & Viney wounded. Sgt Barrett killed.

24   Battalion stayed in all day.

25   Battalion came out about mid day. All tired but triumphant.

August

12   Heard of E's death.

15   6th Av. v. heavily shelled, all behaved splendidly: C coy – 7 hrs heavy shelling.

16   Bn. came out: very tired.

17   Bn. had good rest. Eng post of last 3 days turned up. Many letters about E.

18   Sent for to do liaison with Anzacs. They were making unsuccessful attack on Mogqurt Farm.

23   Crucifix cover shelled all day, dump blown up. Attack by Bucks unsuccessful. Bates killed, Heath missing.

September

2   Inspection by GOC. Jacko a prisoner. Rode to Doullens, met Toddy Wright.

13   Execution at Beauval. Pte of 4th R. Berks shot for cowardice. I loaded <u>all</u> rifles.

22   Crécy. Perfect day. Long ride. Lunch at Canon d'Or. Crécy well worth visiting. Inoculated against paratyphoid.

27   Excellent news. Theipval taken.

28   Rode to Bernaville.

29   Up at 4, to Warluzel. Having billeted there changed to Couillimont. Wet all day.

October

1   To St. Amand, billets poor except HQ's.

4   Am a major. Over to Souastre to look at billets.

5   To trenches via Souastre.

7   Heard from home that news of Mi^9 is practically confirmed.

15   Sunday. Jackson took service (the Oxfords padre, good horseman).

16   Had Coy commanders to dinner to celebrate my crown.

28   Amiens for day. Dale took me in his ambulance. Bought towels & wringers.

November

10   Bn out to huts at Contalmaison. Met Taylor of New Coll in command of 9 Gordons Pioneers.

11   Camp shelled slightly. Weather fine. (Camp just completed by 9th Gordons Nissen huts, good but shelled every night).

13, 16   B. Hamel.

18   To Bn. HQ's in Martinpulch where I found CO going on leave tomorrow.

19 Up to take command in old Bde HQ's.

22 Relieved in the evening by Berks. Shelled as we went out. No casualties.

29 General inspected A, B & C Coys. Afterwards Reid said to him 'Very difficult to keep clean'. He said, 'Yes, very: but these people (ie 5th Glosters) were all right, that was a regiment: the people we saw this morning weren't'.

December

8 Fanshawe inspected camp at 9.30 am: hard on men who had only got in at 1.0 am.

16 GOC's conference at Albert: Fanny in great form.

19 Was to have started on leave but Havre congested. Snow. Brig. Gen did great comb-out.

20 Brig. Gen. round *three* times. My leave put off as I am going on course.

21 'Intensive digging'

22 More 'intensive digging'

25 Service in morning. Excellent Xmas dinner for men: splendid Mess dinner. John Coates came & sang: also others.

27 Off in motor to Amiens. Delays.

29 On to the Donegal at Midnight & so to Southampton. Home. All there except Clare.

31 Church morning. Canon Nash: also evening. In the school which is easier shaded.

1917

[From December 31 to February 11 entries in ink are made in the 1916 diary & then copied into the 1917, larger French diary: & until mid-March entries there are also in ink but thereafter in pencil. This coincides with the protracted Senior Officers' Course which occupied weekdays only for three months.]

January

2 Town with K & children, also Clare & Grace. To Cecil Hotel, quite good. Gaiety.

3 Canadian War Photos good. 'Hoop La' at St Martins. Gertie Millar old but attractive.

4 White Lion Cambridge on Cox's mare. Plenty of foxes. Tea at Whitminster.

7 To Aldershot for Senior Officers Course: sleeping at Tournay, messing at Lille.

21 Sunday. Visit to dock-yards at Portsmouth. Bottomley spoke, very dull. Saw 'Victory', C20 an old submarine. Visited 'Ferret', recently mined. 'Vernon' – electrical apparatus. Whale Island, Gunnery School. Tea with C-in-C Admiral Colville.

February

3 At K's. Chu Chin Chow at His Majesty's. Gorgeous & excellent music.

4 Lunch with Charlie Orde & Frances[10] whom I had not met.

11 Lunch with Helen Maclagan. Everybody short of coal, & finding Devonport's bread & flour ration rather a pinch.

17 Musketry in morning. Travelled to Gloucester with Reynolds of RE. All at home including Penny.

18   Sunday. Church. Lunch at Cottage. Olive much developed & v. intelligent. Audrey v. jolly. Bl subdued but cheery.

19   Musketry in morning. Read of John Orde's death in Salonika.

24–25   Weekend at Folkestone, staying with Gardiners. Chapel at Grange & lunch there. Potatoes & chickens in full swing.

27   News still good. More Hun retirement. Kut recaptured.

March

1   Gommecourt evacuated.

11   Sunday. Church. To Nat Gallery to see Grosvenor House pictures: 'Blue Boy' very fine, also Rembrandt's 'Old Woman'.

12   Trench warfare problems. Bagdad *has* fallen [*it was an unsubstantiated rumour*] [*Pencil entries re-commence*]

18   Sunday. Church. Bapaume captured. To Saintbridge: talked with Violet, Linda & David Verey.[11] To Bowden where Jack, Adela and their children were very affable. Violet showed me E's notebook.

19   Peronne taken.

20   To Gloucester with Florence [*Teesdale*] Bucks lost Warwick, Wiseman & Cooper-Smith: from gas-shell, first two from phosgene, last more from chlorine.

24   To see Uncle Brian at Harrow. Flourishing though rather underfed.

26   Gloucester full of rumours of invasion & revolution in Ireland.

28   To Cheltenham. Lunch with Paterson. P says masters & boys apathetic & little is taught.

April

[1–7   *Returns to France but journey much interrupted*]

4   . . . visited Liverpool Hospital & found out where E. Birchall is buried. A 83 in cemetery. Nicely kept but no flowers yet.[*Took flowers next day*]

6   Off by 7.45 via Abbéville, Amiens & Corbie to railhead between Mericourt & Chuignes.

7   By lorry to supply column: thence to Doingt & on to Bde HQ's at Hamel. Bde took Basse Boulogne, Lempire etc 2 days ago.

9   ARRAS push started.

11   News from Arras still good. 11000 prisoners, 100 guns. Met John Hill who is going to be Staff Captain to 144.

15   Up to line. Slept in culvert: pretty cold & beastly (Lempire 12 miles NE of Peronne, Tombois Farm 1 mile NE of L)

16   Up to Lempire for attack tonight. Objective: Tombois Farm. Rt-D coy, Centre C, Left B. B got in, C & D held up by wire & Mg's. Re-formed & followed B. Also one coy 5 Glos. Success complete. Advanced Bn HQ's. Ellis wounded, died.

17   At about 5 am CO sent me up to see positions. Went up, did some straightening out. Sent patrols out: one occupied Petit Preal Farm where Warwicks were repulsed last night. Wet & trying day. Relieved by 5 Glos.

18   6 Glos blown up

21   Gen Watt (the Jerker) has returned

23   Anniversary of Mi's death. Glorious day: cold wind. Inspection by Fanshawe. Ordered to stand to at 4.15 am to assist in 144 show.

24   Breakfast 4.0 am. Stood to till 3.30 pm

25   Stood to again at 4.15 am, proceeded to Templeux Wood. Up to Left to relieve 6 Glos.

26   HQ's in Lempire shelled fairly frequently & fairly heavily. Relieved 5 Glos in line. Tombois now held by 1 coy with 2 coys stretching down to Gillemont Fm.

30   To billets at Mons en Chaussée. All men in cellars & draughty barns.

May

2   Johnston came to HQ's to be Asst. Adj. He did well at Tombois Farm (headed list of recommendations but someone put Bowen above him: he got MC at Ypres & was wounded August 16).

6   Sunday. Service in half ruined church (this practice was forbidden a week later).

14   Up to line at Demicourt taking over from 7 S. Staffs, 33 Bde, 11th Division.

24   Up to Rt front, Hermies. I had charge of working party making 2 new posts north of Prisoners Cage (became R3). Sniper hit one Oxford & Sgt of party to get him in was also hit.

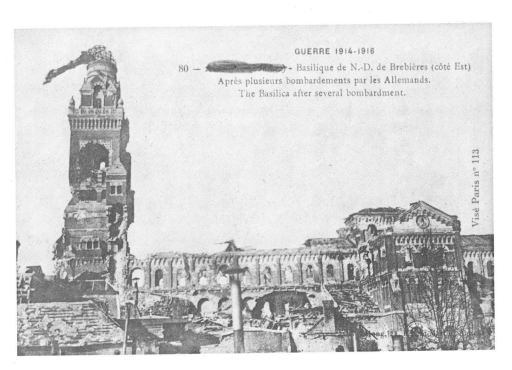

GUERRE 1914-1916

80 — ~~Albert (Somme)~~ - Basilique de N.-D. de Brebières (côté Est)
Après plusieurs bombardements par les Allemands.
The Basilica after several bombardment.

Visé Paris n° 113

Freak effect of bombardment at Albert. Statue of the Virgin
and Child remained poised thus until April 18, 1918

26 Ground round HQ's shelled with about 250 5.9's from 9 to 11. C coy cooker hit & 3 Glosters. To Bde to discuss posts. Joined up 2 new posts, made the tracing myself.

29 With A coy did more work on new post. Back to Velu Wood about 4.0 am. Gerneral in, very well pleased with us.

June

1 Rapid wiring again: wore my 'windy suit' which the tailor has made an excellent fit.

2 Brigadier inspected offcers in 1. Books, 2. 'Windy clothes', 3. Saluting, 4. Rapid wiring.

4 No celebrations! [*ie no Etonian re-union*]

7 B coy did good show at Birdcage. I spent most of the night interrogating 9 prisoners, mostly from E. Prussia.
   [*Diarist records 'Up to line' on 4 occasions between June 7 & 27: during brief intervals of relief goes to see the GOC: has a dental extraction 'quite painless': scores 5 runs in a Sgts v. Officers cricket match: & has a day in Amiens where he visits the Cathedral yet again*].

July

1 Court of Enquiry: I President: took 3 hours.

2 Russian push began. Rejoined Bn at Beaumetz.

3 Round to see Monty Balston at Haplincourt. Found him & Tom! Tom is DAAG 3rd Division. Both flourishing.

4 Marched at 10 am to Bihucourt (Russians have 14,000 prisoners).

9 (To XVIII Corps HQ's at Volkerinkhove). All Coy commanders of 11th Division there. Corps Commander Maxse gave good lecture: the whole course is devoted to the push to come.

14 To 4th Oxfords as 2nd in command.

15 Rode over to Hébuterne, all overgrown with grass, 5 civilian families. Old woman told me that 'gens du midi' who came to protect Hébuterne in first days wouldn't fight & took no interest in the war.

18 Wade-Palmer is a Lce/Corpl. here. He on one side & Ingestre on the other broke my collar bone at football in Dec. '96. [*This must have been at Malvern Link.*]

30–31 3rd YPRES starts. Left Houtherque 11 pm to march to camp 2 miles NW of Poperinghe. Arrived about 2.30 am on 31st. Great bombardment increasing to hurricane about 4.0 am when 5 Eng & several French Corps went over. 2 front systems taken. Rain started about midday & continued all day.

August

3 Bde went forward leaving me as usual on dump, now called 18th Corps reinforcement camp.

15–16 Bde attack Triangle Farm. Partial success. Casualties heavy [*listed under killed & wounded*] in Ox & Bucks. Bde held to have done well.

21 Went to see wounded again but they had all gone. Hospital near Poperinghe had been shelled: last wounded taken out as I got there: everything in disorder.

31 Have been appointed to succeed Knox as OC 48 Div reinforcement camp to my intense disgust.

September

6 [*Lists Staff of reinforcement camp: Col. Nutt knew F at Malvern Confernce*].

7 On FG CM's the whole day as member, Nutt President.

10 Waller relieved me & I go back to Bn.

12 Bartlett off on leave. I took over Bn. We have 17 officers present.
Rest period on billets, during 'big attack on Ypres front, apparently great success'. Bde. Horse Show: Second in jumping, on Clarence.

29 ... after lunch I was summoned to the line to take command of 5 Glosters, their HQ's having been slightly gassed. Relieved by Berks. Our HQ was Cheddar Villa.

October

[*On a blank page, written in ink and thus a later addition, is the statement 'Opposite is the attack by the 5th Glos. Full account in my Army Book 152. They got 1 MC & 2 DCM'. No trace of any Army Books have yet been discovered.*]

4–5 143 show. Up to California to repel counter attack if necessary. Show successful & 143 reported 2nd objective held. No time for reconnaissance. 143 had only got 1st objective: hence v. gallant attack failed. [*Lists of killed & wounded.*]

6 Relieved at 2.30 am.

8–9 Moved to Dambre camp. Another attack, fairly successful.

12 Marched from Dambre to Road camp. Pelting rain the whole way. Tea & rum helped things on.

14 Entrained at Hoputre to Ligny St. Flochel. Then long march to Camblain l'Abbé, NE of Aubigny. Men went splendidly. Adrian huts, very good. (This finished our share of Flanders 1917. General opinion: wet made operations too difficult: also GOUGH was not up to the job: better if whole business had been left to PLUMER who knew every inch).
[*This is a baffling entry as diarist returns to France after leave.*]

November

1 Getting ready. General came round.

2 Up to trenches over VIMY RIDGE: relieved 8 Worcesters.

4 Visited A coy in the sticky left near Avion. Their HQ's were soundly crumped while we sat there, the light being blown out constantly. Wall stopped our leave a week owing to a man wearing a soft cap.

5 To B in afternoon to enquire into accident. Turns out that a pin came out thereby lowering gun which fired two bursts into our trench: killed one, wounded one.

6 All round Coy HQ's & front line. Took just 6 hrs! Out to Petit Vimy, very fine Boche dug out. Our snipers got 4 Boches.

10 Relieved by 6th Glos. Out to Ottawa camp, v. comfortable.

13 The air full of Italy.

14   It is practically certain we go to Italy.

20   [*Cambrai offensive*]

22   Packing up. Went to see 1st half of Bn off by 10.22 from Savy. Slept a bit then to station. 4.30 am on Friday morning passed Arras in distance. Dark when we passed Paris.

24   Journey still going well. At Villefranche eau de vie was put in the coffee. Cloudy but the mountains made a pleasant change. Passed Alise, Dinan, Beaune, Chalon, Macon, Lyon: beautiful moonlight on Rhône.

25   Avignon: not allowed to leave the station but could see the Palais [*des Papes*]. Wandered on to Marseilles which we reached at 6.0 am in sunshine.

26   I woke at Toulon. Hot tea at Les Arcs. Fréjus, Cannes. More tea, sea, beer to Nice. Past Monte Carlo & Mentone to Vingtimille.

December

[*The long journey is apparently over by December 14 but there is little news of significance for some time*]

14   Moved to Tezze & Granella

23   In motor lorry to reconnoitre our possible line. Trenches blasted in chalk.

24   Divisional band played in square. Invited 339 Regt Chasseurs over: they came in large quantities – the officers came to tea.

25   HC in room above chemists. 2 posts, included presents from Billy & Kitty.

1918

[*This year's entries are in a French diary 'Walker pour 1918' and are in pencil with later annotations in ink*]

January

5   Bde inspected by C in C. Great success: men very steady. Gen. Watt & Bde Major Kitson to dinner, latter a great friend of John Christie.

11   My chilblains large but not tiresome.

18 Jan-   [*Leave in Rome, spent in concentrated sightseeing. The account ends quite typically with*
Feb.2   *a 9-point list of 'Things I liked best', a mix of sites, pictures & an opera.*]

February

25   Up to Montello line, north of Nervesa. We are taking over from 1st S. Staffs.

March

3   Rain all day. Berks took over. We went down pretty wet.

8   GOC came & turned out HQ's on alarm. Threatened to stop leave because he found man with long hair.

9   Leave stopped but Greenwell & Boyle already gone. GOC furious.

23   First news of big German push.

April

2 Moved to Ganzigliano, training area 12 miles SW of Padova. 22 mile march, 5 fell out.

5 Smoke demonstration. P of W. attended, great success. Met Jim Dun-Waters who is a pack pony expert [*& also a distant family connection*].

7 Sunday. Went to have 2 teeth out: v. inadequate cocaine. However, managed lunch all right.

10 Car fetched me to take over 4th R. Berks at Valle close to Montechio Maggiore where castle is reputed birthplace of Juliet.

23 Marched to Osteria della Granezzi. Sun–rain–snow. No-one fell out.

24–25 Reconnoitred left & right Brigade fronts, in rain & snow. [*Entries which are very terse suggest an imminent action, & indeed there was a raid on S.Ave on May 12, without casualties, in which one prisoner 'Peter Biris, a nice boy' was taken: one MC was awarded. By May 14 the situation had settled down only to erupt violently in June.*]

May

14 Fanshawe up: complimentary on raid.

19 Relieved by 10th Northumberland Fus. Hot march down to Fara.

20 Washed Bn & its clothes in stream & had excellent bathe & bath combined. V. hot. Plain is all green now, vines out, hay cut, v. lovely.

21 Marched to Rovere, arr. 7 am. Rested all day. To Cornedo starting 10 pm.

28 Influenza, called PUO, is playing havoc. We have 20–30 to hospital every day. (from March 28 – June 15 influenza weakened Bn considerably: in all 140 went to hospital. General course: 3 days temperature, 7 days debility).

June

3 Into line opposite Canove di Sotto. Excellent outpost on Hill 972.

4 Howard motored me to Lugo for OE dinner at CHQ. [*Guests listed: regiment, rank & house at Eton*].

11 Lister came to tell me I had DSO.

15 Awakened 3 am by shells. Stood to. To battle positions. Oxford trench on Lemerle. Boche broke through Oxfords, 5 Glos & 5 Warks held fast in pocket. Went to see Bartlett midday. Our D & C moved forward to help Oxfords. Buck of D killed Spent most of day at Bde HQ's on Lemerle. Reynolds is commanding Bde & Tomkinson commanding 144. (Sarah Jane Buck, Dacre Bank, Yorks) [*evidently diarist is to write to next of kin*]. Boche still in our line.

16 Our C & D & Oxfords moved forwards through wood at 4.30 am. Most of Boche had cleared already: remainder surrenderd. About 700 prisoners to our Div.

17 Stopped in Oxfords trench. Great day for souvenirs!

18 Relieved about 3 pm & moved to camp at Serona.

19 Rode to Div HQ's re intelligence etc. Hardly got back when car called to take me to Div HQ's again. Just came in for end of Fanshaw's farewell: – he's been sent home! Terrible blow to the whole Division: quite incomprehensible to those who've served under him.

25 By train to Padova: CO's course.

29 Mid day train to Verona. Hotel Londres. (1902 Verona with F. had forgotten most things. Scaligers, principal doorways heavily concreted & invisible but town most beautiful still. All the best pictures gone to Florence).

30 Visited Roman theatre. S. Anastasia, Duomo. Back to Padua & so home.

July

2   Back to Bn who are at Cornedo again.

4   Fanshawe's successor has come. Walker, DCLI. who has had Australian Div. Rude & unattractive.

6   General came round & packed me off instanter on leave. Rode to Vicenza. Left 8 pm.

8   Arr. Paris 10.30 am. Saw Jeanne de Hénaut who seems flourishing & is much smarter: v. proud of cousin Charles Mangin.

10 Home by 3 pm train. Everyone at home. Rain came: badly wanted.

22–27 Return journey to Italian front.

28 Sunday. Round front line.

30 Relieved by 5th R. Warks & went to Marziele.

31 Endless correspondence on night of 29/30 [*this is blank, as are many days*].

August

3   Rehearsed counter-attack, 8th Worcesters raid. Div commander saw officers.

6   Court of Enquiry [*no details given*].

9   Relieved 6th Glosters in line. They had just finished share in big raid.

10 Smith & Clevely 'censured' by Div Commander, per GOC Bde

13 Took over left front from Bucks. We are due S of Roncalto, 2 mls SW of Asiego

14 Round the line at stand-to. Round the line in evening on right.

16 Brigadier round line: proposes 6 months at home for me. Rather attractive but almost no hope of coming back to same Bn or even Division

18 Another conference

19 Relieved by Bucks.

21 More conferences

23 Relieved by 6th Warks.

24 Getting ready – Bombshell! (This was the sudden order to have our big raid ready for 26th: we had expected it about 30th).

25 Practised forming-up in morning & whole show in evening.

26 Moved to Left: reserved positions on Rt. Bde front. (nr. Kaberlaka). Started forming-up at 9 pm & at 10.40 started for Ave, with Bucks on right. Great success

27 Relieved by 7th Worcesters.

30 GOC Div talked about my going & said he couldn't spare me. Apparently Watt put me in without further consultation after 16th.

September

1   Sunday. Mattins & HC at Granezza theatre.

2   Saw the Bn off to the trenches. Lunched & dined with no. 3 Mess, Div HQ's.

3   C-in-C presented, at Granezza, decorations for the raid. Our lot consisted of 4 MC's, 2 DCM's & 18 MM's. Great speeches etc. I to Fara in afternoon.

4–5   Venice: Grand Canal, St Marks, Rialto. 5.30 train back.

9   Started from Vicenza on leave . . .

22   At home. Sunday. Canon preached: 50 years since he was ordained deacon & came to Hardwicke. F took service in evening.

30   We have details of Belgian push. They have got further in one day than we did in 3 months.

October

11   Heard that I am to command 2/1st Essex Yeomanry in Ireland.

13   Sunday. Canon told me in church that Germany had accepted America's terms. I begged him to be cautious.

16   My leave extended to cover Investiture.

17   Whitminster for lunch. Frampton for tea. Elaine took me to see Hylda & Henrietta[12] both pleasant to look on & Hylda really lovely.

22   Town with May & Clare. Hotels all full. After telephoning about 12 at last Rubens in Buckingham Palace Road took us in.

23   Helen MacLagan to lunch. Di Guise to dinner. 2 shows: Prince Igor & 'Maid of the Mountains'.

24   Received DSO from King at Buckingham Palace. May & Father attended. Sisters left after lunch. To matinee & evening shows.

25   Started at 11 pm for the 2/1 Essex Yeomanry, Curragh.

26   Splendid voyage. Arrived Dublin 10. Washed etc. at Hibernian Hotel.

27   To Curragh. Arrived 4.0 pm & was welcomed by Davison & Gibson.
     [*Entries are in ink from this date*]

28   Col. of Cheshire Yeomanry called, Verdin, who used to stay at Hardwicke.

November

6   To Dublin, stayed at Hibernian. To Nat Gallery which is v. good.

7   To Bray for Ly. Meath's[13] funeral. Didn't catch any of the family. Rumours of Armistice having been signed. Back to Curragh.

12, 13   Racing at Curragh.

17   To Kildangan, Monastereven, to stay with More O'Ferralls [*List of guests*]. Bridge and dancing. Most luxurious house, everything beautifully done.

28   News that we are to be broken up.

December

7   To Bert House Athy. Cousin Marion, quite different to my memory. Violet v. handsome, Irene heavy & silent.

8   Sunday. Walked with Violet in morning. Church v. plain, in afternoon. Rev. Nicholson to tea, rather pleasant elderly chaplain to D. of Leinster.

17   Left Ireland on leave: fair passage.

18   Dreadful train journey, in corridor. Staying with Ketha. To War Office in afternoon.

20   To Wandsworth Hospital to see Oswald Buxton, wounded in Ave raid. He was cheerful & glad to hear the news from Italy.

28   Harold Hanbury, Olive & self motored to Berkeley for a meet at 12. (Bubb's car has just been permitted to resume work). Olive went excellently on Tennis Ball.

30   Started back to Ireland. Travelled via Crewe. Holyhead boat had gone. Came via Northwall. Am living with Shropshires.

31   Very little to do.

1919

[*This year is a critical one for the diarist. After demobilisation he resumes his interrupted teaching appointment at Cheltenham. Since Michael's death in 1916 their father, now aged 78, has continued with County Council work as well as the management of the Hardwicke estate. The diarist begins to assume the County roles which will occupy him for the rest of his life.*]

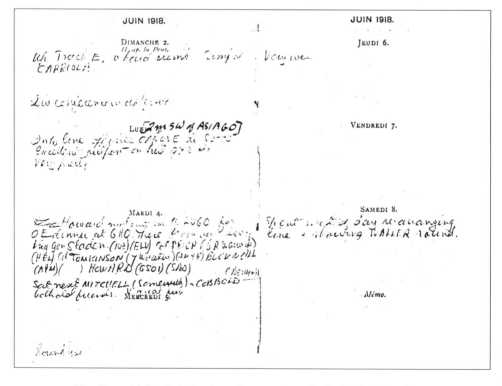

War diary with list of old Etonians who met at Lugo for the fourth of June dinner

January

1   Curragh. Nothing to do.

17   Left Curragh for leave.

19   Sunday. F in morning, Canon evening. [*Father is now officially a Lay Reader*].

24   Lunched at Palace. Bishop wants me to do Secretary to the Diocesan Conference, which of course I can't. Started for Ireland.

February

5   Started on leave again.

10   F, Clare & I to Elmore to see Miss Derrick, engaged to Anselm Guise . . . determined & capable but jolly & forthcoming. Fred Winterbotham & friend flew from Minchinhampton to skate on Elmore Backs.

12   Selby came to look over Velthouse Farm [*on the Hardwicke estate*]. Young, nice & competent. Farm requires tremendous amount of work: fields full of thorns, hedges overgrown, gates very bad, as everywhere.

13   Wrote out election address for C(ounty) C(ouncil) . . . F is 78 & feels that younger men are wanted so I am going to stand.

17   To Town with F. To W.O. to see if there was any chance of going abroad. Met Ted Stewart[14] who said there would be very little chance. He seems much more intelligent than before & very nice.

18   W.O. again, trying to demobilise: told to rejoin before I did that.

20   News that dear Sir Lionel Darell had died of heart failure following influenza. Today F & I went to the funeral at Fretherne. The ugly little church was packed. Bishop Gibson took the service at the grave.

23   Whitminster for tea & supper. Dot & Hilda Clifford came, also Henrietta for a few minutes. Dot is tiny & very Cliffordy. Hilda had not improved herself by cutting off half her hair.

24   Cheltenham with May. Talked to Waterfield, got a demobilisation letter from him

27   Handed in 2 nomination papers for CC [*List of proposers included*]. I am unopposed. Started for Ireland in the evening.

March

6   Received orders to take over 2/1 Ayrshire Yeo.

7   To Dublin to see if my demobilisation has made any progress.

8   Walked in Phoenix Park and saw zoo. To Omagh via Dundalk and Enniskillen.

13   Spent morning watching Assizes open in the Court House. Started for England.

15   Took my seat as CC at Shire Hall. Found a few friends, Jack Birchall, Fred Cripps, Bathurst etc. F introduced me to Mr Hardy of Cheltenham & to Lord Beauchamp.[15] The latter rather humorous on the subject of his brother-in-law Sam Hoare whom I had met in Rome. Francis Hyett re-elected Chairman.

17   Florence drove me into Gloucester for shopping etc. Started for Ireland.

23   Sunday. Church at C of I church. Service distinctly plain but not unlovely. Very few turned to east for the Creed.

25   To lunch came Capt. J. C. McClintock of RASC. who is O i/c Barracks. He turned out to be Tock's younger brother & is very like him but took no great interest in his family.

30   Sunday. Church morning. Called on Kenny in afternoon: he turns out to be a brother of Kenny who was with me in Hanover.

April

5   Started off on leave once more.

7   Olive, age 17, rode over this afternoon & played about with my books. She is developing well & talks most intelligently. She was very much attracted by Inge's *Truth & Falsehood in Religion.* On her return home tonight she asked Blanchie for a 'stiff book'.

8   Standing Joint Committee. Stamford Hutton very strong that magistrates must keep in touch with police matters. Sir John Dorrington started the idea that all CCs should be on SJC. This is of quite unmanageable size but most of the work is done by sub-committee. Beauchamp turned up in a blue uniform with red facings, sword etc: turned out to be the get-up of Lord Warden of Cinque Ports. He has just had a fine row with his outlying tenants: they mobbed the auction on Saturday & refused to allow it to proceed until he withdrew the six months notice he had given.

10   Town. Went to hear Christabel Pankhurst. She struck me as a ranter of the first water, though some of what she said was sound. There is a strong feeling against Wilson now. We suspect him of trying to undermine our power & especially our independence. Added to this there is great impatience encouraged rather basely by Northcliffe, with the long drawn-out negotiations. Tea with Helen MacLagan: her two sons appeared, Michael 5 & Gerald 2. Eric is still in Paris & sometimes interprets for Lloyd George.

12   Rode old Huntsman at Kingscote. Went in to see Frank Gist who is recovering from a lonely & trying winter. M. de Nave[16] arrived this evening. I hadn't seem him since my first leave in Sept. 1915. He will take the family home.

14   County Council. Was elected on to Education & also Local Taxation Cttee. The chief excitement was of course the rates. They have risen to 2.11¼. Meeting lasted from 11 am – 5 pm & wasn't finished when I came away. Started to Ireland.

15   Got into wrong part of train at Crewe. Kind hearted guard forbore to wake me to look at my ticket & I awoke at Preston. Caught train back to Crewe & Holyhead.

16   Back to Omagh where all is much as usual.

24   I went to Curragh races. Lunched with the Shropshires who are being broken up.

26   During 'God Save the King' the gallery [*theatre*] indulged in prolonged hisses.

27   Sunday. Service at the Cathedral [*in Dublin*] rather dull. Very cold. Sleet.

28   Back to Omagh. I have now only about 24 men though I still have 18 officers.

29   Highland Cyclist Bn arrived to take our place. I am living at the club.

May

2   Went over to see General Ward at Enniskillen. He says I may have indefinite leave but can't guarantee that I shan't have to come back. Waterfield wants me back this term which is awkward in many ways. Started to England.

5   Whitminster for funeral of Mr. Teesdale. His age put down as 89: Mrs T said 90.

10   Town. Stayed at Ebury St. [*Many theatre visits, all listed as usual*].

15   Saw Nurse Cavell's funeral pass down Victoria St. Fairly impressive but of the two coys. of the Guards not one man was wearing a medal.

16   To Oxford, nominally for meeting of the Classical Association. Staying in College: SCR very kindly made me an honorary member so I am in utmost clover. Lunch at Grid. Afternoon discussion on the place of Greek in the school curriculum. Reception at Ashmolean. Percy Gardner explained some late acquisitions including a gorgeous bronze head which Farnell says is a genuine Polyclitus. Talked to PG who was friendly but very melancholy. Grenfell showed papyri. Walked with Joseph & visited Edward Bridges whose sister Joseph is going to marry.

17   Myres read a delightful paper on 'Gladstone & Home' & Phillimore a clever but dangerous one on 'Revival of Criticism'. Met Geoffrey Walker who was 'joy-boy' to the 143rd Bde HQs & brought me blankets & comforts the morning after the Glos. attack on Albatross Farm. Everybody amiable, sunshine within & without.

18   Sunday. Chapel & Hall: high table quite full. I sat between Henderson & Henry Oppenheimer: latter a friend of Joseph, a great connoisseur & supporter of National Arts Collection Fund. In SCR had a long talk with Wickham-Legge. He says Clanricarde always boasted of having all Canning's letters etc. & all the historians are panting for them. (I accordingly wrote to Harry Lascelles (*see* note 7) who said my friends must produce an editor who was 'a Whig but not a Radical': they produced Roberts of Magdalen, but I heard no more of the matter. Michael MacLagan was allowed to use some of the material for a thesis. In Oct. 1960 it was announced that Cedric Collyer was using the papers for a new biography)

23   To Grange. They have 34 & seem very happy. No sign of de Winton's return which all agree would be disastrous.

26   To Deal by motor bus, the tunnel having fallen in early in the war [*railway tunnel?*] to see Lucy née Nash & Herbert Harrison. He had about 6 months on the Murman coast: his best souvenirs are the really magnificent outfits supplied by the government.

28   Helen MacLagan down to see the school: she was really delighted & said very nice things about it.

31   Education Cttee. Discussed PNEU scheme with Household.[17]

June

5   To Longney to fix up a lady manager for the school. The parson recommended Mrs Daniel Browning whom I found making butter, quite a rarity nowadays. After much persuasion she consented to act.

10   Town. Tea with cousin Kathleen Brabazon. Winnie Brooke also there.

11   Royal Artillery exhibition. I bought a nice water colour of 'Ammunition carriers at St. Julian 1917' by Lt. A. J. Billinghurst for £14.

12   Met Helen who took me to Mestrovic's exhibition at 'Twenty-One Gallery'. He seems to me to copy archaic Greek masters very closely . . . he gets intense feeling into quiet compositions eg. a lovely Pieta. I don't like his types, eg. the high narrow heads & bare foreheads.

13   Westminster Abbey in morning. Noted Granville Sharp's monument which I had quite forgotten.

16   Biked to supper at Maisemore with Syliva Percival: she has got a beautiful house, Georgian type, done it up well & made a jolly garden. Now of course she wants to leave it for a cottage in the Cotswolds!

17   To Oxford for the voting on the Greek Statute. Travelling part of the way with Sybil Witts: she is working hard in hospital at Leith & looks rather older. I have just become Mrs Witts' trustee. Convocation: listened to excellent speeches, including those by Gilbert Murray & Norwood of Marlborough. Voted 'Placet' i.e. against compulsory Greek. Met Robeson, Girdlestone (orthopaedic surgeon) but couldn't catch Jelf.

18   Met Deed for the first time since 1913. His wounded left arm is still bad.

19   Went to the City & hunted out Young . . . he took me to lunch at Lloyds. Nice place to see but the Captain's Room not so old or attractive as one could wish. Visited Guildhall for the first time . . . went over Bow Church.

20   Battalion dinner 'at the Troc: rather a poor dinner for £1. We had about 35 there including most of my best friends.

24   My first visit to Dartmoor. The party consists of 1/4 Oxfords men: Percival Pickford, Maurice Edmonds, Edward Bridges Son of Poet Laureate & Secretary to the Cabinet, & Hugh Wrong, son of Professor Wrong of Toronto.

26   Edmunds took me around in his car. Ashburton, Newton Abbott, Torquay: went to see cousin Jessie de Polignac whom I had never seen. I had a splendid talk with her for ¾ hr. She is full of life and interest & most amusing. Drove on to Paignton, Kingswear, Dartmouth etc. on to Plymouth & so back to Princeton via Yelverton.

28   . . . at Widdecombe a flag hung out of the school & a short clash of bells proclaimed PEACE.

29   To Naval College Dartmouth to find James Young & Charlie Kitkat. They showed me over the place which is admirably built & organised. I noticed there was no privacy at all, no cubicles & no studies. The boys looked cheery and addressed me as 'Sir' apparently instinctively; then I left by the ferry boat to catch the train for Newton Abbott where I stayed with Maud & Cyril Brackenbury.

July

2   To Inwood, Cookham Dean, staying with the Youngs for Henley.

4   Saw Geoffrey Christie-Miller. Charles Brackenbury is rowing in Winchester Four which eventually won the Public Schools' Cup. Saw Winnie & Hereward.

10   Cheltenham. Lunched with Paterson who detailed the story of Lee & the 'Bath Man Riot' [*a complicated & dramatic confrontation which Waterfield successfully settled with the help of great loyalty from senior boys*]. Exton has suggested my taking the rooms above him at Mrs Leggett's, Devonshire House, Bath Road.

11   To Raikes Hall to hear Will Temple on the Ennobling Bill. I introduced myself to him before the meeting: I had known him slightly at Oxford. He spoke extraordinarily well. Had tea at Boots with F, Temple, Lang the organiser of the meeting & Price.

15   To Oxford for Gaudy, my first. I sat at High Table between Rait & Wickham Legg. I was the only one not a Fellow or ex-Fellow. I had to reply for 'The Army' in a speech which was at any rate brief. Met Hardy for a moment.

16   To Eton to stay with Robeson who has Austen-Leigh's old house. We adjourned to a rehearsal of the Peace celebrations. The boys were formed up by houses in Sixpenny

& then marched off to line the road outside Upper School. Thence to the school yard where they rehearsed the songs . . . a good deal of ragging

17   Elwyn Rhys, Walter's second boy, called on me. A great athlete & a healthy Philistine: very nice manners. Fine service in Upper Chapel. Another practice, this time with Life Guards. Lunch at Rowlands . . . salmon, scrambled eggs, raspberry messes in the old style. Walked about Agar's Plough & discovered Fred Cripps' two jolly boys Joe & Phil, plus a sister.

18   Peace celebration cttee meeting [*at Hardwicke*]. Keen but amicable. The lady-collectors hurled money & notes at me with vague & inaccurate lists of subscribers.

26   Went into Gloucester museum. Some of Grandpapa's birds are still there: Mellersh has designed & arranged an excellent show of Gloucestershire birds: they are mounted in natural positions with characteristic backgrounds. The Roman remains are disappointing & are fewer than I expected.

28   To Grange for concert etc. Elliott is Evelyn Gardiner's successor, gave away prizes & made good but slightly long-winded speech. (W. H. Elliott, broadcaster).

30   Up with the boys. Dinner for Grange Old Boys at the Monaco. We only got about 30 but many more would come if it was better known.

August

1   Motored to Alscott which Jack West inherited about 2 years ago. We were greeted by Olive & Bill, Jill & Mike. Bill is at Sandhurst, Jill is a smart & clever young lady: Mike is a nice rather stolid boy very keen on ships.[18] The house is fairly ugly inside & out but there are some fine pictures & I believe wonderful china.

4   Berkeley Show. F, Grace, Olive & I motored down. Record attendance. Good show of draught horses. Riders not as good as usual & jumpers much less used to the ring. 'For exhibition not competition' were some Gloucestershire cattle. F is secretary of the newly-formed society for their resurrection.

5   Peace celebrations. [*At Hardwick*]. Hardly a spot of rain & a great success. At 3 o'clock we started the women's sports which went off quite well & without quarrelling. This was in Stowell's field, next to the school. The sports over I went to have a look at the Court, where about 120 children were having tea in the coachhouses which were very well decorated. Then back to the school where the second lay of tea was in progress. Short open-air service conducted by James with an address by the Vicar: a 'silent minute' in memory of the fallen. Just before the service, a peal of bells.

6   [*In Town*] Started French phonetics at University College, Gower St.

8   I stayed for a private lesson with Coustenoble. I have about an hour's work to do at home every day. Gracie is up doing dentist so I took her to a theatre.

9   Took Gracie to tea at the 'Old Farm' in the Queen's Road. It is the loft of an old farm building done up as an old furniture shop & tea room.

10   Sunday. St. Peters. Tea with cousin Kathleen Brabazon at 40 Eaton Square.

12   When I started Pelmanism I found my left ear very deaf compared with my right. Also I had buzzing in my ears. So I went to Col. Muecke this afternoon. He looked me over & said it was entirely a matter of my old nose. So he is going to operate on the cartilage. Met Alfred Gilbey [*Col. of the Bucks*] who took me to see his new house.

14   Went over the Clerkenwell property with Cable. Saw the creche, & the parish room that Michael gave. Visited the 'Islington Spa' in Lloyd's Row. Saw St. Helena Row, the worst piece of ours. Like Lloyds Row it has the advantage of not being very high so that everyone gets some light & air. Lloyd Square is the best of the lot. Gave Tom Balston dinner at the Troc: he is fairly flourishing but uncertain about his future.

17   Lunched at Automobile Club as Carlton is being cleaned. I didn't like it much. The rooms are large but crowded: there is a very poor stock of papers: dining room fairly good, & a quite expensive restaurant with foreign waiters!

19   I WAS DEMOBILISED!

24   Sunday. Read lessons in uniform for last time.

25   Town. Duchess Nursing Home, 2 Beaumont St.

26   At 6 pm Muecke came 7 bunged up my nose with cocaine. Half an hour later he took me up to the theatre & removed a lot of the cartilage from my nose. It was a curious performance as I was able to chat all the time. I had a bandage over my eyes to keep out the very strong light that he used. I could feel him scraping & scratching & breaking but there was no pain. I had an uncomfortable night, my nose bleeding considerably.

28   At 7 pm Muecke took the plugs out which made me more comfortable. M turns out to have been at the CCS at Gezaincourt, close to Doullens. He knew a lot of 143 Brigade.

31   Sunday. Sat up in a chair. Head much clearer. Gerald Fitzgerald came to see me. He is contemplating taking a house near Cambridge & studying archaeology.

September

6   Clare had the whole Hardwicke branch of the GFS ie all the parishes round, to a sort of garden party. Our parish girls sang an 'operetta' in front of the palm tree. Afterwards tea etc. This morning Fretherne Court + 750 acres was sold for £39500 to a Mr Daniells, reputed a grocer. £5000 extra was paid for the timber. The Wick Farm had already been sold to Clutterbuck for £5000.

8   F & Clare to Bristol for Poor Law Conference.

12   Sunday School treat. Watched the boys playing cricket. Tea. Races. Billy ran but did not win. Kitty won 1½d!

15   To Dynevor (19) I had not been for about 30 years, certainly not since I went to school. Walter was at the Pant Glas sale & Markie was out but the children greeted me. Elwyn I had met at Eton *see* 17.7.19. Imogen & David I had never seen.

17   Walked with Walter to the Old Castle. The keep, banqueting hall & dungeon are still going strong & the walls have been underpinned. Walter likes the place & knows a fair amount of family history but he is no archaeologist.

18   After lunch Walter took me all over the house. I remembered bits: china passage with the spinets, the kitchen & housekeeper's room. The house is very well furnished with 9 bathrooms etc.

19   Left by the 11.20 after a most delightful visit. I have started a cold in my new nose.

22   Geraldine Chester-Master (20) came with her 16-yr old Billy. She is most amusing: Billy is nice, silent, not very clever.

24 I went down to Bencombe to see McKinley who has just bought the house. He has got the orchard behind it & now wants the 11 acre field & a bit of wood. F offers them at £80 an acre which M says he can't pay. He has given £4000 for the house & about 6 acres.

25 To Cheltenham to recommence my profession! I am living in Devonshire House.

26 Chapel & then meeting of the whole staff addressed by Hardy [*the new Headmaster; Waterfield having retired in July*] He spoke well & nicely. I am to take French on the military side, also bits of History, English, Geog etc. Rather interesting, but I am very much bored at not having any German.

27 Made the acquaintance of my two top sets. Afterwards I had two hours with 3b whom I am taking in English. All very pleasant people – so far. A railway strike has suddenly fallen from the blue [*& continues until October 6th*].

28 Sunday. Hardy preached in the evening: a good sermon on sympathy & hard work. Paterson says the boys didn't understand all of it. It seemed simple if a trifle long – over 20 mins.

October

4 Called on Mrs Hardy. She is delightful & a charming hostess.

5 Sunday. Biked home immediately after school. Took 35 mins from here to Gloucester Cross & 30 mins on: total of 65 mins. Came back in 100 mins with a slight wind against me [*news of strike settlement*].

15 Dined with Headmaster: also there Mr & Mrs Lee. He is a new master, formerly tutor at Magdalen.

19 Biked to Birdlip. Just an hour. The woods look quite lovely, all ruby & garnet. Down the hill to Witcombe but nobody there. Supper with Exton, Paterson there.

21 Exton came up tonight & revealed that he is engaged. He is in some perplexity as to where to live but proposes to come here.

22 To supper with Lady Maidstone (21) at Parabola Rd.

23 Moiseivitch concert. His playing was wonderful but I wasn't thrilled [*no reason*].

25 Meeting of Cttee of Extension of Medical Sservices. I am one of the CC representatives. To everyone's surprise the doctors are apparently satisfied with the financial arrangements. Home. Gracie & May both home, both much better. F & Cecil Elwes came in late having driven into the ditch in Black Cross Lane. No damage. Cecil cheery & much less stiff than he used to be.

28 Public Schools Field Day at Badminton. I umpired . . . whole scheme poor. Harper remarked that the tactics would have been up to date in the Wars of the Roses but antiquated by Wellington's time.

November

1 Over 100 boys at early service which was a special remembrance for the fallen.

2 Sunday. Town. To Muecke to have my nose looked at. He is in bed with trench fever & stiff with inoculations. My nose is going on fine except that there was a small adhesion in the left nostril. This is cut through but he fears that it may form again.

7 H. P. Allen gave a lecture on 'Music & Education': most inspiring . . . he is staying at Hardy's: he tells me that Bevis Ellis, my contemporary at Eton, left him his very

large library of music which Allen has presented to some library naming it the 'Ellis Memorial Collection'. He has also raised £700 to keep it up to date.

8   Allen gave a 'congregational practice' in chapel. He made the boys laugh considerably ... opened their eyes to what singing might mean. At the end they were giving tongue with great force. Called on the Guises at Cheltenham who were officially 'not at home' but received me with open arms. Di looked very flourishing. Sir William is very bad but finds the house nice & warm which is what he chiefly needs. Anselm is doing land agent in Sussex.

10 Attended a meeting of the Executive Committee of the Boy Scouts in St. Mary de Lode Crypt school. They were all very flattering to me because no District Commissioner had ever appeared at a meeting before.

11 Armistice Day. We had the two minutes silence at 11 o'clock in Chapel. The padre came in in cassock only, knelt down & we followed his example. After two minutes we rose, the organ played the Dead March & we went out. Not a word was spoken which made the service impressive & enabled Jews & RC's to attend. Jews stood during the two minutes. For the afternoon Pearson had arranged an extraordinarily successful entertainment for 400 ex-Servicemen. Chapel at 5.30 to which about 200 came. At 6.30 they had tea in the gym. At 7.30 there was an excellent entertainment of which the great features were Marie Hall & Lena Ashwell. At the end the men cheered the boys & masters & everybody.

12 Ever since the 6th I've been taking prep & lights out for Tapsfield who is laid up with very bad eczema. He lives in Thirlestaine Villa which he loathes. Mrs T is pretty & cheery but I don't think she likes the boys enough to be an ideal schoolmaster's wife. T's boys are quiet & well-mannered: the evenings are by no means unpleasant.

22 Meeting of Gloucester branch of Historical Association. St. Clair Baddeley addressed us on Place-names, with reference to the Churn & its group, Cirencester, Cerney etc. I introduced myself to B who spoke very kindly of Michael. After dinner to AMA meeting at Lipson's. About 30 came, mostly from the College. I was put on the local committee & also on the Council.

28 Confirmation. Hardy had made attendance voluntary but then urged the boys to come in such a way which made abstention difficult. The Bishop took it in his usual nice but uninspired way.

December

2   Tea with the Head in order to escort the folk-song party round the big school rooms. They contemplate having the summer school here. Party consisted of Cecil Sharp, his secretary & Mrs Ratcliff.

[Notes on the Ratcliff family supplied by Sybil Witts: marriages of Ronald & Jim. Also on Cecil Sharp. He gave details about collecting folk songs in the Appalachians where a large colony of primitive people carried on the tradition of medieval England & speak Elizabethan English. Sharp's host said to him, 'Do stay, I like you, you are so common'. No schools, no railways, houses dirty & living bad but everyone gentle & hospitable, full of music & culture.]

11 Concert at Town Hall. John Coates 'fair but often out of tune. Max Mossel capable but dull. Myra Hess excellent on the piano.

12 Supper in the school at Hardwicke given by the village to the returned soldiers. I sat on F's right at the 'high table', Canon Nash on his left. Harold Stratton Davies on my right: he was with the 61st Division during the whole war ending up in command of the RE coy in which he enlisted. There were about 100 at the dinner. All very cheery & well-behaved. The dinner was good but short. Sing-song. A fair number played poker. Phelps provided some good beer & the élite were given port in the infants' rooms!

14 Sunday. Col. & two Metford boys in chapel. At Pearson's request Hardy, Seaton & several others including myself attended a parade of demobilised soldiers at St. James.

18 Mark reading, after which Hardy made a very nice speech. Farewell service at 5 pm.

22 Glevum Hall, Cheltenham for a 10–18 dance got up by Mrs Bower.

24 Spent the whole day clearing out clothes etc. from my room. Good riddance of much that had been there for years & years, unused & unusable.

25 Very mild weather. Presents mostly confined to the children. Unfortunately Audrey was seedy & couldn't come up.

27 Biddy again at Kennels. Olive out on Tennis Ball, going well. His Lordship now hunts in yellow.

31 To Town for AMA Council. My portmanteau was not labelled at Gloucester & was put out at Kemble so I only got it on Thursday [*from Wednesday!*] 'Le Voyage de M. Perrichon' at Duke of York's: we had been reading it in school so I asked some boys.

Notes for the War Years

1. Gore, John. Radley, Trinity College Cambridge. Journalist and author. Wrote the official biography of King Goerge V.

2. Showers, Mrs Georgina Hester Cornelia née Somerset. Sister of Bruce and Raglan Somerset and Mrs George Hopkinson. m 1. Lionel Edmee, Comte d'Epineul, who died 1881, 2. Captain Showers, Chief Constable of Essex.

3. Wigram, Col. Rt. Hon. Sir Clive. Private Secretary and Extra Equerry to King George V.

4. Heath, Major-General Henry Newton Charles CB.

5. Fanshawe, Major-General Sir Robert KCB 1917. Commanded 48 S. Midland Division 1915–19. 69 Division 1918–19.

6. Rollestone, John Marcus. Was ordained later and became *Rector of Dursley in 1932.*

7. Clanricarde, Marquis & Earl de Burgh-Canning, Hubert George (assumed the name Canning at request of his maternal uncle). His sister Elizabeth had married the 4th Earl of Harewood: this may have prompted his bequest to the 6th Earl of his large fortune [*& the Canning papers, see* May 18th, 1919].

8. Dundas, Lt. Col. James Colin. Eton, RMA. Military career. *Member of the Royal Company of Archers* [*the King's bodyguard in Scotland*].

9. Michael died at Katia, Sinai in May 1916.

10. Frances Davidson of Dunedin & cousin Charlie Orde were married in November 1914.

11. Verey, David. His mother was Lindaraja Birchall: she married Cecil Verey, Rector of Buckland with Laverton. DV edited 'The Diary of a Cotswold Parson: Reverend F. E. Witts, 1783–1854' among many other works.

12. Clifford, Adelaide Hilda was the widow of Henry Francis Clifford, K.1917: Henrietta Hilda was their posthumous daughter.

13. Maitland, Mary Jane, Lady Meath, wife of Reginald 12th Earl of Meath & daughter of 11th Earl of Lauderdale.

14. Stewart, Edward 'Ted'. Eton. Was in White-Thompson's house with the diarist. See p. 18.

15. Lygon, William 7th Earl Beauchamp. Lord Lieutenant of Gloucestershire 1911–13. Connected by his sister's marriage with Sir S. J. Gurney Hoare 'Sam Hoare'.

16. M. de Nave & the Belgian family. Friends of Father's who seem to have lived at Hardwicke Court for much of the war. During the period 1939–45 members of the next generation were also at Hardwicke.

17. Household, Horace West. Secretary of Education, Gloucestershire County Council.

18. West, Michael. *Lt. Gen. Sir Michael Alston-Roberts-West. Commanded the Commonwealth Division in Korea, 1952–53..*

19. Dynevor. Large estate with house and ancient castle in SW Wales where the Rhys family of cousins lived. *See* note 59, Eton Section for Walter and Markie: their children were Charles, Elwyn, David and Imogen.

20. Chester-Master, Geraldine née Arkwright m. W. A. C. Chester-Master, Harrow & RMC. William 'Billy' was their eldest son.

21. Maidstone, Lady Louisa. Youngest dau. of Sir George Jenkinson. m. Viscount Maidstone only son of 11th Earl of Winchelsea. They lived in Parabola Road, Cheltenham.

Postscript

It was difficult to decide when to finish these extracts. Only about a quarter of the diarist's output has been used and another sixty years of interesting material awaits another enthusiast.

The year 1919 was a watershed in many ways. It marked the end of his relatively free and untrammelled years as a younger son, despite many griefs and disappointments. His mature, adult personality which the diaries have revealed in the making, was established. On demobilisation he returned to his teaching post at Cheltenham College where he remained for twenty years; at the same time he took on a daunting programme of public service to relieve his father and this again increased on the latter's death in 1924.

Colonel Lloyd-Baker was a county councillor for the Wheatenhurst division from 1919, a Deputy Lieutenant of the county from 1922, a magistrate from 1924 and an Alderman from 1936. He became Chairman of the Education, Library and Records committees of the County Council and of many other bodies, such as the Discharged Prisoners Aid Society: a typical kindly action here was to supply a complete outfit of tools to a prisoner who had earlier pawned his own, giving the caveat 'And don't let me see you here again.'

How did he find time for a full teaching appointment? He not only did this but he took on the housemastership of the West Day Boys in 1923 which involved countless visits to worried parents in his own spare time, advising them about their son's problems and possibly their misdeeds with such success that he remained firm friends thereafter with both parent and pupil.

Territorial camps were replaced by those of the College Mission in which he became Quartermaster for many years. He also took an interest in Gloucestershire Boy Scouts: more camps, more meetings— and still more friends. He kept in touch with Army contemporaries at regimental reunions and dinners: at Oxford he started a luncheon club for old Cheltonians which was most popular, and he was present at the inaugural dinner of the Oxford Society in March 1935. Wherever he went, on visits such as those of the Bristol and Gloucestershire Archaeological Society of which he was president, or the Cotteswold Naturalists' Field Club he seemed inevitably to meet at least one old Etonian. He had been invited to return to Gmunden whenever he liked by the parents of his pupil Ernst August in 1908 and this invitation was repeated by successive generations. The Colonel's last visit was made by air in 1976 when he was 93 years old and his host was yet another Ernst August, grandson of his old pupil.

Two people of special impotance in his life were his nieces Olive and Kitty. Olive, after her father's death in action in 1916 and with the diarist in constant danger in Flanders, had been brought up by her grandfather to administer the estate. She always kept a home for the diarist at Hardwicke Court where he had the rooms formerly occupied by his bachelor Uncle Henry. She died as the result of an accident in 1975. Kitty was his beloved prop and stay to the end of his life. Her children and grandchildren and those of her brother Billy whose eldest son Charles is now at Hardwicke Court with his family. were his major interests as he grew into old age. Continuing the family tradition Charles Lloyd-Baker is at present High Sheriff of Gloucestershire and has most kindly written the Foreword to these diary extracts.

Colonel Lloyd-Baker died peacefully at the age of 96 and was buried in Hardwicke churchyard on 21 September 1979.

Joyce Popplewell, North Nibley, 1993

Index

Page numbers in italic type refer to entries in the editor's notes